the brand new house book

the brand-new house book

everything you need to know
about planning, designing, and
building a custom, semi-custom,
or production-built house

THREE RIVERS PRESS · NEW YORK

katherine salant

To Steve, Daisy, Shelley, and Claire
And to my parents Greta and Newell Blair

Published by Three Rivers Press, New York, New York.
Member of the Crown Publishing Group.

Random House, Inc. New York, Toronto, London, Sydney, Auckland
www.randomhouse.com

Three Rivers Press is a registered trademark and the Three Rivers Press colophon is a trademark of Random House, Inc.

Printed in the United States of America

Design by Jan Derevjanik

Library of Congress Cataloging-in-Publication Data

Salant, Katherine.
      The brand new house book : everything you need to know about planning, designing, and building a custom, semi-custom, or production-built house / by Katherine Salant.
         Includes index.
      1. House construction—Popular works.   2. Consumer education—Popular works.
   3. House buying—Popular works.   I. Title.

   TH4811 .S24 2001
   690'.837—dc21

                                                                                          2001023346

   ISBN 0-609-80583-5

   10 9 8 7 6 5 4 3 2

contents

introduction

Building a house looks deceptively simple. You sketch a plan on the back of an envelope, hand it to a builder, and voila! You get your house. Maybe a hundred years ago this was possible. Today the whole process is a lot more complicated. But you don't have to become an expert in home building to get a good house. You do, however, have to know enough to make good decisions—hundreds of them. That is the premise and the intention of this book: to provide you with enough information, on a wide range of topics, so that you get a very good house. And the right house for you.

The key is knowing what questions to ask—both of yourself and others. It also helps to know some pertinent facts about materials (for example, what makes for a good window or a good carpet) and how to evaluate builders, the people to whom you are ultimately entrusting your hopes and dreams and money.

The questions to ask yourself include not only your laundry list of functional requirements—say you need four bedrooms and a large home office—but also your quirks and habits. The right kitchen for you depends on what kind of cook you are: neat or, frankly, a bit messy? Do you catch every spill right away? How organized are you in the kitchen? Do you spread out over every square inch of counter when you prepare a meal, or do you work within a small, confined area?

I organized the book as I imagined you would go about collecting information and thinking about building a new house, starting with nailing down your needs and articulating exactly what it is that has led you to decide to do this. Then there are the big-picture issues: Why do houses cost so much? How much can you afford? Who are the players? Next I consider the broad categories of different types of builders as well as the experts who you should engage to help you.

Along the way, you need to know how to find, evaluate, hire, and work with the many experts—from a buyer's agent to the site supervisor—who will work on your house. I explain how to go about this.

Eventually you will start to focus on specifics such as kitchen cabinets or selecting a hardwood floor or the heating and cooling systems. You'll need to make your own choices or assess those made by a builder. The chapters have been written so that you can read them in any order, no matter when you want to tackle these issues.

At the end of each chapter, "Tips from the Trade" offers specific advice from experts in the field discussed. Each topic is presented in some, but not overwhelming, detail.

Over the seven years that I have been writing about building a brand-new house, I have interviewed experts on every aspect of home building imaginable; their advice is reiterated here. For example, if you decide to work with a production builder, he will sell you a basic house and optional upgrades. Which ones are good choices that can help with resale and which are frivolous? Realtors who work with resale buyers and real-estate appraisers have definite opinions. You can measure a room in a builder's model to see if your king-size bed will fit once it's *in* the room, but can you actually move it there? That can be more daunting than you think—ask any mover. I have.

The furnished models always look terrific because real life never intrudes—no one lives in models to dirty them up. Your new house will never look as good, but a professional house cleaner can offer tips on the details that can make your new house easier to clean. If this is your first home purchase, you may be agonizing over color choices. Interior designers offer some useful suggestions, such as taking a look at your closet to see what colors you favor. Many kitchens in new houses have an open wine rack. It looks good, but wine specialists say you are better off putting the wine somewhere else. And if you want to go the extra mile and add a few things that will make your production house unique, architects suggest some design ideas that would be easy to fabricate out of standard materials.

You've decided that your new home office will be your primary work space, so what do you need to know in planning it? Office designers, acoustical engineers, and specialists in high-speed data transmission all have important things to say. You've already thought about cabinets and flooring and countertops for your kitchen. But who really knows how well the materials will not just look, but last? The installers. If there's a problem, they have to come back and fix it. If you want a deck, do you really want a wood one? Is all that maintenance worth it, just to get the natural look in the great outdoors? When you know the score, a deck made of recycled materials or "virgin vinyl" may have appeal.

At some point you will have to pick a building lot. They may all look the same when you have to pick one, but they won't be when all the houses are built and the grading is finished. One could become a lake with every downpour. You can avoid drawing this short straw by hiring a landscape architect to help you choose a lot. A landscape architect can also develop a master plan for your new yard and help you decide which parts you want to do yourself and which are better left to the experts. For example, a good-sized "starter tree" with a four-to-five-inch diameter can weigh seven hundred to one thousand pounds. You're a tree hugger, but you don't want to pay a bundle for a lot with trees that are diseased or dying; you need an arborist. A house with a view of a golf course sounds great; golf course architects have plenty of tips for how to choose a lot and avoid getting broken windows from errant balls.

Finally you will sit down at the table and negotiate a price for the house and all those options. Buyer's agents—Realtors who represent buyers in a new-home transaction with a production builder—offer some advice on negotiating strategies. Real-estate attorneys point out clauses in the sales contract that should be of more than passing interest, such as "substantially similar." You need to know what this does—and does not—mean.

As you wade into the details of your new-house project, you will eventually get to the less sexy but more critical stuff like heating and cooling. Most likely, you will think about these prosaic matters only after you've considered everything else, so construction considerations are at the end of the book. By this point, numerous aspects of home building that never have captured your fancy, such as framing and joist spacing, may be downright fascinating. And shingle basics can be fun! (No kidding.)

If you're inclined to want more information on the many topics covered in this book, further reading is suggested in an appendix, along with website information and a glossary of terms.

As you go through the process of building a new house, you will be making many decisions large (which floor plan?) and small (which cabinet door handle?). Before you become overwhelmed, remember: You don't have to become an expert in home building to get a good house. You just have to know enough about the subject to make good decisions.

part one

the big
picture

getting started

Thomas Jefferson was a Renaissance man of extraordinarily wide interests. He loved architecture, designed the University of Virginia campus, and spent much of his life building and rebuilding his own house, Monticello. But were Thomas Jefferson to build a house today, even he would find it daunting. At every step of the process, the number of choices can be overwhelming.

In Jefferson's day, housing styles changed slowly. Monticello was unique in its plan and ambiance, but stylistically it was similar to other grand houses built at that time. Today, the number of stylistic options is huge, and with the materials now available, anything is possible. Jefferson could re-create Monticello down to the last handmade nail, build a look-alike largely out of synthetic materials that require almost no maintenance, or build a house that bears no resemblance to anything ever built before.

The choices are not merely matters of final appearance; they also include how the building is constructed. In Jefferson's day, there were only two or three ways to make a window, only small panes of glass were available, and craftsmen built them at the site. Today there are nearly a thousand window manufacturers in the United States. You can have a window with one, two, or even three layers of glass; the frame can be made of wood, man-made materials, or a combination of the two. You can add a coating to the glass and fill the space between the layers of glass with an inert gas to make the window more energy efficient.

Today, Jefferson would need a lot of time just to figure out what he wanted. A big house that seems to go on forever? A little house crafted like a jewel box? How much would either cost? What could he afford? Should he stretch his wallet to the max and eat hot dogs for dinner every night, or stay within limits and leave room in the budget for the occasional steak and a fine wine?

Eventually, he would get to who would build his house, and where he would build it. But at each point in his decision making, he might find himself stopping to rethink the whole picture.

As you embark on your new-house project, give yourself at least as much time as Thomas Jefferson would need and then some. Sifting through all the information; looking at model houses, talking with builders; perhaps hiring an architect, comparing floor plans, materials, and finishes, land costs and location; plus figuring out how to finance this venture; and making all the decisions large and small is time-consuming but necessary. If you short-circuit the process, you could find yourself inspecting your new house at the final walk-through and realize that it's not what you wanted.

Be good to yourself. If you want to buy a house from a production builder (as tract builders prefer to be called), give yourself a month to get your feet wet, at least two or three months to learn who the builders are, where they're working, what their price ranges are, and what their houses look like. If you want to build a custom house, choosing a builder and a design takes time. Besides looking at the finished work of each builder you're considering, you also have to talk with their former clients; this can take you two or three months. If you want to hire an architect, it may take you a while to find one you like, another four to six months to develop the design, select all the materials, and produce a set of construction drawings and specifications—and then you still have to choose a builder.

Once construction starts, a production-built house takes on average about four months to finish, assuming that the weather is decent and the builder does not face labor or material shortages. A custom-built house will take at least six to nine months, longer if the weather is bad, the design is complicated, or you want hard-to-get, unusual materials.

No matter which route you take, you will still face decisions large and small about everything from cabinet selections to carpet colors. And you will have more than one soul-searching moment when you have to decide what to keep and what to give up to stay within your budget.

Keep in mind that price is not everything, and it's not the only thing. The goal is to get the best house you can afford, not the cheapest, and not the most house for the least money. The challenge is to use your money wisely, make prudent choices, and *have fun*. Building a new house is at times confounding. But it is also exciting and exhilarating. The smell of freshly cut wood, the sounds of construction, and the transformation of a site from a big hole in the ground and piles of materials to a finished house is one of life's most satisfying experiences.

settingbenchmarks

When you start looking at models, studying floor plans, and planning your new house, where you live now will be your benchmark, and the basis for all your comparisons. But if you rely on your mind's eye when you are making the comparison, you may find yourself saying, "This house is sort of like the place we have now, but different"—a vague and basically useless appraisal. To make the comparison helpful, take out your tape measure and make a rough sketch of your present house or apartment to take along when you start to look.

Another house that may be etched on your brain is the one you lived in as a child. If your family is still there, ask someone to make a sketch that includes dimensions. If you really like a friend's house or certain rooms in a friend's house, ask if you can measure them.

After you've finished measuring and made your sketch, make a thorough accounting of your house by going through each room and noting its pluses and minuses. This will produce a very specific list of what you are looking for in your new house, and may lead you to consider things that are not in your present house but that you would like in your new one. For example, if you have stacks of books or magazines in too many corners or closets because there's no place for shelving, built-ins could be a high priority.

Some of the items on your list may be those prosaic little details that have become daily irritants, such as minuscule closets. So you don't end up just as cramped in your new house, be sure to measure the closets where you live now, and include the measurements on your sketch. Then measure the closets in any house you get serious about.

The kitchen is one room where you spend a lot of time, so study yours carefully. Are the work areas too small, or ample? Is the storage adequate? Note the number of base and wall cabinets allocated to food storage, pots and pans, and dishware. If you're moving to a smaller house—what the home building industry calls a move-down—you need to make sure that the new kitchen is adequate for a lifetime's accumulation of kitchenware and small appliances. Conversely, if you're moving to a larger house, you're likely to acquire more cooking equipment and dishware in the future, so you'll need *more* cabinets than you have now, not just the same number.

In addition to specific comments for each room, you may also have generalized gripes about your current house. After all, you're moving for a reason. Often these involve storage problems, such as there's no place to put kids' sports equipment. You may have a design gripe (the first thing you see when you open the front door is the powder-room door), or a lifestyle gripe (when you entertain, everybody ends up in the kitchen but there's no place to sit, or, even worse, there's no place for guests to hang out in the kitchen, so you end up alone and feel like a servant).

When you start looking at furnished models or floor plans, you'll quickly discover that no house will have everything that you want. So when you've finished with the pluses-and-minuses list, prioritize the items. What are the "must have, can't live without" and the "no way, no where, no how can I live with those"?

Spending so much time thinking about what you want may feel like you're just standing in place when you could be out there checking all the new-home communities in your area, or meeting with an architect, or interviewing a builder. But the more that you can articulate to yourself what you want in a new house, the happier you will be with the final results. If an architect or custom builder has to intuit what you want, they might not get it exactly right. If you are looking at production-built houses, you will have to decide whether a given house will fit your needs. The more precisely you define those needs, the easier it will be to know which one is the right one for you.

what'syourstyle?

Your new house will have some architectural styling. Most people like the traditional look, so this may be where you're headed. But just as important as the architectural style is your own *personal* style—what you like. Nailing down the characteristics of houses that you like or don't like will help you define your own style and sort out the overwhelming choices that await once you start house shopping. Whether a house is wildly contemporary or strictly traditional, do you like dramatic, eye-popping foyers and houses that make guests say "Wow!"? Or do you feel lost in a huge, two-story foyer? Some houses have big spaces and open floor plans that seem to go on forever. Others have smaller rooms with more contained spaces. Some houses have both. Which one appeals to your temperament and taste?

whatsize?

In addition to the rough sketch of each room of your current house, you need to know the overall size—this too will be a benchmark for comparisons. You can calculate the area in square feet using the dimensions you took for your floor-plan sketch, but it might be easier to call your property tax assessor (property tax assessments are usually based on floor areas). When you calculate the total floor area, do not include the garage, attic, or any other unfinished areas. Regardless of whether it is finished or not, you should also leave out the basement, because by industry-wide convention a basement is not included in a builder's square-foot figure (unless the size is given as "finished square feet above grade" and "finished square feet below grade"). If you ask the tax assessor for the square footage, ask if the basement is included.

To get an idea of what new houses of various sizes look and feel like, visit a number of home builder's furnished models. As you develop the ability to correlate what you see with actual size, you may be surprised to find that only upper-end production-built houses are enormous, and mid-range ones are not that big. According to the National Association of Home Builders, the average-sized new house in 1999 had 2,225 square feet of finished space. Though this is a 44 percent increase over the average-sized house of thirty years ago (it was 1,520 square feet in 1971), and more than 100 percent bigger than new houses built fifty years ago (it was 1,000 square feet in 1950), it's certainly not excessive. Many people would consider a 2,225-square-foot house modest, even small. An increase of a bit more than 10 percent to 2,500 square feet, though, and most people would feel comfortable. A two-story house of this size can include an eat-in kitchen/family room, a small den/study, small formal living and dining rooms, and four bedrooms, including a master suite with a large master bathroom.

You may be able to afford a much bigger house than 2,500 square feet, but be forewarned: Size can be seductive. Beyond a certain point, it doesn't add that much more utility, unless you have an enormous household or you entertain frequently on a large scale. You may be happier scaling down the total size and getting more finishes and features. If you scale down from a 4,000-square-foot house to a 3,000-square-foot one, for example, you will still have a big house, but with the money saved you can do wonderful detailing.

Scaling down from 2,500 square feet to 2,000 square feet probably won't save enough to add in elaborate details because you still have the fixed costs for the kitchen, two and a half baths, plumbing, heating, and so forth.

whatcan**you**afford?

Whether you go for size, features, or some of both, the dollar amount that you can afford will depend on how big a down payment you can make and how large a mortgage you can finance. Figuring out the down payment won't be hard (you know how big your nest egg is), but the mortgage amount depends on a number of factors including your income and credit history. There are mortgage calculators and helpful information available on the Internet, but you should meet with several lenders in your area to discuss your mortgage prospects and get a sense of how a lender arrives at the figure he is willing to lend.

As you wade into the mortgage maze, you will also start hearing about closing costs—additional charges that must be paid at closing, when you sign all the papers, take possession of your new house, and assume a mortgage. The closing costs vary from lender to lender and market to market. In some places, closing costs can be as much as 5 percent of the mortgage amount; in others they may be only 1 percent. That is, for a $150,000 mortgage, the closing costs could range from $1,500 to as much as $6,500.

There are not nearly as many decisions or tradeoffs to make when choosing between mortgage loan packages and lenders as there are in the building of a house (all those floor plans, materials, and location choices), but it's an essential part of the process. The ins and outs of mortgages can be confusing, so you need to allow plenty of time to bone up.

hireexpertise

Buying a house is not like buying a car. The size of the purchase, the number of years of financial obligation involved, and all the choices and decisions you will have to make before you sign on the bottom line make a new-house purchase much more complicated. Another crucial distinction between buying a house and a car is that with a car you can kick the tires first. Before making your final purchase decision, you can see what you are buying and take it on a test drive. When you buy a new house, though, you have to make your final purchase decision and sign on the bottom line before the house is built and before you can see what you are buying.

To make the process go more smoothly, you should engage several experts to help you. A buyer's agent can make the search for a production house go more smoothly. A real-estate attorney can review and modify the sales contract when you've found your builder. A landscape architect can help you pick a lot when you're faced with acres of brown dirt, stakes, and everything looking the same. A private home inspector can monitor the construction to ensure that it is done correctly. An arborist can evaluate the trees to see if the lot premium you are paying is really worth it. Finding all these people to help you will also take time.

fromagreat**idea**toareal**house**

What is a reasonable time line for your new home purchase when you factor in all the planning? If you're buying a production-built house, about nine months. If you're building a custom-built house, eighteen months is more likely.

time table for production-built house

month 1

- Measure your present house, make the plus-and-minus list, prioritize it, think about what style, both personal and architectural, you want.

- Start collecting information about mortgages and financing.

- Check your credit records with the three national credit reporting bureaus to ensure there are no errors.

- Start collecting the names of buyer's agents and line one up.

- Look in the newspapers, and start collecting information on builders and acquainting yourself with the market in your area.

- Start collecting information about attorneys, home inspectors, and landscape architects.

months 2 and 3

- Working with your buyer's agent, tour models, cover the landscape, and focus in on two or three builders (but if there are many builders or many new-home communities in your market, this might not be enough weekends to cover all the ones in your location, price range, and house type).

- Line up your experts.

- Continue to explore your mortgage options.

month 4

- Choose your builder, select all your options.

- With the landscape architect's input, choose a lot.

- Get a lender's approval with specific mortgage terms and amount.

- Hire a home inspector to make inspections at agreed-upon points during the construction.

- Work up and finalize the sales contract with input from the buyer's agent and the attorney.

month 5

- Be ready to break ground.

month 9

- Be ready to move in.

The actual time frame for construction will depend on a number of variables. Weather may prevent the builder from breaking ground until it thaws out. If there are many buyers ahead of you, the builder may not even be able to start your house for several months. The construction part of the schedule is beyond your control, but the rest of it is very much in your court.

(If you want to be in your new house before the start of the school year, you should have the sales contract signed and the builder ready to go by mid-February. Working backward, this means that you should start your new-house search the previous July.)

time table for a custom-built house

month 1

- Measure your present house, make a plus-and-minus list, prioritize it, think about what styles, both personal and architectural, you want.

- Start collecting information about construction loans and mortgages.

- Check your credit records with the three national credit reporting bureaus to ensure there are no errors.

- Start collecting the names of builders and architects and start acquainting yourself with their work. If you have to buy a lot, contact real estate agents who sell land or are knowledgeable about tear-downs.

- Start collecting information about attorneys, home inspectors, landscape architects, and arborists if you want a lot with trees.

months 2 and 3

- Interview builders or architects, depending on whether you want a predrawn design that is tailored to your lot or a never-before-built house that is designed from scratch. Plan on spending plenty of time meeting with these professionals, looking at their finished work, and talking with their former clients.

- Line up your experts.

- Continue to explore your mortgage options.

month 4

- Choose your builder or architect.

- Finalize your lot purchase if you don't already own the land.

- Get a lender's approval for a construction loan and a permanent mortgage.

- Hire a home inspector to make weekly visits to the job site as well as more lengthy inspections at agreed-upon points during the construction.

- Hire an attorney to review the builder's contract and make appropriate modifications. If you hire an architect, have your attorney review the architect's contract as well—the American Institute of Architect's standard architect-owner contract may need modifications for your situation.

month 5

- Be ready to start designing your house. Plan on spending at least four months doing this if you hire an architect. If you work with a builder, the time spent in selecting materials and working up the final plans may be shorter.

month 7 or 8

- Be ready to break ground with your builder.

month 9

- If you're working with an architect, be ready to send the construction documents out for competitive bidding.

- Award the contract to the successful bidder.

month 10

- Be ready to break ground with your builder.

Again, the actual time frame for construction of your custom-built house will depend on a number of variables, including how complicated and unusual your design is. Weather can cause delays. A custom builder works more slowly than a production builder, taking his time to incorporate all the customizing that led you to seek his services in the first place. Six to nine months may be a reasonable amount of time to plan on the construction, but you should discuss this point thoroughly when you are interviewing builders and architects.

In many cases, the first step in turning a dream house into reality is transforming the dream, says architect Carson Looney of Memphis, Tennessee, who has been designing houses there for more than twenty years. In his experience, clients come to their first meeting with strongly held convictions and images of a house that they have been carrying around in their minds for years. As they describe their needs and lifestyle, however, image and function often diverge. To get a livable house, they have to jettison some part of the dream. But after years of wanting a house to look a certain way, this can be hard. Many clients are reluctant to accept the idea that having some of their image but not every piece of it will mean a better house, though most quickly acquiesce when Looney shows them alternatives.

For example, in Memphis, a *Gone with the Wind* Tara-style mansion with four col-umns on the front and a grand, circular stair-case is a perennial favorite. Many clients want this type of house without realizing the ramifications—a circular stair with true Tara proportions can take up as much as eight hun-dred square feet of living area. Looney has found that a smaller stair with a curve and lots of natural light is a close enough approximation for most people. He puts this more modest stair where it works with the other spaces, and not necessarily by the front door. Once clients see the house is more livable with a smaller stair, they willingly abandon the bigger one. If the four columns on the front are really important, Looney tries to keep them in the plan, if at all possible.

Besides the function-versus-image issue, Looney says his clients can have conflicting images—they want things that don't fit to-gether aesthetically. They want the flamboy-ance of Tara on the front, but the sensibilities

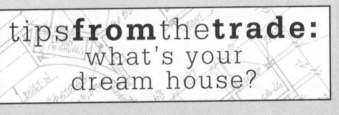

tips**from**the**trade:**
what's your
dream house?

that will define the character of the rest of the house are much more understated. Some clients want to put the four columns on a one-story house, but "You can't squash the traditional Southern house and make it a ranch—that would be like marrying a Cadillac to a VW bug."

The word that comes up again and again in these initial meetings, Looney says, is *balance*—"a word that should be stamped on your sunglasses." Every choice that is made must balance with all the other choices. If you get too focused on one element like the circular staircase, it becomes the tail wagging the dog and starts to dictate the rest of the house. Likewise, too much focus on the façade can also be detrimental because the interior spaces that you will live in everyday will be manipulated to fit behind it. And, he wryly notes, the people who benefit the most from those machinations will be the neighbors—as owners, "What's the joy besides the fifteen seconds when you drive by?"

While he helps his clients sort out what their new house will look like and come up with a plan that meets their needs now, Looney urges them to "look down the road and think about their life in ten years." If unknowns must be factored in—for example, a couple has no children as yet—the clients have to take the architect's word for what they will need. When children are in the offing, this means a house that is less grand.

Day-to-day living also bears closer examination than many clients realize when planning their house. Here again, Looney says he tries to help them mesh their image with reality. A cavernous master suite with a master bath of palatial proportions sounds great, but if the scheme means fifty or sixty feet from the bed to the toilet, this will be a hassle, especially in the middle of the night. Even the prosaic details like a place for the vacuum cleaner and broom need to be thought out, because the once-standard broom closet is a rarity in new houses today.

chapter two: who are the players?

If you're like most people, when you think of building a new house, your thoughts quickly turn to specifics—floor plans, architectural style, kitchen layouts, cabinet doors, countertops. But who's directing the action, putting together all these pieces and making your house happen? As you meander into a hundred different digressions on flooring materials, appliances, a home office, and a decent-sized laundry room, don't lose sight of the person who is orchestrating this: your builder. Choose him with care. Of the hundreds of decisions you will make in the course of building your new house, *this is the single most important one.*

If your budget is tight but you still have a grand vision, you may be tempted to be your own contractor in order to save the builder's markup. This can work well—if you have nerves of steel, tolerate stress well, have no spouse or partner or children, or flexible work hours, or no need for a day job and can get by on little sleep. Otherwise, look for a builder.

While you're doing that, line up the other players on your team. You need an attorney to review your contract with the builder, a landscape architect to help you pick a lot, a private home inspector to check the construction and a buyer's agent if you are planning to buy your house from a production builder. (If you must prioritize, get the buyer's agent first: he or she will help you find a builder. Line up the others by the time you're ready to make a deal and negotiate a contract.)

The other players you should be aware of are the land developer and the site superintendent. If you plan to buy in a planned community, the developer is the visionary who bought the raw land, decided on the site amenities, and set the stage for the home builders—all decisions that will have a pronounced effect on the future value of your house. The site superintendent is the person at the job site every day overseeing your house's construction, stud by stud and brick by brick. You want a superintendent who is knowledgeable and experienced about construction, and someone who can motivate his crews with just the right combination of mother-henning and drill-sergeant strictness.

In addition to lining up the players, you should also know how the building code fits in. The focus of the code is not achieving drama in design, or even a good design; it is the health and safety of the building crew and the eventual occupants—you and your family. The building code will dictate what a builder can or can't do at the micro-level—for example, the allowable distance between floor joists depending on the span and the floor load, or the required fire rating for building materials used for shared party walls between town houses. But the code says nothing about quality of materials and workmanship.

thesinglemostimportant decision:yourbuilder

Deciding who will build your house is your number one priority. A great design, superb location, or dramatic view won't compensate for structural defects or poor workmanship.

assuming the role of general contractor yourself

You might think that this single most important player should be you, that you should be your own general contractor and build the house yourself. This can save you 20 percent or more of the construction cost, so you can build a bigger house with a smaller budget.

Before you jump off this cliff, though, make sure you have the expertise and the stamina. Not only do you need a working knowledge of residential construction, you also need enormous patience, an incredibly high tolerance for stress, and oodles of time.

Coming up with a plan and exercising your flair for design is the fun part. Then you have to build it—the not-fun part. You will have a hard time getting tradesmen to bid your job (let alone get a decent price) because you are a one-shot deal and not likely to offer any further work. You may have to get five or more bids from each trade to get a realistic price for each part of the work. Multiply these half dozen bids by the thirty to forty trades required to build a typical house (imagine phone calls and faxes and meetings for each bid), and you begin to see how time-consuming this project will be. And once you finally nail down a total price for everything and get all the necessary permits, you have to schedule each trade and the delivery of its materials at the right times in the construction sequence. Whenever it rains, you will have to reschedule crews and deliveries and hope they will show up. When each trade has finished, you will have to assess the quality of each subcontractor and decide if their work is acceptable. As you get down to the last two months of building, there will be so many details crying for your attention that you will have to be at the site one or two hours every day that crews are there.

Life is short. Save your health and your marriage, and engage a builder. If you are still not persuaded, realize that you need a builder to get financing—lenders almost never finance a custom-built house unless a licensed, experienced builder is in charge (for more on this, see Chapter 4).

what type of builder?

There are three general categories: a custom builder, a production builder, or semi-custom builder.

A *custom builder* builds one-of-a kind houses, often one at a time. He's willing to build plain or fancy, using unusual materials and crafting unique details. He may provide the design, or you may hire an architect or buy an off-the-shelf, predrawn design from a home-plan design service. A custom builder's price covers only the construction costs; you buy the lot yourself, wherever you want to build. The plus side of working with a custom builder is that you can get exactly what you want. The minus side is that it costs a lot—on average, the *construction* costs are about twice those of a tract-built house, and the lot cost is on top of this (for more on this, see Chapter 6).

A *production builder,* as tract builders prefer to be called, does not offer the anything-you-want smorgasbord; he will build only the plans he offers. Though some will modify their basic house, most do not. The construction materials and finishes will be of his choosing, but you can pick the colors and patterns.

A production builder will not build anywhere; he buys a number of lots in one location from a land developer. Unlike a custom builder, a production builder sells both the house and the lot as a package. Most build one or two furnished models so that prospective buyers can get an idea of the quality and style being offered, but they won't turn over any dirt or start to build any houses until they have a signed sales contract in hand.

The other houses are then built in a production-line fashion, emphasizing speed and efficiency. A custom builder might build only three or four houses a year (and sometimes as many as forty-five or fifty), but a production builder may build anywhere from fifty to fifteen hundred houses a year. These houses may be detailed, but the details will be simple ones that can be easily and quickly executed. Purchasing the materials in bulk and building the same house over and over (so that all costs are known) enables a production builder to sell his houses for much less money than a custom builder, who builds the same house only once or twice and is only building a few houses at any one time, usually on scattered sites.

Most new houses are production-built because they are usually the most affordable. The world of production homes, however, has changed dramatically over the last fifty years. No more one-size-fits-all houses made of ticky-tacky. Production builders offer small, large, and in-between houses, with options that allow buyers to customize their houses to a remarkable degree. And most build in planned communities that offer amenities that can include nature trails, swimming pools, tennis courts, and occasionally golf courses. Furthermore, in major metropolitan markets, the larger production builders may build houses in as many as fifteen different locations.

A *semi-custom builder* is a hybrid of the other two. In most instances, he buys lots, just as a production builder, but sometimes you must buy the lot first. In either case, he will modify the plan extensively and offer a wider selection of finishes, light fixtures, cabinets, and appliances. If you want something that a semi-custom builder doesn't ordinarily offer, he may be willing to get it. This type of builder charges more than a production builder but less than a custom one.

how quickly do you need
a new house?

Time constraints may point you in one direction. Engaging an architect to design your house and a custom builder to build it can easily take a year or more. When the market is hot and demand is high for architects, builders, and tradesmen, the process can take as long as two years, especially if a design is elaborate. If you skip the architect and work with a custom builder who has his own plan, this process can be shorter, but you should still anticipate at least nine months to a year.

On the other hand, a house from a production builder who already has the design and building permits in hand and the subcontractors lined up usually takes about four months, once construction starts. When the market is hot, though, production builders also incur delays.

evaluating the market and builders

Whether or not you decide to buy a house from a production builder, visit a number of builders' furnished models in the area of the country where you are going to build. This will provide invaluable information as to what's acceptable in that market. McDonald's may look the same all over the country, but housing conventions are surprisingly varied. For example, houses in one area may have no basements, while those somewhere else all do. Building a house that doesn't meet local conventions will seriously compromise your resale possibilities.

How you look for a builder will depend on which type you want. With a production builder, much of your search will entail touring and evaluating furnished models. With a custom builder, you will have to look at finished houses and talk with former clients. In either case, the builder's experience is critical. How much is enough? At least three years and preferably five *as a home builder.* A skilled tradesman or a site superintendent will know a lot about the construction end of things, but the management skills are equally important and don't come overnight. Additionally, a builder must have a dependable network of subcontractors and material suppliers to deliver a house on time and on budget. Developing the dependable network usually takes about two years. This network is even more critical in boom times when builders everywhere face shortages of qualified tradesmen and building materials. The builders who keep workers on the job and supplies in the pipeline are the well-established ones, not the new guy on the block.

A national home-building firm may seem to be the most dependable. But a national firm starting up in a new market is in the same position as a small local builder just starting out, when it comes to suppliers and subcontractors. If they've been in business locally for less than two years, any size of firm may have difficulty getting materials and labor, and construction may be delayed. When entering a new market, a national firm also has to learn local building conventions. This takes time. In Florida, for example, humidity extremes, voracious termites, and hurricane wind forces create unique building conditions. A Chicago-based builder can't build his houses the same way when he sets up shop in Florida; he has to learn the local ropes first.

Besides local experience, the next litmus test should be reputation. The serious builder knows the value of a good reputation—future work largely depends on referrals from satisfied customers. Such a builder will stand proudly behind his work and his buyers, and his reputation will be easy to determine. (For more on builders, see Chapters 5 and 6.)

hireexpertise:theotherplayers

For many endeavors you may be inclined to wing it, go with the flow, act on a whim. That's okay when the stakes are low. But a new house has bankrupting potential, and you need all the expert advice you can get. Many new-home buyers do not seek advice in the mistaken belief that hiring an expert is expensive and unnecessary. In fact, the advice can cost far less than imagined and be invaluable.

For production-built houses, you should engage an attorney to review your sales contract, a landscape architect to help you choose a lot, an arborist to evaluate mature trees (if there are any on your lot), and a private home inspector to monitor construction. The costs for all this advice would be about what a builder would charge for the whirlpool tub that most people insist on but rarely use once the novelty has worn off. Engaging a fifth expert, a buyer's agent, will be costless, as the agent's commission will be paid by the builder.

In the case of a custom-built house, the attorney's fees to review your contract with the builder will be higher, but that much more important because you will be putting more money into the project.

If you are going to benefit from these experts, however, they must be engaged and give their input *before* you sign a sales contract. The only exception is a private home inspector, whose services must be noted on the sales contract, but he will not do any work until your house starts to go up.

the attorney

Why bring a lawyer into this? The purchase of a new house obligates you financially for years, if not decades. Getting a clear understanding of the sales contract is only prudent, especially given that almost all contracts are heavily weighted in favor of the writer, which in this case is the builder. An experienced real-estate attorney will help you understand the terms of your contract and evaluate whether it is reasonable or standard for the home-building industry in your area.

You should consult an attorney *before* signing the sales contract. If this means passing up a soon-to-expire "builder's special" (such as a finished basement or a kitchen upgrade included in the base price), you can sign a contract, but write in this crucial phrase: *"This contract is subject to review and approval by purchaser's attorney for [X number of] days. If the purchaser's attorney disapproves of the contract, it will be canceled. If the attorney approves the contract, it will be enforced."* (The number of days should be enough time for an adequate review: at least five business days.) Such a clause will enable you to get both the special deal and the attorney's review.

If you are working with a custom builder, with much more money at risk, you have an even stronger reason to ask an attorney to review the builder's contract. An architect's contract should be reviewed as well. Most architects use a standard form drafted by the American Institute of Architects, but it's a one-size-fits-all document that may require modification for your circumstances. (For more information on engaging an attorney, see Chapter 11; for more on sales contracts, see Chapters 13 and 14.)

the landscape architect

Even if your interest in the yard does not extend beyond keeping the grass mowed, you still need the services of a landscape architect to help you select a lot. A landscape architect is an expert in soils engineering, building design, and hydrology, not to mention plants. He or she can assess whether or not there is sufficient grading to carry rainwater away from the house. If the grading is insufficient, the water can seriously damage your foundation. In most new production-built communities, rainwater is not carried away from a house through a series of underground drains connected to the downspouts. The water is directed through a series of surface channels that collect in a drainage swale. The swale—basically a ditch—can be very shallow, so the untrained eye can easily miss it. But its location and the number of lots that drain into it can be critical. If the lot you are considering is a "collector"—that is, it has a drainage swale that collects rainwater from several adjacent properties—a sizable pond can appear with every cloudburst. In some jurisdictions, the drainage swale can be as close as ten feet to the house, which can seriously affect the feasibility of a deck or patio.

Trying to divine the drainage pattern when you buy a lot is often challenging, even to a professional. The top soil has been removed, and the builder may be in the process of "cutting and filling"—moving earth from one spot to another. Although the builder will have an engineered site plan that indicates what the final drainage arrangement is supposed to be, the actual lot conditions can be significantly different from the plan. A landscape architect can help you sort out any discrepancies.

If you do have landscaping ambitions, ask the landscape architect to evaluate your floor plan. Minor modifications to the house may enhance your enjoyment of your yard when you're looking at it from inside, may make your house feel bigger, and may facilitate the creation of "outdoor rooms." (For more on landscaping, see Chapter 10.)

the consulting arborist

If trees are an important reason for purchasing a lot, you need to have them examined by a consulting arborist—a tree specialist who deals with the long-term care, diseases, and insect-infestation problems of mature trees. Landscape architects certainly work with trees, but their work is more concerned with tree selection and planting than with tree care. Most builders try to be conscientious about saving trees, but few are knowledgeable about tree preservation on a job site. Trees that are damaged during construction usually die slowly—two to twelve years may pass before the damage is evident and the tree dies. By this time, no one makes the causal connection.

An experienced arborist will identify which trees are worth saving. Though most people instinctively want to save the biggest trees on a lot, the less impressive, midsized ones are more likely to survive construction intact. After an arborist has determined which trees to keep and how much of the surrounding ground must remain undisturbed during construction to protect them, the area left for building the house may be drastically reduced or oddly shaped. For this reason, an arborist should be called in *before* selecting or designing a floor plan. (For more on trees, see Chapter 10.)

the private home inspector

Municipal building inspectors look at code-related safety issues. But private home inspectors examine the workmanship and the quality of materials—matters of some importance in the construction of your new house. Though some private home inspectors specialize in new construction, you will be better served by those who regularly look at both old and new houses. They know firsthand how materials in your climate wear over time and which items on a new house can become future problems if not addressed during construction. An experienced private inspector also knows the codes, and he can pick up things that municipal inspectors may miss.

Most new-home buyers hire a home inspector after construction has been completed, but before the final papers are signed. To get the full benefit of an inspector's expertise, however, you should engage his services at three other critical points during construction. The first is after the footings and foundation walls have been poured and the drain tile has been installed and still exposed. The second is after the structural framing is up and the electrical wiring, plumbing and heating, and air-conditioning systems have been installed but everything is still exposed. The third is after the insulation has been installed but before the drywall goes up, which is especially critical if you are building in an area with severe winters. (For more on the private home inspector, see Chapter 11.)

the buyer's agent

If you are buying a house from a production builder, an experienced buyer's agent who specializes in new-home sales and new-home communities in your area can help you zero in on a price range, location, plan type, and community amenities. In areas of the country where there are as many as thirty-five new-home communities being built in a single market, the surfeit of choices can be daunting. Besides helping you find a house, a buyer's agent can also advise you on probable closing costs and get you started in obtaining financing.

How do developers, with so much at stake, choose builders? Reputation and previous experience are paramount, especially in areas of the country such as suburban Houston, where there is no residential building code and no municipal building inspectors to act as an outside check.

Alexandria, Virginia, developer John Cowles looks for candor. "You want a builder who will truthfully convey to purchasers the facts and truths about a community and not misrepresent it. You don't want buyers to come back and say 'I was told this and that.'" To en-

A developer also wants to be sure that the builder is a man of his word. "A developer is concerned that a builder will build what he says he will, X and not Y," said developer Michael T. Rose of Laurel, Maryland. Not only will building Y instead of X anger the purchasers who expected X, it will also devalue the other lots in the project that a developer is trying to sell.

sure that there are no misunderstandings in his developments, Cowles requires every builder to have purchasers sign a disclosure statement informing them that, for example, the project is across the street from a Metro station or the recreation facility will be built at the midpoint of the community, not when it opens.

Once you narrow the field and focus in on one or two builders, a buyer's agent will help you sort through what comes with the basic house and what items are upgrades, which options will enhance resale, and why you should avoid the truly unusual such as fuchsia bathroom fixtures. The buyer's agent will also walk you through the sales contract and help you negotiate the price. Keep in mind, however, that buyers' agents look for different things in a sales contract than real-estate attorneys; agents do not provide attorney's services.

If you want to be represented by a buyer's agent, you should note that nearly all production builders require that the agent accompany you to the model the *first time* that you visit. Some builders are more flexible and will still honor a buyer's agent and pay the agent a commission if the agent faxes ahead or communicates with the builder's sales agent within a short time of your visit. (For more on buyer's agents, see Chapter 11.)

thelanddeveloper

In a new-home community, all your business dealings will be with a home builder rather than the land developer, so it is easy to dismiss the developer's role. This would be a mistake. The developer's decisions affect the entire landscape, from what the exterior of every house will look like to the type and size of houses, the size and shape of the lots, the layout of the streets, the size and kind of trees planted, the number of tennis courts, the presence of amenities such as biking and jogging trails, and even (if the project is big enough) the mix in the local shopping center.

The amenities and the neighborhood character will have a pronounced effect on the future value of your purchase. Accordingly, researching the developer's track record and experience is as important as checking out a builder.

Although you may underestimate the developer's role, the developer is keenly aware of you and your preferences. All his decisions about where to purchase land and how to subdivide it are predicated on the type of houses he thinks buyers will want. Moreover, the developer has to predict housing trends at the time he purchases raw land, which can be five to ten years before he can sell lots. Though home builders are the ones most often asked to predict housing trends, the real visionaries of the future, by necessity, are developers.

In the years spent bringing a project to market, a developer is faced with many critical decisions, but the one most directly affecting you is his choice of builders. A bad choice here becomes a nightmare for everyone involved, and a developer's years of effort can go for naught. Bad builders anger buyers, give a project a bad name, and drive away future buyers. If a builder does not perform, the developer cannot just summarily boot him out because he has already sold him lots. In this unhappy situation, the developer's only recourse is to refuse to sell the builder any future lots, while prodding him to bring the houses already under construction up to par.

checkingout**a**developer

There are a number of tactics to help you make a wise choice:

♦ First, visit the site. If the project has been up and running for several years, the quality and character of the completed neighborhoods will be evident. But you still need to ask the residents if the developer delivered on the amenities as promised in the sales pitch.

♦ Ask the residents about the level and quality of services provided through the Home Owner's Association (HOA), which the developer organized. Depending on where you are looking, the HOA may have greater or lesser responsibilities. In some places, HOA responsibilities are limited to enforcing deed restrictions, arranging for garbage pickup and snow removal, and maintenance and operation of the recreational facilities and neighborhood parks. But in others, such as unincorporated areas of Texas, the HOA may also be providing full-time firemen, emergency response, police, and street lighting.

- If the project is just starting and you see piles of dirt everywhere, that's already a sign that the developer is not well organized. There will always be dirt somewhere, but it should be piled in areas where buyers will not encounter it.

- Check on the developer's track record. How many years has he been in business? Some developers are very experienced as home *builders*, but success as a *developer* requires different skills. Visit some of the developer's completed projects and talk with buyers there. Ask elected officials how they view the developer.

- Talk with the developer's banker. If you check with the major lenders in the area, you'll soon learn the developer's reputation in the financial community. This is important because if the developer flounders and another firm takes over the project, the character may change substantially.

- Ask the developer how he tracks his builders and gets buyer feedback. For example, does the developer have field inspectors who monitor construction progress? If so, how often do they visit job sites? Does the developer periodically contact buyers to see how their experience is going? If a developer does not do either of these things, a builder can underperform, and unsuspecting buyers will continue to buy houses from him.

- Finally, you want a developer who will stand behind you in a crisis, as did developer Mark Montgomery of Rockville, Maryland, when one of his builders declared bankruptcy with ten houses under construction and buyers out $50,000 to $150,000. Promising premium lots at his golf-course community to another builder if he would finish the houses at cost, Montgomery got the houses completed and the buyers lost nothing.

the**site**superintendent

You engage a builder to build your house, but the key person who will make or break your new home is the site superintendent. He's the one who oversees the construction of each house and ensures its quality. As a retired Virginia builder succinctly put it, "A site superintendent can make a hero or a bum out of you."

The site superintendent is characterized by home builders, private home inspectors, and other site superintendents themselves as "the builder's quarterback," "an air traffic controller for builders," "an orchestra director," "a mother hen," and "a skillful diplomat." But exactly what does the superintendent do that makes his performance so central?

If you still think you can be your own general contractor, realize that even a building professional found it much harder than he ever imagined. Two years ago, Rockville, Maryland, architect Richard Donnally

had reached a point in his career where he was ready to live out his dream—designing and building his own house. As a principal in his own firm, he had the freedom to rearrange his work schedule. After twenty-five years of involvement in the building industry, he persuaded his bank that he had sufficient expertise to manage the project. And by acting as his own contractor, he could lower the cost of his custom-built house by about 20 percent and still include all the features and finishes he wanted for his forty-five-hundred-square-foot house.

Designing the house was "exhilarating and challenging." But once Donnally started trying to get it built, he learned the real reason that most people do not do this, and why banks discourage it. "Building a house is much harder than it looks. It's not rocket science, but to do it well requires an incredibly high tolerance for stress because there will be problems every step of the way."

Just getting to first base with a final cost figure was hard, Donnally found. "When I started, I had a good idea of the going rates for labor and materials. I thought I could just get three bids from each type of subcontractor and pick the most realistic one, but I had to get ten to fifteen bids to get one that was reasonable. To get a reasonable price and an honest profit margin for the concrete work— foundation, basement slab, sidewalks, and patio—I had to get twenty bids."

Not only was it hard to get a reasonable price, it was hard to get *any* price. "I would give a sub specs and drawings and then the guy would never call back. The truth is, though your project is everything to *you*, you are a small deal to suppliers and tradespeople. They give preference to the guy building a lot of houses, because he can give them steady work.

"The thing that really drives you crazy in getting bids is that there are more than thirty tradesmen on your job. The granite-countertop guy, the cultured-marble countertop guy, the gutter guy, the roof guy—each one only does that one specific job. You don't realize before you start the number of people you must get bids from."

As Donnally's house went up, he learned another critical fact about bidding. "When you ask for a bid, you can't assume that your bidder will include everything that is required but not specified. For example, I assumed that the guys who hang the interior doors would include the hardware [door handles and latch plates] in their price. They didn't. I had to go out and get these and pay an extra labor charge to get them included. An experienced general contractor would have said, 'When bidding interior doors, include hardware.'

"Some of the confusion about what was included and what wasn't was caused by the lack of detail in my own drawings. In the commercial work that I usually design, everything is detailed and specified, down to the length, finish, and spacing of each screw. We have at least fifty sheets of details and a very thick book of specifications. If you hired an architect to design a house with fifty sheets of details, the fee could be as much as a hundred thousand dollars. You won't get that level of detail in residential projects, so there are a lot of openings for mistakes and use of inferior materials."

When Donnally finally assembled all the bids and started to build his house, the work proceeded in fits and starts. "The subs would meet my price but not show up. Or they would show up for a few days and disappear to do other jobs. I discovered that a mark of a really good sub is not just the quality of his work. He is also really organized and doesn't commit to more than he can handle.

"When one sub didn't show up, I had to cancel and reschedule the others who were to come next. They would go to other jobs and it was hard to get them rescheduled back to me."

One solution to the no-shows was getting the subs who did reliably show up to take on more work. "This was a mistake. I learned the hard way that when a sub is recommended for one thing, don't ask him to do something he doesn't do 100 percent of the time. My framing carpenter said he could do finish carpentry, but he was lousy."

All the no-shows and rescheduling strung the job out months longer than Donnally had anticipated. "My original estimate for building my house was eight months. Then I thought ten months was more realistic, but twelve months was what it took."

Quality control was another issue for this rookie builder. "Some mistakes were easy to spot—my wife, for example, picked up that the sink base was not centered with the window above it. But the average person couldn't tell if you have a proper footing or enough nails in the framing. You can't depend on a municipal building inspector to make sure that these are done correctly. Some are more careful than others, but they

spend only a few minutes at the job site. For the framing and foundations work—critical for the structural integrity of your house—I did a lot of checking and I got a lot of references."

Staying on top of everything was "unbelievably time consuming," Donnally discovered. "At the beginning, I was at the job site only once a week, then twice a week, but the last month, when we were racing to finish, I was there every day for two to four hours. It was a good thing I am a partner in my firm, or I would have been fired. I managed to move my work around and I worked a lot of late nights."

Developing the right management style was another challenge, Donnally found. "You can be tough and mean and get the work done. But if you're too mean, the subs will walk off. A colleague came to look at the job and spoke sharply to one person and he didn't come back for three days. You have to have a sense of humor and be encouraging. You have to be stern. Subs can be like teenagers and never clean up after themselves. I had to get a cleaning service in halfway through construction because there was so much trash and sawdust and debris.

"In short, to run such a project well, you have to be a mix of a drill sergeant and a mother hen. And you have to tolerate stress well. Problems will occur and you must know how to fix them. As a friend said, 'Construction is knowing how to fix a mistake and make it look good.'"

After he finished and moved into his new house, would he do it again? "By doing it this way I saved about a hundred thousand dollars and got the house I wanted. But if I'd had a hundred thousand more, I would have hired a general contractor in a second."

First, he schedules the thirty to forty different trades subcontracted by the home-building firm, and he oversees their work. He orders materials, schedules their delivery, and frequently confers with the on-site sales agent and the purchasers. Before the construction begins, he schedules all the trades in proper sequence over the 90 to 120 days required to build a production-built house, or over a longer period if it is a custom-built house. Work delays—most often caused by the weather but occasionally by a tradesman who did not complete his work, did it incorrectly, or didn't have enough material to complete the job—mean frequent rescheduling. Not only must the site superintendent then reschedule the next two or three trades, he must also tell those due to come two to four weeks later.

And just to make things more complicated, a site superintendent may be responsible for anywhere from three to twelve houses at any given moment, all at different stages of construction. If bad weather forces him to suspend operations, he may have to contact a different set of subcontractors for each house.

Although a site superintendent does not need to have an encyclopedic knowledge of every trade—though many do have this—he must know enough to ensure that the work is acceptable and 100 percent complete, not the 96 percent that many tradesmen are inclined to deliver.

Most crews of tradesmen are not salaried workers; they are hired by a subcontracting firm that pays them by the job. Since this often creates an attitude of "I'll do this well enough to get paid" rather than "I'll do the best I can," the site superintendent has to clarify for each incoming crew what "well enough" means and then check that his instructions are followed. This can be both time-consuming and occasionally exasperating, so a site superintendent will try to get a crew that he has worked with on previous jobs; but with constant rescheduling, this is not always possible. The site superintendent does not usually have the authority to hire and fire crews, but a complaint to his front office generally means that a crew, individual, or firm won't be hired again.

Ordering materials is another important part of the site superintendent's job. He must have the proper materials at the site for each incoming trade, but he can't order anything too far in advance because theft can be a real problem in new developments without residents to observe a site after everyone has left for the day.

How much experience does a site superintendent need before he can handle all this? That depends on the project. With a production-built subdivision, the houses generally have fewer details, and the firm has already built the same house many times. All the glitches in the design will have been worked out. In this situation, the site superintendent does not need years of experience, but he still must have a tenacious personality. If he knows something is wrong, he has to insist that it be done correctly, and he has to have enough gumption to say "No way you can do this on my job." And if a subdivision has houses with many customized details—not uncommon in the higher price ranges—more experience is required. A general rule of thumb in the industry is that after five years, a site superintendent should be able to build anything.

If the project has many houses going up at the same time or if each house is large and complicated, many production builders have both a front-end and a back-end superintendent. The front man takes the house from the initial excavation and foundation work to the installation of the drywall. The back man, usually a more junior person, supervises the dry wall through the painting and all the finish work. Though the first man's job is tougher from a technical standpoint, the second man's work is what the buyer notices, and in that sense more critical.

How does one person, or two if there is a front as well as a back man, stay on top of things? Organization and stamina. In the course of a typical ten- to eleven-hour workday, which normally begins at six or six-thirty in the morning, a site superintendent makes about forty phone calls, spends two hours on routine paperwork, and deals with twenty-five to as many as eighty people as he checks each house at least twice.

As a prospective home buyer, how can you tell if a project has a good site superintendent?

- Cleanliness: Does the site look orderly or is trash strewn about? If the site superintendent is not making each crew clean up when their work is complete—as all contracts stipulate—it's a sure sign that he's not in control of the job.

- Does there appear to be activity going on every day? There may be legitimate periods of inactivity for two to three days and sometimes as long as a week. But if nothing happens for ten days, the job is very likely being mismanaged.

- Meet the superintendent *before* you sign the sales contract. Many building firms set up a formal meeting with both the sales agent and the site superintendent before the job starts and periodically during construction. Asking to meet the superintendent before you sign on is unusual, but a builder should be able to accommodate this.

whenabuilder**says**his**product** "meets the code"

When a builder tells you that his product "meets the code," he is telling you that his houses meet a safety standard, not a quality one. A building code will say *nothing* about the quality of construction materials or workmanship or the useful allocation of space.

- What does he think of you hiring a private home inspector to make periodic inspections? A good site superintendent will be confident and open-minded. As the house goes up, he's likely to say to your inspector, "Just make a list and leave it for me," knowing that he can handle whatever comes up. A less confident and experienced site superintendent may be less sanguine.

- For a production-built project, how often does he talk with the sales agent? The sales agent works with the buyers, but the site superintendent builds the house. If the two don't talk frequently, changes that you want may not get incorporated into the house when they could be done at minimal cost and with minimal disruption.

- Has the site superintendent run other projects for this firm? If so, where? Go there and ask the residents about their experiences with both the firm and the superintendent. If any of the houses are occupied in the location where you want to buy, talk with these residents also. Be sure to ask how promptly the superintendent responded to their queries and concerns—it should be within a day.

queries
for the site
superintendent

- How many houses is the site superintendent supervising? The larger and more elaborate the house, the fewer he can supervise effectively. If you want a large, custom-built, four-thousand-square-foot, million-dollar house with elaborate everything, a site superintendent can't look after more than two or three and do a good job. Even a smaller, less expensive custom-built house will have many details and unique features, so looking after more than three is still pushing it.

- If you're looking at a twenty-five-hundred-square-foot, half-million-dollar semi-custom built house with less elaborate details and finishes, the site superintendent could likely look after as many as ten to twelve at a time if the houses are all at the same site. If the lots are scattered, trying to supervise any more than eight would be difficult.

- If you're considering a production-built house, the lots will all be in one location and there will be far less detailing. An experienced site superintendent can comfortably look after twelve houses; with fifteen he'll be stretched, especially if there are labor shortages (when this happens, many crews will be inexperienced and require much closer supervision).

The code is a health- and safety-driven document, and its primary focus is the welfare of the people constructing and those eventually occupying a structure.

Moreover, depending on where you purchase your house, you may not have any code protection. In Alabama, Arizona, Colorado, Delaware, Hawaii, Idaho, Illinois, Iowa, Kansas, Maine, Mississippi, Missouri, Nebraska, Oklahoma, South Dakota, Texas, and Vermont, the state does not require a residential building code. A local jurisdiction may or may not adopt one. In the other states, some rural counties may not have a building department or inspectors. In all these cases, a home buyer's only recourse is to hire a private home inspector to make periodic inspections during construction.

the residential inspection

The particulars of the residential-inspection process differ across the country, but the process is essentially the same. In the course of constructing a typical single-family or town house, there can be anywhere from five to fourteen inspection visits by a municipal building inspector if everything is installed correctly, more if the inspector has to come back to recheck.

During a building boom, a single inspector can check as many as thirty houses at seven different sites in a single day. Since a municipal building inspector typically spends only five minutes at each visit, he can only certify that the structure is in compliance with the code "to the best of his knowledge." There is always the possibility that something critical is missed.

The jurisdiction that issues the occupancy permit has the responsibility to force a builder to fix any code problems that come to light within a fixed period after completion, usually one year. In many states, a building department has an additional twelve months to monitor the project and ensure that the problem is fixed.

A reputable builder will correct any errors immediately. If he drags his feet, many jurisdictions can take him to court, and some have additional "incentives" to elicit prompt compliance—for example, fines that can start at five hundred dollars a day.

Though only five to fourteen inspections, each only a few minutes' duration, may seem barely adequate, the system generally works well. A reputable home builder knows that in addition to the legalities, a code-compliant house is good business—a huge number of sales come by referral.

The code addresses a finite range of issues, and most of a residential building department's dealings are with the building permit holders—that is, the home builders. But all building departments receive complaints from home buyers who mistakenly believe that their builder has wronged them in a way that the department should remedy. A classic buyer freak-out: cracks in the basement slab caused by normal settlement and shrinkage as the concrete cures. This is not under the purview of the building department. Nor is *this* misunderstanding: Some years ago a woman called a Maryland building department to complain that her builder wasn't mowing her lawn.

Building inspectors also get complaints that may be legitimate, but they are powerless to do anything because the problem is a quality issue, not a code one. A common such complaint is rattling dishes—every time the new-home owner walks across the floor, the dishes in the cabinets rattle. The new homeowners explain that this problem did not exist in their previous house, which was built forty years ago when lumber was much less costly and home builders routinely oversized the structural framing members. The floors didn't bounce and the dishes didn't rattle because the builder put in more and larger floor joists than were structurally required. With today's volatile lumber prices, however, most builders construct a floor with less wood than they used forty years ago. The floors are closely engineered for actual floor loads, and the focus is on building a floor that meets structural requirements, not aesthetic ones. The result: the floors are as strong or stronger than those in older houses, but the builder may use the smallest allowable floor-joist sizes and place them as far apart as possible. As a result, even a dog weighing 50 pounds walking across the room can cause the dishes in the cabinet to rattle.

When home builders shop the competition, what do they look for? Telltale signs of quality in the model and at the job site, and glitz that will inveigle a buyer to look further and make a return visit. While some of these telltale signs are only evident to a professional, there are a number that any home buyer could check.

tips**from**the**trade:** how do home builders judge each other?

For most builders, the note-taking starts as they head down the street toward the model or a custom builder's show home. Of course, the house has to look good. But Fairfax, Virginia, builder Bill Barber's first question is this: "How is the house sited? I never like a house below the street—I don't want water in it."

Pulling up in front, the analysis begins in earnest. Newark, Ohio, builder Vince Ghiloni looks for the small but telling details that indicate how much care a builder takes. "I look at the size of the light fixtures by the front door and garage. Larger ones look much better and they don't cost much more than little tiny ones. I check the downspouts. Is there a plastic splash block or did the builder go to the extra effort and expense and put in drains to carry rainwater away from the house?"

Once in the house, most builders start with the glitz and the gimmicks, because when these are well done, they definitely help with sales. As Mendocino, California, builder

Frank Fanto observed, "It's the sizzle that sells the steak, not what you're chewing on."

Inside the house, Ghiloni looks at the big picture: Does the floor plan work? Is there good traffic flow? He also examines the details: Is there large trim around doors, windows, and wall bases? "A larger four-inch trim around a door just looks better than a two-and-a-half-inch trim piece, and the cost is only five or six dollars a door. I feel the trim surface to see if it's smooth or full of flecks and painted in a hurry. Stair-railing spindles are 1⅜-inch or 1¾-inch. The cost difference is small, but the extra ⅜-inch gives the railing much more strength."

Drywall is hard to get completely perfect, and buyers will have to live with a certain amount of imperfection, Barber says. But the ceiling shouldn't have any sags, and large wall expanses that are flooded with sunlight should be done with extra care so that waves and bumps don't show.

Fanto, a custom builder himself, pointed out that production houses may not have the level of detail and workmanship found in a custom house, but the basics should work. The models always look good, but a nearly completed house—not the model—is usually a better indicator of the standards. "Try everything," he advises, "especially the things you wouldn't notice until you moved in—all the faucets, outlets, appliances including running the dishwasher through an entire cycle. Operate all the windows. Shut all the doors—if the latches aren't lined up properly, they won't stay closed."

But, as Fanto notes, "The quality of finish work in a house, however, is just the icing on the cake. It doesn't say much about its struc-tural integrity." For assessing those nuts and bolts, a look at the job site speaks volumes. Builder Randy Rinehart of Charlottesville, Virginia, advises, "Not only do the conditions at a job site indicate how conscientious the builder is about customer and employee safety, it also shows how good a manager he is, and, in turn, how well the house is being built. For example, are food wrappers, wood scraps, and pieces of drywall and electrician's wire lying around the house or yard? Or is there a Dumpster and a clean job site so that the next trade to come on the job can do its job quickly and efficiently? Are the construction materials protected and stored properly? If it's an all-brick front, are windows protected so that the glass won't get scratched with mortar?"

Another telling detail at a job site is a builder's sign. "If there's no sign, I always ask, does this person want to stay in business? And more immediately, without a sign, how can a guy deliver materials to the job site?" Ghiloni said.

Focusing in on the house itself, Columbia, Maryland, builder Allan Washak mentioned one quick test that can be a good quality indicator. Engineered floor joists (the framing members that hold up the floors) that are partially made of oriented strand board (it looks like particleboard with big chunks) may look cheap, but they're actually much better and more expensive than a sawn piece of lumber that comes straight from the tree. Dimensional lumber, as this is called, is full of sap and cracks. It will shrink the first year the house is occupied, causing the floor to move slightly. Doors can become hard to open and nail pops and cracks will appear in the drywall.

Windows are another quality indicator. Many buyers think a wood window is the gold standard, but Ghiloni said the real test is how energy efficient and maintenance-free it is. An argon-filled window with low-emissivity (low-e) glass is more energy efficient, and the low-e glass helps to keep carpets and furniture from fading. A wood window that has an exterior cladding of vinyl or aluminum will never need painting, but "an unclad one must be painted every three to five years, a maintenance headache for the next one hundred years." Many of the telling framing details, however, are hard to assess. Fanto suggested hiring someone who is educated, such as a general contractor, to look for you.

And while you can tell a lot by looking at a builder's work, Barber concludes that the final test should be how you feel when you meet him face to face. "You must meet and like the builder—you will be married to him for one and a half years."

how much will it cost?

In 1950 the average new house in the United States cost eleven thousand dollars and had a thousand square feet. Today the average new house is more than twice as big with twenty-two hundred square feet and, at two hundred thousand dollars, costs about eighteen times as much.

Since the price of everything has gone up exponentially over the last fifty years, the huge price increase for houses is part of a larger picture. But compared to all the other purchases that you will make in your lifetime, a house is by far the largest. Yet you still end up asking yourself: Why do houses cost so much?

The single largest expense for any house is the land it sits on. So where you decide to build your house will have the single biggest impact on its price. Of course, the size and shape of your house will also affect its cost. A simple box with a single-pitch roof is the cheapest and most energy efficient house you can build, but most people think it's boring. And with all the rooms that people want to put in houses today—three or four bedrooms, a family room, a home office, formal living and dining areas, a two-car garage, and even a home theater—the simple but efficient box would be enormous and look like a beached whale. The more you depart from the basic box shape, though, the more it will cost you. An L-shaped house with a family-room wing out the back and a formal living/dining wing to one side of the entry foyer will have attractive interior spaces with windows on three sides. But all those extra walls, foundations, roof area, and windows will quickly drive up the cost. Even a more modest extension from the basic box such as a second garage bay will make a house cost more. The sprawling L-shaped plan would also need a big lot, which will add to its cost.

With a production-built house, the builder picks the lot size, house size, house shape, all the materials and finishes, and names his price. As a buyer, you have no control over these choices. But you naturally ask: Is this product a good value? Most buyers apply a cost-per-square-foot test, but this is not the value benchmark that is generally assumed, and using it to compare builders is not as informative as you might think. No two builders work in exactly the same way or use the same materials. Two houses side by side that are built by two different builders may look the same, even to the point of having almost identical floor plans. But take a closer look. Builder A has hardwood flooring everywhere and Builder B offers it only in the foyer. Builder B's house will cost less and have a lower cost per square foot. Which house is the better value? There's no one right answer here—you will have to decide for yourself.

With a custom-built house, you pick everything, so you have control over costs, and even how you get a price. If you are working with an architect, the traditional way to get a price is to invite several builders to competitively bid on a set of contract documents—written specifications and drawings. The idea here is that as a consumer you are better served by competition. In fact, though, you may be better served by engaging a builder when you engage the architect. As the architect designs the project, the builder, who know prices to the dollar because he's in the marketplace every day, monitors costs. This avoids the enormous effort of designing a project, sending it out for bids, and then getting prices that are over your budget, leaving you either to redesign and scale back or to scrap the project altogether.

When a custom-built house does come in over budget, many owners decide to purchase some of the materials themselves to save the builder's markup and avoid redesigning anything. This may sound like a sound strategy that avoids painful choices. But it can easily backfire, not save the money you expect, and lose the builder's goodwill.

The hard truth is that as you go through the process of getting a price for a custom-built house, you will constantly bump up against the three constraints that affect all jobs—budget, quality, and quantity. You can have any two of these, but not all three. If you want a four-thousand-square-foot house and Brazilian cherry hardwood floors throughout, the budget must be very large. If you still want the cherry hardwood floors but can spend only a hundred thousand dollars, be prepared for a very small house. If you want a large house, but your budget is fixed at a hundred thousand, you will have to settle for builder-grade carpet and a base-grade sheet-vinyl flooring for the kitchen and bathrooms. As the production builder makes his choices, he faces these same constraints and goes through the same budget-quality-quantity trade-off.

Where does the money go? Although the finishes and fixtures that warm your heart can make a house more expensive, the far less sexy "sticks and bricks" form the bulk of construction costs. And, as noted above, the single most expensive item is not the house at all but the land, which averages about one quarter of the average sale price, according to the National Association of Home Builders (NAHB). In many markets, though, the land cost is typically closer to a third of the total sale price.

How about the other two-thirds to three-quarters of the total sale price? Here's how the NAHB breaks down the costs:

- The most expensive item in the house itself is the structural framing and sheathing—about 20 percent of the total sale price. How rooms and the overall building envelope are sized, however, can make some difference here. Production builders, who have honed building efficiencies with scientific precision, minimize waste by having overall building dimensions and room sizes conform as closely as possible to standard sizes for framing lumber, plywood, drywall, and other building goods.

- In areas where basements are common: excavation, foundations, and backfill costs account for about 9.6 percent of the total sale price.

- Windows, on average, account for 4 to 6 percent of the total. Since substituting cheaper windows will not force clients to otherwise modify a design, builders say they are an inviting target when budget overruns occur.

- Plumbing fixtures make up 5 to 6 percent. These are also manufactured in standard sizes, and a seemingly innocuous change can quadruple the cost. A standard five-foot bathtub might be two hundred dollars, but a nonstandard, five-foot, six-inch tub with the same finish and color could be eight hundred dollars.

- Drywall is 5 to 6 percent. Most buyers give short shrift to this essential, but nationwide, drywall shortages have both driven up its cost and delayed construction.

- The heating and air-conditioning system, another essential that rarely captivates buyers, accounts for 4 percent.

- The electrical work, another 3.8 percent.

- Kitchen cabinets and flooring, the two items that most buyers spend the most time agonizing over, account for only about 5 percent of the total. This flooring figure, however, assumes a mix of carpet, hardwood, and ceramic tile or sheet vinyl in the bathrooms and kitchen. Eliminating carpet altogether and installing hardwood everywhere would, of course, increase the proportion of the budget for flooring.

- The other line items such as gutters, light fixtures, basement slab, and an asphalt driveway fall into "the little things that quickly add up" category.

thecost-per-square-footmyth

You want the best value for your money. If you're like most buyers, you will typically assess this by comparing builders on a simple cost-per-square-foot basis. Unfortunately, this figure doesn't tell the whole story. If it's low, you're not necessarily getting more for your money. If it's high, you're not necessarily getting gouged. But it's understandable that you would make these inferences. In our current Era of the Major Discount, every shopper routinely encounters a wide range of prices for the exact same item.

The home-building arena, however, requires a different mindset. No two builders work alike, create identical products, or even use the same materials. To make a fair and accurate comparison of Builder A to Builder B, you have to look beyond their prices and cost-per-square-foot figures to the product. It also helps to have a grasp of the many variables that affect a builder's cost.

building shape, style, and size

Design can affect cost dramatically. As noted earlier, the cheapest house is a box. But most buyers, especially those who seek out a custom builder, want character and style. All those corners on the exterior and a multi-gabled roofline, however, will cost you. If a builder usually offers a two-story house with thirteen or fourteen corners and you want to add ten to fifteen more, the cost can easily go up by 30 percent. More complex designs with as many as sixty corners will raise it even more.

The style can also affect its cost. A simple, spare look is always more expensive than a traditional colonial look or a Spanish mission style because any flaw will show and the workmanship must be more exacting. Even simple light fixtures cost more than gaudy ones.

Custom builder Randy Rinehart of Charlottesville, Virginia, said his clients frequently want dramatic two-story spaces to add flair. But they seldom realize that these drive up the cost, especially evaluated by the square foot. "For what you pay to get the volume and the look, you might as well put a floor in there and get usable space on the second floor. The cost is almost the same."

Even when the square-foot figures are the same, some plan configurations cost more than others. While you may know that a one-story house costs more per square foot than a two-story house with the same floor area (because the one-story has a larger foundation and roof area), you may not appreciate more subtle distinctions that affect cost. For example, moving the master suite down to the first floor will raise the cost, unless you eliminate other first-floor functions such as a formal living and dining room, because your builder will end up having to add a master suite wing on the back. This will increase the cost for the foundation, exterior walls, and roof.

Adding or subtracting floor area will affect the price, but not as much as you might think because many of the fixed costs—heating and cooling, plumbing, electric wiring, appliances, and a garage structure with a paved driveway—must be factored in no matter what size the house is.

Finally, materials also affect cost. There is a choice and price range for nearly everything—the only constraints are taste and budget. Do you want hardwood everywhere? Only in the foyer?

analyzing the cost-per-square-foot figures

The cost-per-square-foot figures can give some useful information if you interpret them carefully. After you've calculated the cost-per-square-foot figure for two production builders with seemingly identical houses side by side, try to figure out what accounts for the difference.

For example, if Builder A's standard kitchen cabinets are white with vinyl-wrapped raised-panel doors, and Builder B has oak cabinets with flat-panel doors, Builder A's costs are higher. If Builder A offers a bigger master bathroom or a soaking tub as standard, his cost will be higher. Builder A's costs may also be higher in less obvious ways: He may use a 90 percent–efficient gas furnace instead of a 78 percent–efficient one. Or he may

When a project comes in over budget, custom builder Vince Ghiloni of Newark, Ohio, says that clients often try to shave a few feet off the end of the house, believing that this will save enough money to keep the rest of the design intact. This rarely lowers the cost as much as his clients expect because only raw square footage is being eliminated. For example: The plan was a two-story, 3,000-square-foot house that priced out at $105 a square foot; shortening by 2 feet, and hence eliminating 160 square feet of space, will not reduce the total project cost

tactics to reduce the cost

proportionally at $105 × 160 square feet, or $16,800. The cost reduction would be closer to $5,000. If the clients were willing to nix a full bathroom with a tub/shower, sink, and toilet, which is much smaller in floor area (only about 60 square feet), they would lower the cost of the project by nearly the same amount, about $5,400.

Conversely, Ghiloni also pointed out, extending this same 3,000-square-foot house by 2 feet (and hence adding 160 square feet of space) would add only about $5,000 to the cost, not a proportional $16,800.

use cast-iron waste pipes instead of plastic ones, so that when a toilet is flushed it won't be heard all over the house. Or he may include a better grade of windows. Builder A's house will cost more per square foot, and you may decide that it's the better value.

When comparing custom builders, you won't have two production-built houses side by side that you can compare. But it is helpful if you have a plan that you can show each builder and then ask what it would cost to build. If you don't have any plan as a basis for discussion, the builder will try to elicit what you want in the way of style, room count, finishes, and amenities. Without knowing what your budget is, however, the builder has no way of knowing whether or not what he is suggesting is realistic for you. Unfortunately, many buyers fear that if they tell the builder what they can afford, he will overcharge, so they don't give a straight answer. Their hesitation is understandable. But many exasperated builders point out that if clients are not forthright and forthcoming with a budget, much time is wasted designing and pricing a project the clients ultimately can't afford.

"What is the sense of pricing out a house at half a million dollars if you only have three hundred thousand?" asks Vince Ghiloni, the custom-home builder in Newark, Ohio. "Everyone has a fudge factor. If you have a maximum of three-ten to spend and say three, this is certainly close enough."

Another problem with the money discussions is that most people don't know what things cost, so they don't know what quality a given cost-per-square-foot gives them. How does a house costing a hundred dollars per square foot differ from one costing two hundred per square foot?

The ANSI Z765–1966 standard applies only to single-family dwellings—detached, free-standing houses or attached town houses. It does not apply to multi-family structures such as condominium complexes or apartments. The standard is also limited to over-all dimensions; it does not cover interior dimensions or rooms that are typically measured from interior wall to interior wall. But it does give figures that you can use to compare Builder A and Builder B. The major distinctions among space are "finished" or "unfinished," and "above grade" or "below grade":

- A "finished" area is defined as "an enclosed area that is suitable for year-round use." The finished-area calculation also includes all walls, both interior and exterior. "Unfinished" areas most commonly include garages and unfinished basements.

- "Above grade" includes all floor levels that are entirely above the ground. "Below grade" includes all floor levels that are partially or entirely below the ground. When a house is built into a hillside, the entire structure will receive the "below grade" designation.

The area is measured at the floor level, so that two-story spaces such as entry foyers and family rooms can only be included in the calculation once. Some of the standard will strike you as nitpicky—for example, a fireplace and chimney can be included only when the hearth is at floor level. But seemingly minor differences of twenty-five to fifty square feet here and there can add up to a substantial amount. (See Resources for information on getting the ANSI standards.)

To help buyers correlate size, design, finish quality, and cost, most custom-home builders show them finished houses to clarify what is realistically attainable with their budget. When the "realistically attainable" is a plain-Jane house, however, staying within a budget during the planning process is often a constant struggle, because few clients can resist the temptation to start dressing things up.

howmany**square**feet?

Before you start comparing Builder A's house to Builder B's on a cost-per-square-foot basis, ask how the square footage was calculated. Unbeknownst to most new-home buyers, the home-building industry adopted a standard method for calculating square feet only in 1996, and it is not yet in universal use. The conventions for calculating square-foot figures still vary regionally, and even within the same market by various builders. Some builders include only what you can walk on, excluding regular-sized closets but counting walk-ins. Others count two-story spaces twice because the entire volume is finished space that must be heated and cooled.

Even when builders in the same market are consistent in their measurements, their notions of square feet and buyers' notions are likely to differ. Most buyers think this means "useable space." But most builders calculate it in terms of the total area occupied by the building, and this can be substantially different. For example, using the builder's approach, 150 to 200 square feet of a two-story house billed as "2,200 square feet" can be solid wall.

To further complicate matters, Realtors and appraisers have used methods for calculating square feet that differ from the builders'. To bring some order to this picture, the National Association of Home Builders Research Center in Upper Marlboro, Maryland, organized a committee and developed the square-foot measurement standard. The committee, which included builders, architects, lenders, appraisers, estimators, Realtors, and building-code and other government officials, produced a written standard, "Square Footage—Method for Calculating," which was approved by the American National Standards Institute as ANSI Z765–1966.

The American National Standards Institute (ANSI) acts as both a referee for any organization that wants to form such a standard and as a repository for such standards. ANSI standards cover everything from how to measure square feet in houses to silver levels on photographic film.

Ask if the builders you're considering use the ANSI standard, and, if not, what method they do use. Then be prepared to wait several days for an answer, as the question will very likely have to be passed back to the firm's construction personnel.

the**bid**

When you commission an architect to design a custom-built house for you, how will you arrive at a price? Traditionally, the architect prepares a set of construction documents—drawings and written specifications—and invites builders to bid on the job; this is called a competitive bid. The theory here is that competition among builders for your job will give you the best price. In fact, by the time construction is completed, the cost to build your house may be much higher than the bid price.

Knowing that prices often rise, during construction, many experienced custom-home builders refuse to competitively bid. They know that if they give a realistic price, they won't be the lowest bidder. What homeowners rarely appreciate, however, is that the builder who doesn't "low bid" to get the job is acting in the homeowner's interests as well as the builder's:

◆ The builder needs to make a decent profit to stay in business and finish your job. Every homeowner's worst nightmare is the contractor who bids low to get the job and then walks off halfway through because he didn't have the money to finish it. At that stage, it's nearly impossible to find someone who will step in and finish; the final price is always a lot higher than the one the homeowner assumed at the outset.

- The more adventurous and unusual the architect's design, the more it becomes a never-before-built prototype, and the more likely that unknowns will crop up. The builder who puts in enough slack to cover those unforeseen but inevitable costs will not likely be the low bidder.

- The architect's carefully prepared construction documents—highly detailed drawings and specifications—that form the basis of competitive bidding can have omissions, which the bidding contractors know will eventually have to be added. If a builder bids low to get the job, he can make up his margin in what's called change orders. The contractor is supposed to confer with the architect when he spots an omission during the bidding period, but this doesn't always happen. A change order for an item that was not in the original contract means an additional cost for the homeowners. On the other hand, the conscientious bidder who adds in the omitted items will often lose out to the low bidder. Said one Washington, D.C., builder, "Many times I look at plans to bid and know things are left out. If I'm thorough at bid time, I will lose the job because I put in things that are left out. For example, I see that the specs don't include enough wiring, and the job will need more amperage. If I put in twelve hundred dollars to heavy it up and the architect doesn't analyze my bid, the client will pay for change orders later."

If builders refuse to competitively bid, how do they get jobs? By a negotiated-bid process. The cost to build will be comparable to that of a competitive bid if all the construction documents are complete, but the cost is arrived at quite differently.

Rather than prepare all the architect's construction documents and *then* bring in a builder, the builder is selected while the project is still at the initial design stage. The builder works with the owners and the architect to monitor costs and to keep the project within the bounds of the budget. This also avoids added design costs for scaling down and redesigning a project if the bids come in over budget.

Besides the obvious advantages for the builder—he can get the job without spending forty to eighty hours working up a bid that may not be chosen—there are also advantages for the homeowner:

- During the design process, owners have access to someone who knows costs almost to the dollar. Architects who specialize in residential construction may have a good sense of cost, but the builder, who is buying materials and building on a daily basis, has constantly updated information. The builder's input enables owners to know what their aesthetic decisions are costing them, and so helps owners make reasoned choices—for example, should extra dollars be allocated to a more elaborate roofline or fancier kitchen cabinets and appliances?

◆ With every budget, there are choices and ranges of quality for nearly every item. With a negotiated bid, this can be explored. The builder can demonstrate the advantages of using a tradesperson who might be a little more expensive, but the quality of their work is better.

◆ No one can afford everything. With a negotiated bid, the builder can help a client make cost-saving substitutions that won't affect quality. In a bathroom, for example, high-quality plumbing fixtures can vary tremendously in price.

◆ When the builder works alongside the architect, he can often suggest alternative ways to achieve the same effect that are less costly to construct.

◆ With a negotiated bid, the house will be finished faster. There is no bidding period, which usually takes about four weeks. More important, the builder has already worked the job into his schedule and lined up his subcontractors. "When the design is finished, you can roll right into construction," noted Potomac, Maryland, builder Guy Semmes.

◆ With a negotiated bid, the builder usually works with an "upset limit" (a fixed price for the job set by the owner) or on a "cost-plus" basis (the cost of the job plus his profit and overhead). With the fixed price, the builder does not keep open books, but delivers the house for the agreed amount. With cost-plus, the books are open and the builder discusses all job costs with the client. The "plus" factor of the "cost-plus"—the profit and overhead figure—can vary depending on the cost of construction and the scope of the work. In the Washington, D.C., area, the range is about 15 to 20 percent for new construction. But this can vary from one region of the country to another.

Despite the benefits that accrue to homeowners who derive a price by a negotiated bid, most do not opt for it because they fear that they will pay too much without the element of competition. If you count yourself among this group, look at several bid sets when you interview each architect. If the one for a $500 thousand house has thirty-eight pages of drawings and fifty pages of written specifications, it's thorough. There may still be a few omissions, as even the most conscientious architect can overlook something. But with thorough documents, the omissions are likely to be minor. And every job, whether the bid price is negotiated or competitively arrived at, will have a few change orders, because nearly everyone changes their minds and wants something a little different when they see their new house begin to go up.

falseeconomies

If the design of your new custom-built house comes in over budget, you might conclude that you can recover the bottom line if you purchase some of the big-ticket items yourself to avoid paying the builder's markup. Then you won't have to make some hard choices and reconsider, for example, those longed-for but pricey skylights that open and close by remote control. But most builders hate it when owners supply materials. Besides the fact that they make less money, such an arrangement creates headaches for all parties, causes delays, and rarely save owners as much money as they assume.

If owners insist on supplying some of the big-ticket items to save a buck, most builders are very reluctant to take on the job. From their perspective, such a cost-cutting tactic reflects a fundamental misunderstanding of what the builder's markup covers: profit and reward for his efforts and, more critically, his time and overhead to do a very complicated job correctly. The builder orchestrates the construction process. He arranges for the purchase and delivery of several hundred items in a precisely ordered sequence. He schedules thirty or more subcontracting trades to work with the materials as they are delivered, and he supervises the subcontractors to ensure that their work is done correctly. The delivery of each material must be coordinated with many others; it has to arrive at the right time, intact, and with all the required parts so that the subcontractor can do his job. What seems like mere scheduling is a time-consuming process— a contractor can spend half his work day just overseeing delivery of materials.

"Among the general public, construction is perceived to be so simple that anyone can do it. But what I know and offer I didn't find beneath a rock," says custom-home builder Frank Fanto of Mendocino, California.

Though purchasing a plumbing fixture or kitchen cabinets seems easy enough, most owners don't know what needs to be ordered. With plumbing fixtures, for example, they buy the plumbing fixture, but they don't get the accessory parts needed to install it.

Then the headaches begin. "If a part for something that an owner purchased is missing, who will run out to get it? If the plumber goes to get the part, he will charge for this. If I get it, I won't get paid for my time—that's part of what the markup covers," observed custom builder and remodeler Steve Perlik of Vienna, Virginia.

Even such seemingly straightforward purchases as bathroom tile can become headaches because owners don't know what trim and accent pieces are required. "It's time-consuming for an owner. After the second or third trip to the tile guy, owners begin to appreciate the know-how of the general contractor and his network of subcontractors that the markup pays for," said Silver Spring, Maryland, builder Jim Boyd.

Besides covering the time spent in trips back and forth to suppliers, the builder's markup provides him with some margin to cover losses when materials are damaged at the job site. "If an owner purchases kitchen cabinets and the builder installs them, what happens if one is dropped and damaged? If I purchased them, my markup can help cover the replacement cost of the one that was damaged. If I drop the owner's cabinet and have to replace it, I'm even worse off," Perlik said.

Besides the likelihood of slowing down the job and irritating the builder, clients don't save as much money as they think they will when they purchase things themselves. As Boyd explains, "The client says, 'I can get a designer discount.' But how well is the person connected? The average person doesn't have access to a professional discount. Besides, the discounts are like used cars—there's no standard discount. The client won't get as good a discount as the builder will get unless their uncle owns the store."

bringing in your own subcontractor

Besides purchasing materials themselves, some owners try to save money by using subcontractors who are friends. For the builder, an owner-supplied sub can be worse than the owner-supplied items. Among other reasons, if the friend is moonlighting, he will do extra work only on the weekends, and this slows down the job.

The friend can also be less competent or experienced than the homeowner realizes. Besides this, Boyd observed that most subs will pick the easiest way to get a job done, and this can make it difficult for the next tradesperson. A homeowner won't know this, but a general contractor will. "That fifteen-dollar-an-hour electrician roughs in outlet boxes all right, but oftentimes he doesn't pay that much attention to where he's putting them. If he places them too close to the doors and windows, the trim carpenter can't trim, or must cut the trim to fit around the box. Another example, the bathroom cabinets are ordered and installed, but they are too close to the toilet joist and the plumber says, 'No way I can put the toilet in there!'"

Boyd's advice: At the outset of the job, owners have to accept that "certain things cost. The plumber will get forty to forty-five dollars per hour; the owner pays fifteen percent more for me to get the guy there on time and to do the job right."

After the job is finished and the house is built, owners may discover yet another reason that purchasing items themselves doesn't pay in the long run: The builder will warrant and repair items that he purchases, and part of his markup covers his time for this. But if the owner-supplied skylights that are supposed to open and close with a switch won't work properly, the builder can say with some justification, "That's not my problem."

If you are planning to build a Really Big House, make sure you and your pocketbook are ready. You're not simply transiting from a smaller house to a bigger one. When you move from a 2,500-square-foot house to a 5,000-square-foot one, you're making a quantum leap in terms of size, finishes, and cost. Your twice-as-big-new house won't be *twice* as expensive to build. It will be about *four times* as expensive.

tipsfromthetrade:
why do *really big* houses cost more money?

How can this be? Firstly, the cubic volume of the bigger house will be about 2.5 times more because the rooms won't look right unless the ceilings are higher—at least nine feet. The vastly increased volume requires a much more sophisticated and expensive heating and cooling system.

With bigger rooms, higher ceilings, and more wall surfaces, you need to increase the scale and the level of the detailing. The single crown molding that enhances the relatively small rooms of a 2,500-square-foot house with 8-foot ceilings will disappear in larger rooms with higher ceilings. You'll also need more and bigger windows. But to rein in your utility bills, these windows should be argon-filled, with low-emissivity glass.

Then come the inevitable upgrades: better floor finishes, a trophy kitchen and a master bathroom, a state-of-the-art sound system and entertainment center, and anything else that you want—and think you deserve—in the palace of your dreams.

The *building* cost will also be higher because you will have to hire a custom builder. For a twenty-five-hundred-square-foot house, you would be fine with a production-home builder. But a twice-as-big house requires much more elaborate design and detailing than most production builders can deliver, and none as yet are building houses of this size.

Where do you end up cost-wise? Though rules of thumb can be dangerous, on average the construction cost per square foot of a 5,000-square-foot house is at least twice that of a house half as big. If the current *construction* cost of a production-built 2,500-square-foot house in your area is about $80 per square foot, it would be at least $160 per square foot for a 5,000-square-foot custom-built house. The total construction cost of the smaller house would be about $200,000; for the large one, about $800,000. (Note that production builders sell the house and the lot as a package; they do not separate out the construction cost unless asked for this information.)

Furthermore, as you get into the planning of your large house, you're likely to want more elaborate detailing and finishes, at least for some rooms. You're likely to find that the $160-per-square-foot budget is too modest. If you want to have intricate wood detailing with unusual woods like red birch or walnut, the materials will cost more and require an unusually skilled carpenter. This will drive the cost up closer to $200 per square foot, or a million dollars for a 5,000-square-foot house. You should also note that these costs cover only the house. The land cost would be added to this because custom-home builders do not sell lots, they build on your land.

Even if your budget exceeds a million dollars, be forewarned: It won't cover everything on your wish list. Chicago architect Philip Hamp, who has designed a number of large houses, observed that "Everybody has a budget. It could be three million or three hundred thousand, but it's still a budget. The clients have to draw the line somewhere and make some hard decisions."

When you're looking for ways to cut your budget, don't skimp on design costs. With a big house, every design flaw will show. "From the entry foyer, you don't want the major view through the house to be the seam between the fireplace and the wall, or the first thing that catches a visitor's eye to be the powder-room door," observed architect Bill Sutton of Vienna, Virginia.

Would-be owners of large houses also need to think about how they will live in a big house—both their day-to-day living and formal entertaining. In many cases, couples building large houses are empty nesters. "Two people in an eight-thousand-square-foot house can feel cavernous," Sutton cautioned.

"For the day-to-day aspect, elements like back stairways become important. You can be in the kitchen/family room area and go up to the master bedroom without going through the formal areas that can sometimes feel like museum spaces. For formal entertaining—whether it's 10 guests for dinner or New Year's Eve for 150—people always migrate to the kitchen. You have to design it so that it feels right with only household members, a somewhat expanded crowd of ten to twelve, or a much larger number of New Year's Eve party-goers," Sutton said.

chapter four financing

You can ask the simple question "How much house can I afford?" But you can't get a simple answer. The price that you can afford is determined by the size of the mortgage that you can get.

This sounds straightforward enough, but computing the mortgage is another matter, which will depend on a number of factors. Your income is a central one, but most lenders also want to know how you spend your money, and what other debts you have that could affect your ability to pay a mortgage. They want to know about your car loans, credit-card debt,

Include the optional upgrades or options when you calculate how much production-built house you can afford. The house offered at the base price will be very basic, and you will likely want to get some options, unless you are looking at the high end. For example, if you qualify for a $160,000 mortgage with a 5 percent down payment, the total price you can afford would be $168,000 (a midpoint to lower end in most markets). But if you want to get some options, the base-price range that you should be looking at is not the full $168,000; it should probably be $155,000 to $160,000, which gives you room to add the upgrades.

don't **forget** **the** options

student loans, property taxes where you want to buy a house, the amount of down payment that you can make, the amount of equity you have in the house you own now (if you own one), and your credit rating as reported to the three national credit reporting bureaus. Lenders are also interested in any extenuating circumstances in your life that could affect your credit rating and your assets such as a recent divorce, a job layoff of several months that occurred two years ago, or a medical emergency that gored your credit.

After all this data is sorted out, and a lender goes through all the calculations, he will come up with a dollar figure that he's willing to lend you. Since every person's financial profile is a little different and every lender interprets all this data a little differently, three lenders could come up with three slightly different answers. The bottom line here, however, is that a mortgage figure plus the amount of money that you put down as a down payment will determine what price of house you can afford.

lenders and loans

Before you get very far in your search for a new house, you need to meet with several mortgage lenders and discuss your prospects. You may be under- or over-estimating what you can afford. When you meet with each lender, explain that you are just starting out and gathering information. Any lender should be happy to talk with you.

You will discover that every lender offers a slightly different interest rate on their mortgage loans. Interest rates are calculated to an eighth of a point. If the going rate is "around 8 percent" you could hear quotes of 8.125, 8.25, 8.327, and 8.5 percent. The lenders also offer a startling array of loans. The standard thirty-year fixed mortgage that your parents may have had still exists, but lenders also offer fifteen-year fixed mortgages, ARMs (adjustable-rate mortgages with interest rates and payments that change over the life of the loan), intermediate ARMs, balloons, and buydowns. The terms of these various

There are numerous websites that have mortgage calculators and detailed mortgage information. In fact, it is possible to do the entire mortgage transaction over the Internet. But just as you need to go out and look at the new houses in your market to get a sense of what's out there, you also need to meet with two or three mortgage lenders to get a sense of how lenders think and interpret financial data before you surf the web. The lending formulas make the lending seem hard and fast, but a lender's decisions are also nuanced and take into account personal information that won't show up on a credit report such as late payments due to a divorce, being out of work, or horrific medical expenses.

types of loans can make a difference in how large a mortgage you can qualify for, and, depending on your situation, which is the right choice for you. Since each lender may offer a slightly different version of each type of loan, make sure that you ask about a standard thirty-year fixed loan so that you can make an apple-to-apple comparison between lenders.

There are a number of factors besides the loan terms that may make one lender look better than another, such as closing costs. These are the fees that a lender charges to make the loan and are an important source of a lender's income. The list of closing costs can be long, and the charges can be as little as 1 percent to as much as 5 percent of the total mortgage amount. If you are borrowing $160,000, this would mean you might be paying $1,600 to $8,000 in closing costs.

check your credit

Before you start to meet with lenders, you should check your credit rating with the three national credit reporting bureaus. You certainly know if you generally pay your bills on time, but there can be errors in the records. Since your credit rating and credit score will greatly affect how a lender will assess your credit worthiness, you need to make sure that the records are in order (for information on how to contact the credit report bureaus, see Resources).

Besides all the usual ins and outs of getting a mortgage, you will have additional factors to consider if you are building a brand-new house. If you are working with a production builder, the builder himself will offer financing. It is often very competitive with conventional lenders such as full-service banks or mortgage banks, but not always. You still need to shop around and compare what builders are offering to what other lenders are offering. If you're building a custom-built house, you will have to get both a construction loan to cover the cost of building the house and a permanent mortgage after the house is done.

Before you meet with several lenders, as a very first step, you might go to a bookstore and get one or two books on the subject, especially if the mortgage process already sounds intimidating. (See Resources for some of the many helpful books that have been written on this subject, as well as how to check your credit.)

howmuchhousecanyouafford?

If you have cash in hand—a lot of cash from, say, an inheritance—you can just plunk down the money and buy the house. But if you have to borrow money, the answer is not so straightforward. How much money a lender is willing to lend you depends on how much debt he thinks you can carry and still repay the loan, and his calculations can be a cumbersome process.

When a lender considers your income, he's not just looking at the gross annual figure. Twenty-five years ago, a lender's rule of thumb was that a household's mortgage debt burden should be about 2 to 2.5 times its annual income—that is, a lender was willing to lend you 2 to 2.5 times your annual income. In response to the vastly different levels of consumer indebtedness, however, today's mortgage lenders focus on your *gross monthly income* and your other debt. Their rule of thumb is that your monthly mortgage payment should not exceed 28 percent of your gross monthly income. Also, that your monthly indebtedness for *everything,* including your mortgage as well as car payments, credit cards, property tax, and home owner's insurance should not exceed 36 to 40 percent of your gross monthly income.

For example, if Household A's annual household income is $50,000, its gross monthly income before taxes is $4,167, and 36 to 40 percent of this would be $1,500 to $1,667 for total monthly debt. The 28 percent for the house would be $1,166, and the money left for other debts would be $334 to $501.

If Household B's annual household income is $75,000, its gross monthly income before taxes is $6,250, and 36 to 40 percent of this is $2,250 to $2,500 for total monthly debt. The 28 percent for the house is $1,750, leaving $500 to $750 to pay other debts.

As you can see, this formula doesn't leave a lot of room for high credit-card balances, big car-loan payments, or student loans. You may think this is not very realistic, given the way that people live and spend their income—or how *you* live and spend your income. Nonetheless, this is how a lender sees it.

The next step in calculating how much house a household can buy is going from the monthly mortgage payment a lender thinks you could make—$1,166 and $1,750 in our two examples—to how large a total mortgage amount he will offer that results in these levels of monthly payments. This will depend on mortgage interest rates, which are

A further consideration that you will face in getting a mortgage for your brand new house is that you have to get a loan approved at the time you sign a sales contract with the builder, but you don't sign all the papers and assume a mortgage until the house is built. This could be anywhere from four to nine months later. It may only take four months to build the house, but the builder might not start for five months or he could be delayed by weather. If the interest rates go up in the interim, your monthly payments do, too. For example, on a $160,000 mortgage, if the interest rate goes from 8 to 9 percent, your monthly payment would increase 6 percent on a 30-year fixed. If the lender determines that you can't meet this with your income and current debt load, you could lose your financing for that loan and not be able to buy the house. Furthermore, the builder to whom you paid a deposit will almost certainly state in his sales contract that in this event he will not be obliged to return your deposit (see Chapters 11–13 on purchasing and contracts).

Since rising interest rates are always a possibility, when you make your initial calculations and apply for a mortgage, you should not put yourself too close to the edge of your limit. At the time you get the loan approval, the lender will guarantee the interest rate for thirty to sixty days. However, your house won't be finished for ninety to one hundred twenty days or even longer. You can either let your rate "float" and lock in on a rate much closer to the date that you will close, or you can pay to lock in your rate at the time you get the loan approved. With many lenders, you can pay to get a lock-in on an interest rate for as long as a year. But the longer you want to secure the lock, the more you will have to pay. For example, for a twelve-month lock you usually have to pay a full point (1 point is 1 percent of the loan amount, or $1,600 for the $160,000 loan).

always fluctuating. For Household A, if the current interest rate is 8 percent and they want a thirty-year fixed rate, the monthly payment would be $1,174 and the amount they could borrow would be $160,000. If the interest rate on the loan becomes 9 percent, they could borrow only $150,000.

For Household B's $1,750 monthly mortgage payment, when the interest rate is 8 percent they could borrow $240,000 with a thirty-year fixed loan. If the interest rate was 9 percent for the same thirty-year fixed rate terms, they could borrow only $220,000.

If you have a superb credit rating, however, you may qualify for a mortgage amount that is a higher percentage of your monthly income.

These amounts, however, are the total amounts that you can *borrow*. When you buy a house, you will have to make a down payment. The amount varies with the terms of the loan, but let us say it's 5 percent down and you want a mortgage for the other 95 percent. If $160,000 is the maximum you can borrow, this is 95 percent of $168,000; so that is the price range you should be looking in. If $150,000 is the maximum you can borrow, the house price would be $157,500. If you can borrow $240,000, the house price would be $256,000.

However, this is the total price for everything. With a production-built house, the basic house may be pretty basic, and you may want some upgrades. So for Household A, a base price of $155,000 to $160,000 would leave them with $13,000 to $8,000 for upgrades. On the other hand, they might decide that they want space above all upgrades, so they will buy the biggest house they can get with their $168,500.

other factors: property taxes and equity

Before you can make your final calculation, you also have to add in the property taxes that you will have to pay on your new house. In some jurisdictions, these can be very high, which would leave you with less money per month to pay off a mortgage (the 36 to 40 percent of your gross monthly income that is used to calculate your mortgage also includes property taxes).

On the other hand, you may own a house now and have equity in it (the difference between what you paid for it and what it's worth today if you sold it), which you want to apply to your new-home purchase. This also affects the lender's assessment of your mortgage qualifications—you can afford more. If both of these households had $50,000 of equity in a house that they already own, this would, of course, affect their mortgage prospects. They could either put down a much bigger down payment and pay a smaller mortgage or buy a higher priced house.

down payment

If you have extraordinarily good credit, you may be able to get a conventional mortgage with no down payment. You will still have to contribute 3 percent of the mortgage amount toward the closing costs, but this can be a grant or a gift from relatives. Otherwise, the minimum down payment that you can make for a conventional loan is 3 percent, but you may qualify to buy a house with no down payment by getting a Federal Housing Authority (FHA) loan or a Veterans Administration (VA) loan. Some states also have special loan programs to help first-time home buyers. If you make a down payment of less than 20 percent for a conventional loan, however, you will have to pay for private mortgage insurance (PMI), and this will be included in the calculation of how much debt burden you can carry. The amount of PMI a lender will require depends on the type of loan you get and the size of your down payment. For a thirty-year fixed-rate $160,000 mortgage, with a 5 percent down payment, it would be about $105 a month in addition to the $1,167 that you are already paying. If you were making a 19 percent down payment on the same thirty-year fixed mortgage, the PMI would only be about $55 a month. In either case, once you have paid down the principal to 80 percent—that is, you owe only $128,000 because you've paid off the first $32,000 of the loan—you will not be required to pay the PMI.

loan application

If you bought a house ten years ago, you will already have some familiarity with the mortgage-seeking process. But you will be pleasantly surprised to discover that the procedures have been streamlined to a remarkable degree. You no longer need to bring in a shoe box of documents including twelve months of bank statements and canceled checks. You may still have to fill out long and detailed forms, but the lending decision can be made within minutes because today most mortgage lenders use an automated underwriting system to evaluate your application and credit. The required documentation is mercifully short—many lenders only want a W-2 form, an income tax return, a bank account statement, and your most recent pay stub. Bring these items with you when meeting with a loan officer, and, after all the data has been entered into the automated underwriting system, you may get a loan approved in less than ten minutes.

yourcredit

When you meet with a lender, he will want to know your income. But he will be even more interested in your credit record, because he wants assurance that if he lends you money, you will repay him. This is a critical factor because your ability to get a mortgage depends on your financial history. Whether you can get a mortgage loan or not, the amount that you can borrow, and the terms and rates under which the funds will be lent will depend in large part on your track record in repaying past loans, including auto loans and credit-card payments.

credit scores

Your repayment track record can be quantified into one number called a credit score. When a lender calls up your credit records from each of the three national credit reporting bureaus—Equifax, Experian, and Trans Union—he will order a credit score from each one. The scoring is calculated using a statistical model designed by Fair Isaac & Company in San Rafael, California, and everyone in the mortgage business refers to the credit scores as "FICO scores."

Each of the three credit reporting bureaus applies Fair Isaac's statistical model differently, so each gives a different FICO score. Lenders generally request two or three scores and use either the lower of two numbers or the middle of three, and lenders also interpret these scores differently.

FICO credit scoring does not focus on income or assets but on your recent credit history and your track record of paying loans and credit card bills on time. In other words, paying these bills promptly or even early will help your score; late payments will hurt it. The FICO scoring model also includes how much credit you have available and how much you have used. Maxing out on the allowable amount you can charge to a credit card and maxing out on the number of credit lines you may get can lower your score.

When the FICO score was first used by mortgage lenders, the sheer number of credit inquiries into your credit record would have affected the score itself. Your friends and relatives who have gone through the mortgage process may caution you from talking with many lenders for this reason. For instance, if you were a careful consumer who shopped ten different car dealers looking for the best price, each one would check your credit. By the time you reached the tenth dealer, your score could have been sufficiently lowered that you couldn't get a loan. Likewise with mortgage lenders; the more diligent you were in checking out lenders and rates, the worse off you were, FICO score–wise.

The FICO model was then modified for car-loan and mortgage inquiries so that within a thirty-day period all such inquiries will show up in your record as a single inquiry.

"a paper," "a+ paper," and "b paper"

FICO scores range from 300 to 900, but scores at the extreme ends of this range are very rare, said Craig Watts, FICO consumer affairs manager. Most people score in the 600s and 700s; the magic cut-off number is 620. Generally, if you score 620 or above, you can qualify for "A paper," meaning a loan at the best terms; some lenders, however, require a FICO score that is close to 700 to get the lowest interest rate and the lowest down-payment requirement. When you talk with lenders, ask each one what FICO score is required for "A paper."

If your FICO score is really high, a lender might consider it an "A+ paper" score. In this case, he might decide that you qualify for a higher mortgage amount than he would ordinarily give to someone with your income and debt load. Before you borrow to the max, however, you should consider how comfortable you will be with the higher payment and how it will impact your lifestyle.

With a lower FICO score, you can still qualify for a mortgage, but you will have higher down-payment requirements and you will have to pay a higher interest rate. For example, if your FICO score is 600, a lender might consider you "B paper"—that is, you could still qualify for a mortgage, but not on the best terms. Instead of getting the 8 percent "A paper" rate on a thirty-year fixed mortgage, you might get a 10 percent rate.

After thorough analysis of statistical models, Freddie Mac and Fannie Mae, two quasi-federal government mortgage investing corporations, determined that the lender's risk—that is, the probability the person

why is **620** the **magic** fico **score?**

your present employment, your monthly income, your marital status and age, and your occupation. Your score may also be low because of errors in the report, or because you were laid off for two months, borrowing the money will repay it—is significantly better if the FICO number is 620 or above. Their analysis also showed that when FICO scores are below 600, the chances of default increase dramatically. Although only 15 percent of consumers have scores below 600, they account for 50 percent of all consumer defaults.

or you incurred an enormous medical expense and were late in some of your payments. If there is a good explanation that you can document for why your scores were low, a loan officer will take this into account. But if your scores are low because you have been irresponsible in paying your debts, this will work against you.

Mortgage lenders are quick to say, however, that the FICO score is not the sole determinant in making a mortgage decision. The FICO score does not take into account other pertinent information such as the length of

The FICO scores may sound onerous, but they have actually made mortgage-lending decisions much less subjective. Many people who couldn't have qualified in the past are now getting mortgages.

With a $50,000 annual income and $1,166 monthly ceiling for a mortgage payment, you could borrow only $130,000. You would also have to come up with a much higher down payment—possibly as much as 20 percent, or $31,000 to buy a $155,000 house.

Rather than pay such high interest rates, you may be better off cleaning up your credit before applying for a mortgage. But this cannot be done in two weeks—it may take you a year or more before you can qualify for "A paper."

disclosing your fico scores

In the past you were not told your FICO scores unless you were turned down for a loan. The Fair Isaac's (the firm that developed the FICO scoring model) rationale for this was that interpretation of the scores can be very confusing. But many consumer advocates complained about the Kafkaesque secrecy of credit scoring—getting a loan depended on a score that wasn't divulged to you. Both the U.S. Congress and some state legislatures proposed legislation to require that the scoring be disclosed. As of July 1, 2001, California law requires that lenders must disclose your scores to you, and this will soon become the norm everywhere.

In response to consumer advocates, FICO itself now allows consumers to pull their scores directly off the Internet. Working with Equifax, one of the three national credit reporting bureaus, FICO will give you a credit report and a FICO credit score along with an explanation of your score. However, you can only get the FICO score as calculated by Equifax. The other two credit reporting bureaus, Trans Union and Experian, use the Fair Isaac model differently. Their FICO scores can differ from Experian's by ten to sixty points (for information on how to get your scores, see Resources).

The FICO scores may also become less of an issue for borrowers in the future because Fannie Mae has removed them from their automated underwriting system and replaced them with actual data taken directly from the borrowers' credit report. Whatever method is used, however, the intent will be the same—a lender wants to evaluate your ability and willingness to pay off loans.

what if your fico score is 0?

Frugal consumers who have never used a credit card or borrowed money won't have *any* credit score. Should you fall into this category, you need to apply for a credit card, use it sparingly, and pay bills on time or early, so that you create a credit track record and a credit score. This might seem unfair—why shouldn't you be rewarded for your frugality? Unfortunately, the credit-rating system is set up to reflect the spending habits of the occasionally extravagant majority rather than the frugal minority.

typesoflenders

There are numerous institutions that lend money for home mortgages, including credit unions and savings-and-loan associations, but the three most common ones are banks, mortgage banks, and mortgage brokers. Both banks and mortgage banks have their own funds to lend. A mortgage bank lends funds only for real-estate mortgages, whereas a full-service bank makes all types of loans and offers other services as well, such as checking and savings accounts. Mortgage brokers do not have their own funds to lend; they sell or broker mortgages for other lenders. Mortgage brokers make their money on the "retail markup"—that is, they offer you the same rates and terms as a bank or mortgage bank, but the lender who is actually lending you the money is charging a slightly lower interest rate. The broker makes money on the difference. In effect, a mortgage broker buys wholesale and sells retail.

Another important difference between the banks or mortgage banks and the mortgage brokers are the barriers to entry. The banks and mortgage banks are highly regulated, but mortgage brokers do not generally receive the same degree of oversight. In some states a mortgage broker is not even required to be licensed, or license require-ments are minimal.

Nevertheless, there are many excellent mortgage brokers with years of experience. Many of them have worked for banks or mortgage banks and have contacts throughout the industry. The really aggressive mortgage brokers may represent fifty or more lenders from all over the country, and they are well positioned to get you an extremely compet-itive rate. But watch out for the less-qualified and less-scrupulous ones who may over-promise and under-deliver. They may promise a great rate and a low estimate of closing costs, but then jack up the closing costs and the loan rate just as you are preparing for closing, when it's too late to find another lender. If you do not close when the seller or builder says your house is ready for occupancy, you can forfeit your deposit and lose your house. Even worse, a bad mortgage broker may not be able to get the mortgage funds lined up for you on the promised date and therefore just not show up at the closing.

When you meet with a mortgage broker, ask how long he or she has been in busi-ness and for a list of the lenders represented, as you would ask a builder or anyone else for references. If the broker looks promising after your initial interview, randomly call two or three of these references. With every mortgage lender of any type that you meet, you should ask for a list of recent customers and randomly call three or four. Should the lender refuse to give you any references or names of former customers, cross him or her off your list.

How do you get the names of several lenders to go and talk with? Ask your friends and relatives which lender they dealt with, or look in the Yellow Pages. You will find that mortgage brokers generally do not identify themselves as such, for example, if you look in the Yellow Pages. When you call to inquire about a company, you have to ask if the firm is a mortgage broker or a mortgage banker.

When you visit a new subdivision and ask the residents about their experiences with the builder, also ask which lender they used and if they would use the same one again.

The mortgage-lending business is ferociously competitive. But an interest rate that sounds too good to be true probably isn't true—the lender may charge more points or add more junk fees (see below). If you call a lender for a quote and it differs from what you read in the newspaper, however, it does not mean that you are being stiffed. Mort-gage rates fluctuate from day to day and even within one day. By the time a rate comes out in the newspaper, it is already two or three days old and may be out of date.

closingcosts

In addition to coming up with the down payment and securing a mortgage, you will also have to pay closing costs: the fees charged by lenders to process your loan, secure the funds, and attend to all required legalities, such as affixing document tax stamps to the warranty deed and getting it properly recorded at your local county courthouse in their property-records department. The closing costs will be due at the closing, the time when you sign all the papers and assume both the mortgage and ownership of the house.

After you and a loan officer have discussed your mortgage prospects, a realistic price range for a new house, and down-payment requirements, ask him or her about their closing costs. These can be substantial, and can range anywhere from 1 to as much as 5 percent of the total mortgage amount. Your down-payment money, which is also due at the closing, is in addition to the closing costs.

Some of the closing costs are fees that are legally required, such as the document tax stamp, but some are "junk fees" the lender tacks on to make more money on the loan. When mortgage interest rates are low, the lender will make less money on the loan and will be more inclined to pad his fees. When the interest rates are higher, the lender makes more money so he has less reason to pad the closing costs. As a general rule, the higher the mortgage rate, the lower the closing costs should be, and vice versa.

There is no set amount or formula that lenders use to calculate the closing costs. Each lender calculates this differently and charges a different amount for closing, so this is an important point of comparison between lenders. Standard closing costs generally include:

- an appraiser fee (an independent third party inspects the property to make sure it is worth what you are paying and they are lending)

- required taxes (many jurisdictions have a document stamp tax, for example)

- a charge for a credit report

- flood certification

- title insurance fees

- discount points

- tax service fees

Typical junk fees are:

- "administrative fee"

- "processing fee"

- "closing review fee"

- "document preparation fee"

- "application fee" (this is not a standard charge, and many in the mortgage industry consider it to be a junk fee)

Some lenders claim to omit fees that they simply call something else. For example, they advertise "no origination fee" but instead charge a "funding fee" or a higher interest rate. Mortgage brokers may also charge their version of junk fees. A mortgage broker makes money by selling mortgages for other lenders, and the broker's profit will be folded into the cost of your mortgage. Some tack on additional fees that can be called "loan brokerage," "loan origination," or "one-time add-on fee."

making the apples to apples comparison

To make a comparison of mortgages between lenders and not get lost in the details of all the different loan packages that each offers, ask each loan officer for the interest rate on a conventional thirty-year mortgage with zero points. He or she will immediately follow this with quotes that include a rate plus points, for example, "8 percent plus 2 points." A point is 1 percent of the mortgage amount. A lender uses points to raise its yield on a loan without raising the interest. To get the rate quoted, you will also have to pay 2 (2 percent of the total) points; nearly all lenders charge points. For example, if you are borrowing $160,000, 2 points would be $3,200 and it would be due at closing. (If you are borrowing $240,000, two points would be $4,800.) Many lenders also charge an origination fee of 1 percent, which would be another $1,600 (or $2,400). You can see how the closing costs begin to add up. As with the mortgage interest rates, points will be quoted to an eighth of a point, so a lender could say 2.125 points, or 2.375 points, and so forth.

Some lenders lump the origination fee in with the points when they give you a quote, but many do not, so you have to ask when getting a quote whether it includes both. You can avoid paying the points, which would lower your closing costs and reduce the amount of cash that you have to bring to closing, by folding them into your mortgage. But you will have to pay a slightly higher mortgage rate and a higher monthly payment than was originally quoted.

Many buyers have the income to qualify for a mortgage but they don't have a lot of cash to bring to the closing table. These buyers get a "zero discount" or "premium pricing" mortgage with no points. Even if you do have the cash available to pay the points at closing, there can still be advantages to going the zero-discount route, especially if you plan to live in the house less than seven years.

Suppose that a lender tells you that to get the 8 percent interest rate on the thirty-year fixed $160,000 loan you must pay 1.125 points, or $2,000, at closing. If you elect to pay zero points, this amount is folded into your mortgage and you pay an added $41 a month. It will take you about five years to pay off this added amount to your mortgage. If you plan to move in less than five years, you are better off paying zero points because you will be selling your house before repaying all the extra that you borrowed.

Even if you plan to stay in the house indefinitely, there are still advantages to the zero point option. The $41 extra that you are paying is tax deductible, along with the rest of the interest you are paying. With the extra cash in hand you can buy some of the furnishings that your builder does not supply, such as window treatments. Or you can invest it or put it in a CD and make money on it while you pay off the points. In addition to the points, all the other closing costs can be folded into the mortgage, but this will increase your monthly payment.

good-faith estimate

Within three days of formally applying for a loan, a lender is required by law to give you a "good faith estimate" that lists the specific dollar amounts for all the closing charges. Bear in mind, however, that this is an *estimate only,* and these can be higher when you actually close.

While you are still shopping around for a lender, however, you should ask for an itemized list of their closing-cost charges with the percentage amount where applicable (for example, the document stamp is .01 percent of the sale price of the house), plus an estimate of the total closing costs based on the amount of money that you want to borrow. If the lender will not give you a list of his closing charges or an estimate of what they might be until you plunk down a three hundred dollar application fee, move on.

When the lender gives you this list, ask for an explanation of each one and ask which charges are legally required and which are "customary charges." This difference should become clear as you compare closing costs at different lenders. The legally required charges will be on every list, but the customary charges will differ.

The legally required closing fees must be paid, but all the others are negotiable. After you have assessed the loan package that each lender is offering, go back and ask which fees each is willing to waive or reduce to get your business. When business is hot and many people are looking for loans, he may not budge on anything. When business is slow, however, he may talk. Even if you don't get any break on your mortgage, making such an inquiry sends a signal that you are a knowledgeable consumer who knows what you are doing.

Another question to raise is whether the lender is willing to guarantee in writing that it will not charge any more closing fees than the ones listed at the time you make a loan application. This will protect you from arriving at closing and discovering that fees have been added that were not previously disclosed. The required good-faith estimate is just that, and is not binding on the lender.

builder-lenders

When you buy a brand-new house from a production builder, the builder will invariably offer financing—that is, a mortgage if you qualify, just as any other mortgage-lending institution would. The builder will do this through his own mortgage banking company, his own mortgage broker, or a designated lender; the interest rates and terms are usually competitive. To induce you to use his financing, the builder may also offer you sizable monetary incentives—usually several thousand dollars.

The largest national home-building firms—including Pulte Homes, Ryland Homes, US Home, Kaufman and Broad, and Centex Homes—own subsidiaries that are full-service mortgage banks with their own funds to lend. Smaller, regional home-building firms are more likely to have a lending subsidiary that is a mortgage broker, not a bank. The smallest building firms may also have their own mortgage broker, but they are more likely to have simply a relationship with a local bank. Whatever the arrangement, the builder-lenders offer buyers the same enormous variety of loan programs that other lenders offer.

You should certainly shop the competition and check out other lenders before you sign on with the builder's lender, however. The builder's on-site sales agent may assert that the builder-lender's rates are "competitive," but you should check for yourself. The sales agent may also assert that buyers *must* deal with the builder's lender, but in fact you are free to get a loan from any lender. The only constraint is that in doing so you forgo the builder's contribution toward closing costs.

Some builder-lenders have programs and coaches to help first-time buyers save up enough money for a down payment, which is often the biggest hurdle to home ownership for first-timers. Some builder-lenders even have counselors who work with buyers to clean up their credit.

Another plus with builder-lenders is that they're very attuned to two situations that frequently occur in the financing of new houses: delays in construction that affect the closing (and hence the timing of a lock-in on mortgage rates); and a buyer's desire to add ten thousand dollars worth of options after the initial loan amount has been approved.

builder-lenders and rate locks

A builder-lender will be in frequent communication with a builder's sales agent, often learning of delays before the buyer does and adjusting the lock-in and closing dates accordingly. If you use a different lender, you will have to monitor this yourself and make sure that the lender is kept informed of any construction delays that could affect the timing of the lock-in. Otherwise, your lender may lock you prematurely into a rate that may expire before the house is finished.

Even a builder's lender is not infallible, however, and he can lock in the mortgage rate too soon. When this happens, some builder-lenders will extend the lock because they have a vested interest in selling you the house. When you meet the builder's lender, ask what they do when this happens.

Even when construction proceeds in timely fashion, months will pass between signing the sales contract and the builder finishing the house. Since there is always the possibility that interest rates can go up in the interim, some builder-lenders will approve a loan at the highest rate for which you can qualify, so that if the rates do go up, you can still get a mortgage.

With most mortgage lenders, you can lock in your mortgage rate at the time your loan is approved without charge for thirty to sixty days. Some builder-lenders, however, offer a rate lock-in period that is as long as eighty-nine days, so be sure to ask.

builder-lenders and adding options

As your house goes up and you finally see what it looks like, you may decide to add things. Rather than seek approval for a bigger loan at this later stage, many builder-lenders will get approval for a higher mortgage initially. "They ask for $300,000, we get $310,000 or $320,000," said Deborah Still of Pulte Mortgage. The loan adjustment is easily managed because the builder's sales agent simply calls the builder-lender. If you use another lender, you must inform him that you want to borrow more money and then check up to make sure that you are qualified to do this and that your lender has adjusted the mortgage and the good-faith estimate of closing costs accordingly.

Some production builders, however, require that you pay *cash* for any upgrades you wish to add after your loan has been approved and construction has begun. When you discuss terms with the builder's lender, ask about their policy on change orders. If you don't use the builder's lender, ask the sales agent about the builder's policy on change orders with other lenders.

Buyers can benefit from the quality of service that the builders' mortgage lenders have a strong incentive to provide. Since a home builder can supply many customers to a lender, it's in the lender's interest to have everything go smoothly. As Donna Veronick, a vice president and area manager for US Home Mortgage, described the situation, "We have two customers to keep happy: We must please both the buyers and the builders. And the builder is not happy if the buyers are not happy."

switching lenders

If you initially decide to use a lender other than the builder's, and later change your mind, your builder-lender will usually welcome you back with open arms—even if it's two days before closing. Moreover, you may still get the builder's incentives that were initially offered.

The opposite can also be true. You can start with the builder-lender, but find it's advantageous to switch as your house nears completion because another lender offers a better deal. When your house is about thirty to sixty days from completion, plan on a second round of comparison mortgage shopping. In some areas, builder-lenders may inflate their loan rates above the prevailing market rates as your house nears completion. This means that you will be paying for the builder's financial incentives such as the $1,000-title insurance policy yourself, explains Dallas mortgage banker Lonny Coffey. "The perception is that you get value with the builder's incentives, but if he inflates the rate you're not getting value, you're paying for it."

Although the builder is obliged to give you the closing-cost incentives as stated in his sales contract if you use his lender, he is not obliged to give you a competitive interest rate on the loan, nor is he obliged to state that the rate he offers may not be competitive, Coffey adds.

When you get quotes from other lenders on your second round of mortgage shopping, ask for the market rate with zero points and the market rate with the same number of points your builder lender is charging, as you did when you first looked for a mortgage. To make an apples to apples comparison, make sure that you are comparing the same type of loan and loan program that your builder-lender is offering. Then, *because mortgage interest rates are always negotiable,* go back to your builder and ask for the better rate or you will walk. In many cases, the builder will oblige because he will see that you are an educated buyer and he doesn't want to lose you, Coffey says.

If he won't, make the switch. Loan approval and the preparation and assembly of all required loan documents can be done in less than four days (though most lenders prefer to have about thirty days). Starting your second round of mortgage shopping when you are about sixty days out gives you enough time to get everything in place without unduly stressing yourself or your lender.

Some builders may write into their sales contract that once you sign on with their lender, you can't switch to another one to get a better rate. This point is negotiable. To give yourself the opportunity to shop around and possibly switch as your house nears completion, add a clause to your sales contract that states: "The buyer will use the builder's lender if he can match the competitive rate the buyer can get elsewhere at the time of closing." If you also add that your alternative financing will be "at no added cost or risk to the builder," the builder will be more amenable.

Because the builder knows that inexperienced buyers can end up with unscrupulous lenders who can derail a closing, he may insist that you seek this second round of alternative financing from a lender that he knows is reliable. In that case, a builder usually gives three or four choices, and these must be listed on the sales contract.

Whether you stay with the builder's lender or switch, when you get the lock-in rate, *you should ask for it in writing, along with a written itemized list of all the closing costs.* This is simply a good business practice.

While some builders inflate their loan rates to cover their incentives, there are some who will still extend their financial incentives if you find a lender who offers a better deal and want to switch, as long as the other lender is one who they know to be reliable so that your switching will not delay closing.

As you work your way through the mortgage maze, keep in mind that the builder's financial incentives to use his lender are very market-driven. When the market is slow and buyers are scarce, some builders are willing to let you apply their financing incentives to a mortgage obtained from another lender. But you have to negotiate this at the time you sign the sales contract, not when you approach closing and find that you can get a better deal somewhere else.

"Portability" with a builder's financial incentives can be especially advantageous when the builder-lender's closing costs are not competitive. For example, if the builder-lender charges $1,000 more in closing costs for a $200,000 loan than other lenders, you're only saving $500 when you use his $1,500 incentive. If the builder's $1,500 financing incentive is portable and you can use it with a different lender whose closing costs are $1,000 less, you could save $2,500 ($1,000 because the other lender's closing costs are less, plus the $1,500 from the builder that you can apply to the other lender's closing costs).

Should the builder refuse to let you apply his financing incentives elsewhere under any circumstance, and you know when you negotiate the sales contract that you will not be using his lender, try to apply the dollar amount of his financing incentives toward an upgrade or option (such as an outdoor deck) when you negotiate the sales contract.

financing a custom-built house

When you buy a production-built house, the builder takes out a construction loan and pays interest on it while your house goes up. You only have to apply for a permanent mortgage, which you assume when your new house is finished. If you are building a custom house, however, you will have to apply for a construction loan as well as a permanent mortgage.

The construction loan requirements dictated by lenders may prevent you from acting as your own general contractor to save the builder's markup and to construct a bigger house. Unless you have all the money in hand and don't need any financing, you won't get a construction loan. In financing a custom-built house, almost all lenders will insist that you hire a licensed, experienced builder to supervise construction. Moreover, lenders will not lend you money if you want to work with just any builder. If you want to engage one whom the lender has not worked with before, the bank will check him out—some banks more thoroughly than others. For example, Bank of America Mortgage, the fourth largest mortgage lender in the United States, not only reviews a builder's work experience, his credit, his own banker's reference, and how well he pays subs and suppliers. This lender also reviews his current inventory to ensure that he can handle your job along with the others on his docket. "If the builder's credit profile indicates an inability to pay debts, subs, and suppliers in a timely fashion, we will not make the loan," said Corina Zamora, manager of construction lending for Bank of America Mortgage.

As many custom builders have a few spec houses for sale on the side, the number and status of these unsold houses in a builder's inventory is a particular concern, added Vicky Olsen, division risk manager for Bank of America Mortgage. "If I saw a builder with five houses unsold, I would ask why. If there's no financial liability and there's a good explanation and the builder's paying his bills on time, I might go forward. But usually five unsold houses means there's a problem. You will see late pays to creditors and other red flags."

loan terms

The construction loan and the permanent mortgage are commonly combined so that you have only one closing and one set of closing costs. When the house is completed, the construction loan is rolled over into the permanent loan. But the construction portion of the loan has a higher interest rate than the permanent portion, usually one or two points above the prime interest rate. During the construction period, you do not have to pay the principal, only the interest; but the dollar amount of interest payments increases as the construction proceeds. For example, for a $450,000 construction loan at the rate of 11.5 percent (assumed for this example to be 2 points above prime), your initial monthly interest payments (when the bank has paid out only 20 percent of the loan amount to the builder) would be $862.50. But as you get closer to completion and the bank has paid out the 80 percent of the loan amount, you would be paying $3,450.00 per month. Construction delays early on are irritating, but as you get closer to completion, they can really cost you.

down payment

The down-payment requirements for a construction loan for a custom-built house follow the same parameters as a permanent mortgage. The amount required varies with the loan type, but as the total cost of the project increases, so does the down payment. Sometimes you can borrow as much as $400 thousand with only 5 percent down, but most lenders require a higher down payment at the $300 thousand mark. Above that, the down payment generally rises to 10 percent, and at $500 thousand it goes up to 20 percent. Above $750 thousand, the down payment usually tops off at 30 percent, but most lenders have an upper limit to what they will lend—Bank of America, for example, draws the line at $1.5 million. Above that you have to pay cash.

The total cost of a custom-home building project includes the lot cost as well as the construction. If you are buying the lot at the same time that you are building on it, the construction loan would include both. If you have owned the lot for six months to a year, depending on the lender's specific requirements, you can apply any equity that has accrued toward your down payment. It is unlikely that the lot value would have appreciated much in such a short time. But if you have owned it for ten years, its value may have appreciated significantly, and you may have enough equity to cover your entire down payment. That is, if your total project cost is $440,000 and you have $44,000 of equity in your lot (10 percent of $440,000), you won't have to put down any additional cash for the down payment; you can then apply the entire $400,000 loan to the construction of your house. If, on the other hand, you are buying the lot at the same time as you are building the house, you would have to come up with the down payment in cash. More important, this could affect your construction budget. If you can spend a total of $440,000 but the lot costs $75,000, you would only have $365,000 to spend on the construction. In addition, $44,000 in cash for a down payment would be required.

Your existing house, if it has appreciated significantly, can be another source of down-payment money. To use it, however, you will have to take out a home-equity loan, because most lenders require that you bring cold cash to the closing table.

Should you sell your existing house during construction, you can apply the funds that you net from the sale to the principal of your permanent mortgage when your loan rolls over from the construction phase. If you net $100 thousand, for example, you can reduce the principal on your permanent mortgage by this amount (reduce the amount you are borrowing from $400 thousand to $300 thousand). You can then greatly reduce the repayment period, or greatly lower your monthly payments over the same period. But you will have to address this when you are negotiating the loan. You may find that it is beneficial to have two closings—one for the construction portion of the loan and a second for the permanent mortgage. At the second closing, you would add the funds from the sale of your old house to your down payment. This will reduce the amount that you are borrowing, and hence the size of your monthly payment. Since the closing costs of lenders vary, you may find that the total closing costs for two loans and two closings with one lender are less than the closing costs charged for one closing and two loans with another lender.

When construction is completed, the finished house will be worth more than the total cost of the sticks and bricks required to build it. (For example, your $440 thousand house could appraise at $500 thousand.) When you move in, you will already have a hefty chunk of equity in your new house.

cost overruns and construction delays

The lender will base your loan amount on its appraiser's assessment of your proposal— your lot value, plans, and specifications. If you hit bedrock while excavating the basement or decide later that you really did want to add the forty-five-thousand-dollar bonus room over the garage, you will have to come up with the cash yourself. To avoid any unpleasant surprises once you start excavating, some lenders, such as CTX Mortgage (a national mortgage company based in Dallas), require a soil report before approving the loan.

Cost overruns are always a possibility on a custom home-building project, so most lenders will insist that you have a sterling credit record and other assets that you can draw on to cover them.

A six-month time frame to build your house may be reasonable, but with nation-wide shortages of skilled construction labor and materials, nine to twelve months may be more realistic in some places. Since it's easier to finish early than ask for an extension on your construction loan, apply for a longer loan period than you think you will need.

draw schedule

Rather than give you all the construction-loan funds at once, the lender will pay out a portion at the completion of each phase of the job. The construction loan is usually broken down into five payments, or draws, but it can be as many as ten or as few as three, depending on the lender and the builder. And before the lender writes any check, it will send out an inspector to verify that the work has been done.

During your initial meeting with all lenders that you are approaching about financing for your custom-built house, you should ask who is doing the actual inspection. You need to have a professional inspector or a retired builder to do this, not an "internal" inspection that could be a clerk who does a drive-by. If the clerk doesn't verify that the work has been done or is clueless about what he is looking at, the builder could be paid for work that hasn't been performed. If the builder then skips town and blows the money in Vegas, you are out of luck. Of course, this would not happen with a reputable builder. Still, it is prudent to protect yourself by insisting that a professional verify that the work has been performed before any checks are issued.

Though a builder-owned mortgage company sounds as if the builders have their hands in both pockets—they sell you the house and then loan you the money to buy it—a major reason that builders have their own mortgage company or a preferred lender is "to control the deal." In explaining why his firm set up its own

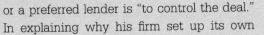
tips**from**the**trade:**
why the builders
are the lenders, too

mortgage company, here's how Tom Bozzuto, chairman of Bozzuto Homes (a medium-size home-building firm in the Washington, D.C., market), described the situation: "Every time we sold a house, a mortgage company made money for something we could do just as well. We're making the same money that a third party would, but we didn't do it just to make money. Just as important to us was keeping control of the process. Our customers would go through the mortgage process with no difficulty, then they got to the closing table and needed more money to close and take possession of the house. Or two days before closing, it turned out that their credit was not okay, or they had a relative 'who does mortgages, I want her to do mine,' and it delayed things."

Home builder Allan Washak of Columbia, Maryland, further elaborated: "The product I build, I own until you settle and move in. I'm trying to protect my financial interest in that house. I also want to protect our customers—their interest is just as important. I want to make sure that our buyers have a sound mortgage from a reputable lender. My concern is the buyer who looks up on the Internet, gets baited and switched and taken advantage of by a lender that promises teaser low rates but adds on thousands of dollars in closing fees and prepays."

And then there are the no-shows—the lenders who don't show up at the closing. One builder who now has his own mortgage company said, "I've had unsuspecting buyers sign up with flaky lenders who offered great rates but didn't show up for closing. We had to deal with a moving van on the street full of furniture, crying children, distraught parents, and we had to scramble to find alternative financing."

Another reason that builders cited for having a single designated lender was logistics and overhead. A medium to large builder may close on fifty houses a month, and all of them will be in the last few days of that month. If the builder has to deal with fifty different lenders and make sure that all the loan documents are in order, it can be a logistical nightmare that requires several full-time employees to coordinate. Even the small builder who builds only thirty houses a year prefers to deal with only one lender instead of thirty.

While builders clearly benefit from having their own mortgage company, so do buyers, because the priority of the builder's mortgage company is to sell houses and secondarily to sell loans. As Bozzuto said, "We are principally in the home-building business. It is not unusual for our mortgage company to say we will take a little less money on this buyer to make sure that the sale did happen." And not just one house. "We want to sell their first house, their last active adult-community house, and their two houses in between," said Deborah Still, executive vice president and chief operating officer for Pulte Mortgage.

Besides generally offering favorable rates in an industry that is ferociously competitive, the builder-lenders may have lower closing costs than conventional lenders. They do not usually charge a loan application fee, which can often be several hundred dollars, and charge only their cost—about twenty dollars—to obtain credit reports from the three major credit reporting bureaus (many lenders charge fifty to seventy-five dollars for this). As with other lenders, however, all the fees applied to closing costs that are not legally required by law are negotiable, so you should ask.

the production-built house

chapter five

About fifty years ago, many home builders bought large tracts of land, subdivided it, built roads, laid the utility lines, and then constructed the same one or two houses over and over in a production-line fashion. The builders' emphasis was on simplicity and speed; the houses were small and modest, but the buyers didn't care. After a nearly twenty-year hiatus caused by the Great Depression and World War Two, people were willing to buy any house they could get.

Because the home builders developed tracts of land, they were known as "tract-builders";

the communities they created by subdividing land into many small lots became known as "subdivisions." The speed and simplicity of building led to huge developments of similar-looking houses, which were famously characterized as "little boxes made of ticky-tacky" by folksinger Pete Seeger and frequently described as "cookie-cutter houses" by the culterati.

Understandably unhappy with the song, the carping, and a sobriquet that many home buyers still associate with boring and substandard houses, tract-home builders today prefer to be called production builders. Their emphasis is still on speed, and they still build houses in a production-line fashion. In nearly every other respect, however, the home-building business has changed dramatically.

Rather than the one-house-size-fits-all attitude common to production builders in the fifties, variety abounds. Town houses, once found only in cities, are offered all over the suburbs, and range from the very large and luxurious to the very small and modest. Single-family detached houses likewise range from very large five- or six-bedroom, three-car-garage villas to modest, two- or three-bedroom one-car-garage (or no-garage) bungalows.

Lot sizes can also vary. The very large house might be on half an acre. Or, bowing to many buyers' time-pressured lives and acknowledged aversion to yard work, it could sit on a small lot with a modest fringe of land running around the house. Smaller houses may be on a quarter acre, but in many markets smaller lots are the norm, and houses may be separated by only ten feet or less. But mindful of the cookie-cutter criticism, the houses will all have varied facade treatments.

The variety of housing and lot size is partially a matter of targeting different pocketbooks. The large and luxurious town house is designed and priced to appeal to older, affluent buyers who are fed up with yard work but still want the grand lifestyle. The modest town house, which will invariably be in an outlying suburb where land costs are lower, is designed and priced to appeal to younger, first-time buyers who are more willing to commute long distances.

The variety in offerings also reflects another important market reality: There are many different types of households today. Some are still the nuclear family—mom, dad, and two or three children—but there are also childless professional couples, empty-nester couples with adult children who are no longer at home, families with grown children still at home, multi-generation households, blended families with older teenagers and younger children by the second marriage, and so forth.

While production builders now offer a variety of lots, house sizes, and floor plans, they still aim for speed and ease of construction, and their designs are simple. Even within the paradigm of the simple box, however, production builders and their architects have produced some ingenuous variations. The builders have also filled their houses with amenities that were once found only in expensive, custom-built houses—granite countertops, huge master bathrooms with large soaking tubs, separate stall showers, and double vanity sinks, for example. Aesthetically speaking, however, production-built houses will rarely display subtleties of view and light because they are designed for a specific lot size, not for a specific site.

The way that houses are sold has also changed. Fifty years ago, builders operated with a "build houses and buyers will come" approach. Today a builder will erect one or two furnished models to show prospective buyers what he is selling, but he won't turn over any dirt and start to build anything until he has a signed sales contract in hand. These days every builder also offers optional upgrades that are showcased in the models; it is often hard to discern the basic house underneath.

The character of production-home building firms has changed over the last five decades. There are still many small, locally owned firms, but in many markets home building is dominated by large national firms that build all over the country and enjoy such economies of scale that they can purchase building materials by the train load. The smaller, local firms do not have that kind of buying power, but they use their lower overhead and fewer layers of management to advantage. They are generally more nimble and can respond faster to changing design trends. To compete with the big guys, they are also more willing to change a floor plan to accommodate buyers. The big firms, however, have more resources to experiment with important but less sexy issues like energy efficiency and indoor air quality.

And, of course, the size of production-builder subdivisions has also changed. You can still find stand-alone subdivisions of a hundred houses built by a single builder in a suburban location. But in most metropolitan areas, you are more likely to encounter either a much smaller development of twenty to thirty houses on a few acres that are closer to the city center, or a much larger development of several thousand units on several hundred to several thousand acres in the outlying suburbs.

The smaller, close-in development is very likely to be built on land that has been converted from industrial use. Its principal attraction is location, and it will have few, if any, site amenities. The larger developments, generally called master planned communities or planned unit developments (PUDs), are nearly always built on converted farmland. PUDs often have as many as ten builders, and they offer a variety of housing including single-family houses, attached town houses, and apartment condominiums. Within each broad category of house types, there will be a range of sizes and prices. "Build-out"—the point at which all the houses in a development are completed—will be five to seven years in the smaller PUDs; in the largest ones, house construction may go on for twenty to thirty years or more.

Though large, the PUDs are not wall-to-wall houses. The amenities usually include biking and hiking trails, tennis courts, swimming pools, a community center, a shopping center, and frequently, a golf course. Large stands of trees and vegetation are often left untouched. Some of the larger PUDs have a commercial area with both retail and office space where many of the residents work, commuting by foot or bike.

Most PUDs have a traditional suburban street layout with "feeder streets" and cul de sacs. The houses are generally clustered by house type and price. In some of the newer PUDs, land developers have opted for a Traditional Neighborhood Design layout, sometimes referred to as the New Urbanism. In this arrangement, the houses are set close to one another and to the street, which New Urbanists regard as a communal living room and not merely a conduit of traffic. Two-car garages with their large doors, often the most prominent feature on the front of a new house today, have been moved to a rear alley in keeping with New Urbanist thinking that such huge expanses of blank wall hinder social interaction among neighbors (some New Urbanists doubtless think they are also ugly). Still other PUDs offer a mix of the New Urbanism with rear alleys and rear-loading garages in some sections and front-loading garages and cul de sacs in others.

With all the variety in house type, size, and community, which one is right for you? The total amount you have to spend will certainly be a controlling factor. But when you start to look, you will find that you have choices regardless of budget. In many markets, $200 thousand, for example, will likely buy you a modest town house nearer the city center or a much larger single-family house farther out. Between these two extremes there will be a range of choices—an increasingly larger town house as you move farther out or a smaller single-family house as you move in from the outlying suburbs.

It may take you some weeks or months to sort out how you want to spend your $200 thousand. Once you make that determination and zero in on a house type and location, you may find that there are four or five builders at as many locations that still meet your criteria. At this point, though, the houses will be similar and the distinctions more subtle.

As you tour models, you will quickly realize that base-price houses without the optional upgrades are pretty basic. With your $200 thousand budget, then, do you go for more space and fewer options or more options and less space? Eventually you will decide, based on the size and needs of your household, what is right for you.

If you have a larger budget—say four to $500 thousand—you will, of course, have more choices. In many markets, with a budget of this size you could also consider a custom-built house. What are the advantages of this? You can pick and choose everything from the floor plan to the doorknobs, but the cost of construction, on average, is about double, so you will get a smaller house. You have to buy a lot and find a builder. The entire process takes at least twice as long: A year from the start of negotiations to the finished house is not uncommon. A production builder can complete a house, start to finish, in about four months, barring bad weather and shortages in skilled labor and materials.

Another possibility is a semi-custom builder: They offer more plans than do most production builders, they will make more extensive changes to the plan, and they will give you more choices in materials and finishes. If they don't have the cabinet that you want, for example, they will give you an allowance—a fixed amount of money—and you pick out your own cabinets. The same-sized house will cost more than a production builder would charge because the builder is doing more work, and all that customization will slow things down, so the construction will take longer.

assessingthemarket

Before you can start touring new home communities and builders' furnished models, you have to know where to look, who the builders are, and what the prices are. Until recently, the best source of information was a local newspaper's real-estate section, but now we have the Internet. With a few clicks of the mouse, you can access information on new houses in almost every market in the country. Much of this data, however, comes in highly abbreviated form, such as "$271,900, 4 BR, 2.5 Bath, 2 Floors, 2,416 square feet." If you know what you are looking for, the websites are an invaluable tool. If you're just starting out, though, a newspaper real-estate section is still the best place to become familiar with builders, planned communities, and price ranges in your market. And such sections remain the best and quickest way to keep abreast of what's new—grand openings of new models in existing developments and in new communities, close-out sales, and special offerings such as a finished basement included in the base price.

With careful study of the ads in the real-estate section, you will get a sense of the price range for new houses in your area as well as some correlation between features such as number of bedrooms and price. You will also start to recognize the names of the builders. To become familiar with all the major players in your market, however, you need to read the section for about a month, because many builders do not advertise every week.

With one or two weeks of reading, the purchase of an up-to-date road map with all the newest streets, and some homework on your part as to what you can afford and what price range you should be looking in, you're ready to visit the model home parks in several planned communities. You will soon get a clear idea of what a "4 BR, 2.5 Bath, 2 Floors, 2,416 square feet" house actually looks like, and see that every builder's version is a little different. But knowing what "$271,900" looks like may take a while. That's because as you circle the new houses in the newspaper ads that fit your range, you will find more than one house type and size in your range—a bigger or smaller single-family house or a bigger or smaller town house. The key variables are location and land cost. If you plot the new developments on your new map, you will see that as you go farther into the outlying suburbs, the size of the house increases.

When you begin to visit the models and start to factor in all the trade-offs between one site and another, you'll find that price and size aren't the only considerations. For example, the distance to work—a bigger house and an extra five hours a week of commuting time versus a smaller house, two hours less a week of commuting, and more time to help kids with homework. Then there's proximity to public transportation—if it's good, can you get buy with only one car? Where are the shopping and other amenities located—will you have to drive twenty minutes every time you need a gallon of milk?

With all these field notes swirling around in your head, you're ready to hunker down over a computer for several hours of website research. When you start to surf the web, you will find numerous local and national websites devoted to the sale of new houses. Three of the largest national ones are NewHomesDirect.com, NewHomesNetwork. com, and homebuilder.com. When you type in a state and city or county, each of these sites allow you to select price ranges, basic features including the number of stories, bedrooms, and bathrooms, and the car capacity of the garage. You will find different listings on each site, so you should check all three. The national websites also have daily news feeds and a host of other consumer information germane to the new house—hunting process.

Some local markets have their own new-house websites. In the Washington, D.C., area for example, buyers can click to NewHomesGuide.com., which lists every builder and every development within a fifteen-county, three-city area. To find out if your market has a website with a comprehensive listing of new houses, check HousingGuides.com. Most of the HousingGuides.com sites also offer a free subscription to their monthly publication. Though more cumbersome to use, these are handy when touring models.

You should go back and forth among the newspaper, the web, and model-home tours. While you're out in the field, be alert and open to the serendipitous discovery—the smaller builder who "piggybacks" on the advertising of other builders but doesn't advertise in the newspapers or on the website himself. Often these smaller builders have unusual houses that are worth a look.

landvalues

As you tour the models in different communities, you will begin to see some repeats—that is, you will see the same or nearly the same model offered by the same builder in several locations. Of even greater interest, the prices are not the same at each location because the builder paid a different amount for the land that each one sits on. The difference in land cost from one location to another may be ten thousand dollars, though in some metropolitan areas it can be as much as a hundred thousand.

When you begin to narrow your search, you can use this fact to your advantage. If you see a particular house that you like, but the price is a real stretch, ask the sales agent if the builder sells it in other locations and what the prices are there. Since land prices can vary substantially over short distances, you may not have to go as far as you think to get the house you want.

Why does the land cost make so much difference in the sale price of the house? It is the largest single expenditure for *any* house. For a production-built house, the land

As you peruse the ads in the real-estate section and the home builders' websites in your area, it helps to know the meaning of a few key phrases:

learningthe **language** of **home**builders

- The "base price" refers to the basic, stripped-down house with standard features and finishes, no options, and built on the least expensive lot, which is usually smaller, has no views, and may be located near a busy intersection.

- License is often taken in listing prices—"low $100,000s" can mean $105,000 or $120,000.

- Builders usually advertise a range of prices for a particular location, but the lowest priced house is rarely the model. If the least expensive unit is the one that interests you, call ahead and ask the sales

agent if there is one under construction that you can see. The builder may also show the house as a furnished model at another location.

- Directions to a "sales center" can mean a trailer surrounded by mountains of dirt, earth-moving equipment, and plenty of construction activity, or an actual finished and furnished model. *Always* call ahead to find out exactly what is available to see.

- "Grand opening" can mean the ceremonial first spade in the ground or the finally finished model, so call ahead to confirm what is intended.

- The ad may say there is a model to visit, but in fact it may not be finished and open for public view; call ahead to confirm.

accounts for a quarter to a third of the sale price. This will not show up on your website search, the newspaper ads, or the builder's sales brochures, because production builders sell the house and the lot together as a package. However, newspaper ads and website listings often include the model name—for example, the "Devonshire," or the "Berkeley." When this information is given, you can track the price at different locations.

baseprice**and**options

The furnished models all look fabulous. Much of what you see, however, is not included in the basic house or the base price. Most of the embellishments that add a certain je ne sais quois—the bay windows, the maple hardwood floors, the granite countertops, the raised-panel cabinet doors—are optional extras. Even minutiae like the size and type of trim around the doors and windows can be upgrades (the upgrade can be wood instead of plastic, or a wider piece of trim). Unfortunately, the extras are rarely labeled as such, and this makes it hard to distinguish between the options and the basic house.

The simplest way to bring some order to this confusing picture is to ask the on-site sales agent to go through the house with you and point out the options one by one. If the agent is busy with another buyer, ask her to give you an option price list if it's not included in the sales brochure. This will not list *all* the options shown, but it will give you a good idea.

The price of the enhanced model will be much higher than that of the basic house, so ask the sales agent for the price of the model as shown. Don't faint when you hear the answer—in many areas of the country builders routinely add seventy-five to a hundred thousand dollars worth of extras.

Since you want to know what something closer to the basic house that you would buy will look like, ask the sales agent if there are any nearly completed houses for other buyers that you can see. No buyer will have gotten all the options, so this should give you a good idea.

After you've seen ten to fifteen models and carefully noted the options, you will be able to separate the extras from the basic house more easily, and also to pick up on the extras that different builders throw into the basic price or periodically offer at a reduced rate, such as a brick front or Corian, an expensive, synthetic solid-surfacing countertop material for kitchen and bathrooms.

As a general rule, houses priced from the lower end to the middle range of your market will be very basic, so all those embellishments will be extra. At the upper end, buyers can afford more and expect it, so a higher percentage of the finishes and features shown in the model will be included in the base price. There will still be subtle differences. For example, at the higher end, the standard cabinet doors in the kitchen will have raised panels, but they will not be solid wood; the solid-wood door will be an upgrade.

thevalueofoptions

Everyone, including the on-site sales agent and other prospective buyers, has an opinion about options and resale. Who's right? Which options are frivolous and which are prudent choices that add to the value of the house and help with resale? The short answer: only those items that future buyers also want and will be willing to pay for. If that $2000 master-bedroom closet organizer, $500 jade-colored marble fireplace surround, and $650 polished-brass fixture package for the master bathroom don't interest future buyers, you will be spending money now that you won't recoup when you sell your house. Unfortunately, many buyers learn this truth only after they lose a bundle at resale. This is especially true at the low end, where buyers have smaller budgets and are more conscious of every cost.

choose the functional over the cosmetic

How can you avoid options that will cost you in the future? As a general rule, choosing the functional over the merely cosmetic, and neutral or innocuous over the unusual or exotic, will pay off at resale. Real estate appraiser William C. Harvey of Great Falls, Virginia, advises buyers to focus on the functional because "the further away an item is from function, the less it's worth." Even when an option is functional, Harvey points out that it may be worth less than you think. Individual taste is also a factor that affects value. For example, a hardwood floor is usually a plus, but staining it too dark or too light a color can greatly reduce its appeal at resale, because many people don't like either look.

Similarly, taste can also affect the value of items that are included in the base price. If you select unusual colors that have a limited appeal—for example, fuchsia wall-to-wall carpeting—you'll have fewer takers when you try to sell your house, or buyers will subtract the cost of replacement from what they are willing to pay. If you're in doubt on what constitutes "unusual taste," go with Harvey's "nine out of ten rule": If nine out of ten buyers will like something, it's a good choice. But if only one out of ten does, it's not. He suggests that if you have a yen for the exotic, exercise it with your furnishings, not your house.

The options that add the most value are the ones that increase usable space, such as finishing off a basement, especially in a town house. If a walk-out basement is an option, get it too. The immediate access to the backyard and the larger windows and sliding glass door that lighten up the space and make it feel less like a cave make the walk-out worth its extra cost.

A fireplace is another good bet, but don't go overboard. One will add value, but more than one generally will not, and a fireplace is worth more in some locations than others. For most buyers, the family room is the desired spot. A fireplace in the living room is less sought-after, and having one in a master suite is definitely frivolous unless the house is at the very high end.

For buyers willing to tamper with tradition, gas fireplaces have definite advantages over wood-burning ones. Though more expensive to install, gas fireplaces provide more heat and are more practical—you don't have to haul logs around or clean up ashes. For an extra $250 or so, some builders offer a remote starter for a gas fireplace so you don't even have to get up to turn it on.

If your option dollars are limited, the one room where some upgrading nearly always pays off is the kitchen. A bigger side-by-side refrigerator, a gas stove, and more expensive cabinets with upscale door fronts and hardwood or tile flooring will always interest future buyers of your house.

how many options is too many?

Your total budget is certainly a factor here, but you also have to consider your house in the context of the neighborhood. If you get more options than most of the others in your subdivision, you're "over-improving"—that is, future buyers may not be willing to pay substantially more to buy your house with all its options than they will for the house across the street that doesn't have as many. They will pay some additional cost, but not 50 percent more. This is one reason that it is *never* a good idea to buy the builder's model with all the upgrades in it unless you are offered a *very* substantial discount.

The difference between adequate and overboard options is a fine line. There's also the opportunity cost to consider. If you get bay windows, a breakfast room bump-out, or hardwood floors, you may not in fact get substantially more money at resale than your neighbor across the street who didn't get these extras; but you may sell your house much faster, which can be worth a lot in reduced stress.

The best way to get a sense of what is considered the "market standard" for your neighborhood (albeit a builder's upgrade above the standard basic house) versus what is considered a luxury item that won't pay for itself is to look at many resale properties, Harvey says. If you look at houses three to six years old (close in time to the current new house market), you can see for yourself what is expected for your price range and what is overdoing it. For example, in most markets now, two sinks and a separate shower and a tub are standard in the master bathroom, but separate his and her commode compartments cross the line into excessive.

A good way to gauge the middle ground between under- and over-improving in specific communities is to look at several finished or nearly finished houses. If people are already living there, you can ask which options they got.

Before you make your final selections and sign on the dotted line, you also need to recognize that options can have non-monetary value, and evaluate them by this criterion as well. If an option will significantly enhance your enjoyment of the house while you live in it—if, say, after a hard day at the office, a soak in a whirlpool hits the spot—then it may be a good investment for you. Just don't expect the next buyer to pay for that particular upgrade.

touringmodels

When you walk into a builder's furnished model, the first thing you will notice is the furnishings and finishes. But don't let these be an undue influence or a distraction. You may like or hate the faux blue maple cabinets in the kitchen, but look beyond them to the kitchen itself. When you stand at the sink, can you join in conversation in the breakfast area, the family room, or the dining room? Do you need a kitchen sink placed so that you can watch your children playing in the family room or in the yard while you are fixing meals? Are there enough cabinets for your cooking equipment and tableware? Is there enough counterspace to prepare a meal?

If the spaces are different from your own house, think about how you would actually use them. A cavernous master suite with a huge bathroom can be appealing, but how much time will you actually spend there? Will a sitting area in a master bedroom be more useful than a fourth bedroom?

If a house is smaller than twenty-four-hundred-square feet, you will have to make some compromises on room count and room size, so pay particular attention to the must-have rooms on your own list. Are they present in this house and truly acceptable? There may or may not be a home office; if the plan includes both a family room and formal living and dining rooms, the formal areas will be small.

This may sound as if touring each model will take a lot of time, but after you have toured several, you can be thorough and quick. As you pick up speed, though, don't try to see too many houses in one day. Once you've zeroed in on your price range and general location, the sizes of the houses and the floor plans will be similar, and the differences between them are likely to be subtle and hard to keep straight. Looking at more than five houses in one day is pushing it. If you bring the kids along, plan on looking at fewer than this. One way to help you keep the different models straight is to videotape them or take photographs, but you should ask the sales agent before you start to click away.

If you plan to look at a large number of models, you will soon have a stack of sales brochures. You need some way of organizing this material, as well as a system for helping you remember the models that you especially liked and the individual details that you might want to add to your house.

the sales agent

Don't avoid contact with the builder's sales agent for fear of being trapped into signing a sales contract. A good sales agent will have a wealth of information about the product that can be useful to you, and she or he knows that buyers *always* visit three or four times before they get serious.

When you first enter a model, the sales agent will try to engage you in some small talk. She's trying to find out if you're a browser or a buyer, and she's trying to get a sense of what you're looking for and how to be helpful. She will nearly always offer to take you through the house. If you take the guided tour, don't hesitate to ask the agent to point out all the options and any decorator items that were added to enhance the model presentation but are not for sale.

After the tour, ask for the price of the model as shown. There may be as much as $100 thousand worth of extras, but if you ask the agent to identify a few of the big-ticket items, you're likely to find that much of that $100 thousand is easily accounted for. In many markets today, a lot premium (an upcharge for a lot with trees, a view, or some other amenity), a sun-room addition, a breakfast-room extension, and a third garage bay can easily add $75 thousand to the base price.

You should also ask which options have been the most popular with buyers. If you end up buying a house in this community, you will want to get some of them as well. When resale time eventually comes, you will have a harder time selling if you took the plain-Jane approach and your house is less attractive than the others on the block.

If you prefer to look by yourself and ask questions later, the agent won't be offended. And don't be embarrassed to admit that you're just whiling away a weekend afternoon and want to look mainly at the window treatments. Browsers have friends who may come to take a look and end up buying. Being up front about your intent is especially helpful when there are other people in the model, including serious buyers.

Most sales agents suggest that you go through first and get a sales brochure with floor plans afterward, but you may find that it's easier to look at the model with a road map in hand, and the floor plans are also handy for taking notes. If you have a rough sketch of the floor plan of your present house, you can compare it to the builder's floor plan as you walk through.

the sales information card

Invariably, the agent will ask you to fill out a sales information card. You are *not* obliged to do this, but giving your name and checking off how you heard about the project—newspapers, website, drive-by, or a friend—gives the builder useful marketing information. Giving your address ensures that you will get updated information about new models, price changes, and new financing.

The sales information card also requests somewhat detailed information about your income. If you find this intrusive, and many people do, you don't have to fill it out. But eventually this question will have to be addressed. If you haven't already talked with a mortgage lender and don't know how much financing you are likely to get, or even if you can afford the model that you are looking at, a good sales agent should be able to calculate the figures in her head in about half a minute.

tapping the agent's expertise

Besides giving the house a careful look, ask the agent about the features that you can't see. For example, does the builder have an unusual energy package?

Very few houses are a perfect fit, so ask about the builder's policy on making any alterations to his standard plan. Some builders won't change a thing, but others are more accommodating as long as the request does not require major surgery.

Both the builder and the sales agent want to know what you think, even if it's negative. The builder wants the feedback, and explaining your reactions to the agent will help your own cause. If the agent understands clearly why you didn't like this particular house—you want a large dining room and the one in this model is tiny, or you feel "lost" in the large, two-story family room—she can direct you to another house by the same builder that is closer to your needs or style. If you hated the kitchen cabinets, the builder probably offers seven other styles to choose from.

Feel free to ask the sales agent how this builder's product compares with others nearby—she'll certainly know. But be wary if the sales agent starts to criticize the competition. Not only does this create an unpleasant atmosphere, it may also be a way to gloss over the shortcomings of her own product. A good sales agent will offer a straightforward assessment of the other builders nearby. But as the comparisons are being made, make sure that apples are being compared to apples. If the square footage the same? Are the standard items the same? Does one include a fireplace in the base price and the other offer it only as an option? Is the fireplace gas- or wood-burning? What size and brand of whirlpool tub is offered?

Should you decide this house is very promising and return for the second or third time, also factor in how you feel about the sales agent. During the sales negotiations and the four to six months of construction, you will be working together very closely. Sales agents are usually quite affable, but if you don't feel comfortable, it will color your entire purchase experience.

the**model's**furniture

Study the furniture as carefully as you study the house. All of it has been selected to show a space to best effect, but not necessarily to show how real people with real furniture would live in it. Don't blithely assume that your own furniture will work as well as the decorator's did—you need to look very carefully, especially if the house is small.

kitchen

The rooms to study hardest are the ones you'll use the most, particularly the kitchen. If eating in it is an important part of your lifestyle, you need to make sure that there really is enough room to eat. If there isn't, you will resent it every day you live in the house. Is the table in the model sized for a cocktail bar, a quick in-and-out fast-food restaurant, or real people enjoying a leisurely breakfast and reading the paper?

Some houses have a breakfast area that is furnished to imply that the space can also be used as an informal sitting area; if the eating table is shoved up against the sofa, though, you know it's really one or the other. Many kitchens have a "planning desk" that's next to the eating area. The desk can be handy, but make sure that you have enough room to sit at it without banging into the chairs of a nearby breakfast table or vice versa.

For Arthur Morrisette, Jr., who has been in the moving business for close to fifty years and now heads Interstate Van Lines in Springfield, Virginia, the most important question to ask when touring a furnished model is "Will *my* furniture fit?" Morrisette transports household goods all over the country. He frequently encounters logistical problems with new houses, both large and small, and in all price ranges including luxury ones costing nearly a million dollars. In some instances, his crews have had to remove door frames, window frames, and even bricks to get the furniture inside.

When Morrisette's vans pull up in front of a new house, the first problem confronting his crews is the front-door. Standard front-door openings used to be thirty-six-inches wide, but thirty-four-inch or thirty-two-inch ones are not uncommon today. Though a seemingly minor downsizing, the two- to four-inch difference is critical for a mover. Many furniture pieces must be turned and angled this way and that to get them through the doorway. With a narrower width, it's much harder, and furniture or the door opening or both can be damaged.

Worse still, entry foyers are also getting smaller, and this leaves the movers even less room to maneuver. When a closet or wall is directly opposite the front door and the foyer width is less than five feet, it's a tight squeeze. When this condition is coupled with a thirty-two-inch door opening, Morrisette said that extra-large pieces, such as the currently fashionable ten-foot long sofas with big round arms, are nearly impossible to get into the house.

Once over the threshold, the main living areas in most new houses do not present a problem, but the hallways leading to bedrooms are invariably narrow, a seemingly efficient allocation of floor space that makes the movers' job more difficult.

Stairs in new houses are another headache, especially ones with a U-shaped configuration. Though this type of stair may be very efficient space-wise, it's murder on the movers. Besides contending with the narrow width of the stairs—rarely wider than thirty-six inches—and the sharp turns, the movers also have to maneuver around the stair rail. Not surprisingly, the walls in the stairwells frequently get scuffed as the furniture is being carried up the stairs.

While the stairs get smaller and steeper and the hallways narrower, master bedroom suites are ballooning. In new houses today, the master bedroom often includes a sitting area and enough room for a king-size bed with a sizable headboard, a large armoire or triple dresser, and a large entertainment center with a drawer base and television niche. Getting such large furniture pieces into the master suite, however, can be difficult to impossible. With tight stairways and narrow halls, the only way to get a king or queen mattress into the master bedroom is by bending it. If the mattress has coils inside, the bending can break some of the springs. In many cases, Morrisette's crews have had to saw and fold king or queen box springs in half before they can be carried up the stairs and into the master bedroom.

One sure indication of the relative difficulty of moving furniture into a master suite is the size of the furniture shown in the model. If the room is big but all the furniture in it is modestly sized, moving in bigger pieces was probably too hard. If the furniture is big, but the hall is narrow and the stairs are steep with one or two turns, Morrisette suggests asking the builder how he got the furniture into the room. In some instances, it has appeared to him that to do this the builder must have put the furniture in the room while the house was still under construction, and then finished the house around it.

Morrisette's final words of advice: When you've narrowed down the field to two or three builders, assess each one's model from a mover's perspective. The question to ask is not "Will this piece of furniture fit in this room?" but "Can I get it *into* the room?"

If the kitchen is small with only modest cabinet storage, you may need to store eating and serving dishes in a dining-room buffet. If so, make sure that the one shown in the model—if there is one—is big enough to hold things and not just for looks.

dining room

Whether the house has a separate dining room, a dining alcove, or a designated dining area in the living room, be sure to check out the table and chairs. Is there enough room for everyone to get in and out of their chairs and for you to move around guests? If you're not sure, have your spouse or partner sit in a chair while you try to move around him or her. If the table shown is narrower than what you have now, you may have to replace your own; but if you like everything else about the house, this may be an acceptable compromise.

Smaller houses usually show a table set for six. For hosting larger gatherings, can you extend the table easily? Removing furniture from the living room to accommodate the longer table may be acceptable for Thanksgiving and other important holidays, but no one wants to do this on a regular basis.

living room

As you survey the living room, look to see if a large portion of the space also doubles as circulation. If so, adding more furniture than is shown in the model may not work, especially if what you want to add is a coffee table in front of the sofa. Many model homes do not have coffee tables in the living room for just this reason.

bedrooms

When you move onto the bedrooms, red-flag the crib. Sometimes it can simply be a decorator's way of saying that a house will be suitable for a young family, but in smaller houses a full-size bed may be a tight fit. While you're in the room with the crib, see if there is a good spot for a changing table. You will use it many times a day if you really do have a baby, but this essential piece of equipment never appears in furnished models.

A bedroom that is furnished as a study can be the decorator's way of saying that this house would work for a professional couple, but this too can mean that the room is too small to be comfortably used as a bedroom.

The master bedroom will always be bigger than the other bedrooms, but it can be the trickiest one of all, furniture-wise. There will always be a double bed, but the decorator will select a size that shows the room off best. If your bed is larger than the one shown and won't fit, think about whether you are really willing to downsize (most people are not). To give the impression that the master bedroom can also be an adult hideaway, many decorators will add an armchair or a chaise longue by the window but leave out a dresser. The adult-hideaway concept can be appealing, but make sure that you still have room for your clothes.

real people and their furniture

Of course, seeing a house that is finished and occupied will give you a much better idea of how real people and their furniture will look. If you are looking at a large project in its final construction phase, you can often find a house for sale by a homeowner who bought in early and had to relocate. If you see that your furniture will fit and the owner's taste is similar to yours, this may be a better deal than a brand-new house. The owners are competing with the builder for buyers and will have to sell at the same price, even though they may have spent several thousand dollars on window treatments (curtains and blinds that do not come with the house), a deck or patio (which is almost always an optional extra), and landscaping (if it's more than just a few bushes, the owners added it at their own expense).

watchoutforthelittlethings

When Kitty Kallen led the charts with "Little Things Mean a Lot" in the early 1950s, she wasn't singing about houses. But the "little things" about a house that never capture your attention when you tour a model can become major irritants after you move in. Some of them can be avoided with advance planning, some not. But identifying them at the outset avoids the unpleasant discovery later.

Much of the excitement of buying a brand-new house is getting to choose the paint colors, cabinets, countertops, and floor finishes. With a production-built house, you'll find the selection of these items large enough to personalize your space. But the choices are limited and they do correlate with price. As the price goes up, so does the number of choices.

With paint colors, production builders usually offer no choice at all. Although model homes frequently have unusual, eye-catching color schemes, the builder's goal is to make his model house stand out from the competition and to give buyers an idea of the decorating possibilities. In reality, most production builders offer only one wall color—usually an off white—and one trim color.

As any interior designer can tell you, however, even with only one wall color, you can create very different looks with different carpets. Two award-winning interior designers who work with production builders all over the country—Lita Dirks of Englewood, Colorado, and Susan Gulick of Herndon, Virginia—say the trick is to select one that looks right with your furnishings. The key here is "neutral." If you stay in the neutral zone, the walls and carpet will work with any decorating scheme, including the one you have now and the one you will have ten years from now. If you want to add some excitement and bright colors, put them on the less expensive room accessories such as draperies, pillows, and artwork, which you can afford to change from time to time.

Neutral walls and carpeting do not automatically translate into a dull and boring interior. There is an enormous gradation of neutral colors with both warm and cool tones. Which end of the spectrum to head for depends on personal taste and the climate where you live. In the northern regions of the country, with long, cold winters—especially ones with a lot of cloud cover—pick a neutral with a yellow, orange, red, or orange-red base. In climates with dreary cold winters, these will warm up the space and create a "cozy envelope." In areas with a warm climate, choose a neutral that has a cooler cast with undertones of grays, blues, or greens.

But, our experts hastened to add, correlating color tone and climate is not a hard-and-fast rule. The tone should also complement your other furnishings. If you're not sure whether to head for the gray/blue/greens or the yellow/orange/reds, look at what you have. You will find a thread of color choices in your furniture, dishes, place mats, and napkins.

Should this be your first venture into interior decorating and you don't as yet have any furnishings, Gulick suggests looking in your closet: "If you look over your clothes, you will find color themes you may not be aware of."

Ideally, the carpet color should be close to the wall color so that the two will blend together and create an interior envelope. But if the builder's standard wall color is an off-white, a neutral carpet that closely matches it could be a maintenance nightmare. If prudence dictates a darker color, try to stay in the same color range as the walls. Though it's tempting to get a different colored carpet for each room, using only one for the entire house will make the house feel bigger.

- *Linen closet.* In many new houses, the hall linen closet is minuscule, with shelves barely adequate for washcloths and pillowcases. The builder isn't mincing on the details—it's just that the closet's central location on the second floor always makes it the ideal spot to put the air ducts for the heating and cooling system.

  You may be able to install shelving for your sheets and towels in the master bedroom's walk-in closet (the house will surely have one) and add shelving in the closets of each secondary bedroom for linens to be used by the occupant of that room.

- *Space for two dressers.* In furnished models, the master bedroom often looks luxuriously big, but look again. When you start to catalog the furniture in it, you may find only one or no dresser at all. You can only cram so much into the closet, especially if you are planning to put linens there. If you have two dressers, will they fit? Will purchase of a single, larger dresser that you can both share be adequate? Can you store clothes in another bedroom? Or is it time to pass on this house?

- *A place for cleaning supplies.* If you have small children, you need a place for cleaning supplies that is out of reach. You can put child locks on the cabinet doors below the sink in the kitchen and store them there, but the one time you forget to close them is the time your three-year-old will decide to take a look. Most builders provide a small cabinet above the refrigerator that would serve this purpose, but it will also be hard for you to reach. A handier place is a wall cabinet above the washer and dryer. If your builder does not provide this in his standard package and your budget is tight, ask if he can get a cheaper cabinet for the laundry than the ones he's using in the kitchen and bathrooms.

- *Broom closet.* Old houses always had a broom closet, usually in the kitchen, but new houses do not. Can you put your vacuum cleaner and broom in the front-hall closet and get coats in there too? If any members of the household play sports, is the front-hall closet big enough to hold sports equipment as well?

- *A place for backpacks.* Almost every school child in America now carries a backpack, which they generally dump at the front door. A specific place to put them would perhaps break the kids of this bad habit. One possibility, which would also solve the coats-and-sports-equipment storage problem, is to install a bank of cabinet "lockers," one for each member of the family, in the area by the door to the garage. Though cubbies are not a standard cabinet type, it is relatively easy to fashion an open cubicle with cabinets above and below, using stock cabinet parts.

the **character** issue

Production builders offer plenty of options that will individualize a house, but these aren't enough for some buyers. They still want that unique detail or two that will add character and subtly differentiate their house from others on the block. If this is your situation, here are a few suggestions:

entry area

An easy place to make a change that will be apparent as soon as you walk in the front door is in the shape of the openings from your entry foyer into a living room, dining room, or family room. For a not-so-subtle 1930s retro look, make the top of the openings elliptically shaped arches.

To add some stylistic consistency without overdoing it, you can add the same elliptical arch shape or semicircle to glass-paned doors on the wall cabinets in your kitchen (many stock cabinetmakers have glass-paned doors with this detail) or to a transom window over a doorway or larger window. You might also consider windows with semicircles at the top for a larger space, such as a family room (many window manufacturers make these).

For a more subtle and contemporary look, increase the width of the openings to the rooms off the entry foyer and run the height of the opening all the way to the ceiling. This will make the space feel more open and the rooms feel bigger. Since it requires nothing extra, the builder may be more amenable to this idea than to other suggestions. To add some subtlety and an even more contemporary look, make the corners of the larger openings rounded instead of square. Carrying the rounded corner detail throughout the house will help to tie together the design of the whole house. Though subtle, it will make your house feel different from your neighbor's.

To create a focal point in your entry, hallways, or stairs, architect Jerry Messman of Tampa, Florida, suggests a shallow niche made from drywall. Even if the niche is only two inches deep, it will be noticeable, and it's a nice way to highlight a painting or a set of photographs.

room dividers

Though walls are the conventional way to separate functions and define spaces, you can also do this with columns. In many parts of the country, columns have been widely used over the last ten years; some critics would even say they're overused. Still, when used

When Mies van der Rohe, one of the great architects of the twentieth century, uttered his famous maxim "Less is more," he was talking aesthetics and the beauty of simplicity. When Louise Rafkin, a professional house cleaner and the author of *Other People's Dirt,* praises simplicity in design, she's being practical—elaborate window and door trim and triple crown moldings are hard to clean.

detailsthat**lessen** the**cleaning**burden

Rafkin's secret to cleaning success: Focus on the details and minimize the number of surfaces where dust can collect. Since dust falls downward, Rafkin starts with where it lands—the floor. Hard surfaces such as tile or hardwood are much easier to keep clean than carpet, especially in an entry foyer or a mudroom. Her favored floor treatment, which she has in her own house, is hardwood with area rugs under furniture areas.

Besides the cleaning issue, Rafkin dislikes wall-to-wall carpet because it wears and tears at different rates. After a year, the carpet under a couch will not look the same as the carpet in a heavily trafficked area, and both collect dust. But acknowledging that wall-to-wall carpeting is the least expensive way to finish a floor and what most people will choose, she advised—"for peace of mind"—a mottled carpet in a neutral color with a little texture. Carpeting with higher, denser pile can have a rich, silky look, but every footprint shows, especially on a floor that has just been vacuumed.

Even if your budget dictates carpeting for most areas, Rafkin would still get hardwood for stairs. Though carpeting looks good here, it is nearly impossible to vacuum. A vacuum cleaner can't get in the cracks, and a battery-operated handheld type doesn't have enough suction.

Turning her attention to where the wall and floor meet, Rafkin characterized elaborate, traditional ogee-profile wall bases with their curves and small indentation as "dust collectors." They look great on move-in day, but before long, someone will have to bend down and clean out the dust and bugs that will have collected there. A clam-shell profile wall base with a shallow curve at the top is simpler, less expensive, and a "dust resister." A straight wall base with a squared off top gives a clean, utilitarian look, but dust will still collect on it. A wall with no base at all—which Mies would have loved—is also a bad idea because the wall will get nicked by a vacuum cleaner.

Central vacuum systems are offered by some builders as upgrades, but Rakfin has found that the long hose is cumbersome to drag through the house, and the suction is not great if you are vacuuming any distance from the central motor.

Though most dust ends up on the floor, it also lands on things higher up, such as chair rails and elaborate ceiling trim, which can look skuzzy when dust and cobwebs collect on it. Dining room chandeliers are another of Rafkin's' "no way" details because you have to "clean, clean, clean." A plate rack or a bookshelf running along the top of a wall, however, is one detail that Rafkin likes. "You can take a certain amount of license because you can't see the shelf from the floor—the dust collecting there is out of sight." Open shelving that is closer to eye level, on the other hand, is a "nightmare" and one that Rafkin frequently encounters as many homeowners have books, art objects, or children's artwork that they want to display.

Windows are another cleaning issue, especially when they are high up. The sixteen- to seventeen-foot-high window wall looks great in the two-story family room in the builder's model. But most of those windows will be hard to reach, Rafkin pointed out, and she predicted that anyone who buys a house with such an arrangement will end up hiring a professional window washer with special equipment to clean them both inside and out.

In the kitchen, Rafkin recommended forty-two-inch-high wall cabinets that go to the ceiling instead of shorter thirty-inch ones that leave an open area between the top of the cabinet and the ceiling. The taller, more expensive cabinets increase storage capacity; more important, installing them avoids a distasteful, periodic confrontation with the dust and grease that collect when the area above the wall cabinets is left open.

While master bathrooms are getting bigger than ever, they're not any easier to clean, Rafkin noted. Walk-in showers—so big that you don't need a door or curtain to keep the water from going everywhere—are a "bear to clean" because the no-door feature means larger areas of tiled walls to wipe down. The smaller shower stalls with clear glass that are also popular look great, but they spot easily. If you don't wipe them off every time you use the shower, the walls quickly look grimy.

As you plan your new house, Rafkin concluded, it's also helpful to keep in mind that it will probably never look as good as the builder's model, even if you build one exactly like it. The model looks perfect because no one lives in it, and the builder has an army of people to fret over every dust ball.

selectively, a column can be eye-catching. If a round, prefabricated wood column proves to be too expensive or you don't like the look, you can easily construct a square column out of two-by-four-inch framing lumber and cover it with drywall.

To avoid a toothpick effect, the column needs to be big enough to look right. If the first-floor ceilings are nine feet—now the norm for new houses in most areas of the country—the column should be ten to twelve inches on a side. To create a simple capital at the top of the column, you can use stock wood trim.

doors

A sliding glass door on the rear of the house that opens onto a deck or patio from a kitchen or family room is standard in most markets, but substituting a pair of French doors for the "slider" will give a more tailored, upscale look.

In the past, builders have not offered this on smaller houses, because the exterior doors had to swing in for security reasons; if the space was tight, the doors could easily hit furniture every time they were opened. (The doors had to swing in so that the hinges would be on the inside. If the doors swung out, the pins would be on the outside, and could easily be removed). Now several manufacturers make outswing French doors (the doors swing out instead of in) with concealed hinges that eliminate the security risk.

The now-standard nine-foot ceilings are a relatively easy way to make a smaller space feel larger. To make it feel grand as well as big, architect Margaret Rast of Vienna, Virginia, recommends eight-foot-high doors instead of the six-foot, eight-inch high ones that most builders use. She also suggests wider trim along the top of the higher openings. If you use a wider, thirty-six-inch, interior door as well, when you pass though the doorway, "You'll feel like you're really walking through something," she says.

trim

If you can't get wider or higher doors, replacing painted wood trim around doors and windows and wall bases with exposed maple or oak can make these conventional details, like the rounded corners, pull the whole house together. If you do this, a more expensive, clear grade of wood will look better.

cabinetry

If the trim and floor are oak or maple, try another wood type for the cabinet doors in your kitchen and bathrooms. Merrilat, a stock cabinet line used by tract-builders all over the country, offers cabinet doors in cherry and hickory, as well as in the standard oak and maple.

A built-in look, often the hallmark of an architect-designed, custom-built house, can be achieved in bedrooms, home offices, and family rooms by using stock cabinet bases or drawer bases and wood countertops to match instead of plastic laminate or Corian. A bank of stock-cabinet bases and wood counters topped with open adjustable bookshelves along a family room wall, for example, offers an opportunity to embellish a room with some of your favorite things that really will make you feel good—family photographs, children's artwork, objects passed down from your grandparents or collected on trips, and books.

windows

Andersen windows, a brand that many production builders use, makes Andersen Art Glass—eleven stained-glass designs including four by Frank Lloyd Wright. These can be incorporated into any Andersen window and used as a decorative element. For example, the stained glass could be used in a side window next to a front door, as a transom window above the front door, for a stairwell, or in a powder room.

A large number of windows that fill a space with light is a common feature in new houses today, so whatever you buy will likely have these. To get a more traditional as well as a more custom look, Messman suggested putting a six-inch drywall strip between windows that are lined up together. Separating the windows gives a sense of the thickness of the wall and, if you're going for a more traditional look, it's more authentic, because old houses didn't have large, uninterrupted expanses of glass.

flooring

Inlaid carpet with a hardwood border for a living, dining, or family room adds a more tailored look. It's also a cost saver because you are only getting hardwood for the periphery of those areas.

makingthefinalcut andchoosingyourbuilder

In buying a production-built or semi-custom house, most of your time will be spent touring and evaluating furnished models. Eventually, though, you'll winnow the list down to two or three models and two or three builders. At this point, you need to check out the bona fides of the building firms behind the houses, and make a return visit to the projects for a closer and more thorough look at the merchandise. (See Chapter 2 for more information on evaluating builders.)

the houses

When you make the return visit to the models, ask to see two or three nearly completed houses for other buyers. The furnished model will always look great, but nearly completed houses will be a better indication of the workmanship that you can expect. You may have looked at other houses on an earlier visit when you first saw the model, but this time give the nearly completed houses much more scrutiny. Are the walls bulging or plumb? Are the cover plates for the outlets and light switches square or crooked?

Try everything. Open and close all the doors (these are routinely removed in models to make the house and rooms look bigger) to see if the latches line up properly, and if the doors stay shut. Open all the windows. Try all the faucets in the bathrooms and kitchen.

Send someone upstairs to flush the toilets while you listen below. Plumbing in new houses can be noisy because most builders use plastic waste pipes, which are noisier than the more expensive cast-iron pipes in older houses. The house won't be furnished, so there won't be any drapes or furniture to dampen the sound. But if the flushing toilets sound like Niagara Falls when the house is empty, they will certainly still be audible when you move in. If you want to be thorough, flush the toilet in the model, which will be furnished, for comparison.

Another noise issue in a new house can be rattling dishes in kitchen cabinets. In older houses, this was rarely an issue because lumber was cheap and builders put in more and larger floor joists than were structurally required. With today's volatile lumber prices, however, builders use less lumber. They engineer the floors for actual loads, and in some instances install the smallest allowable floor joists placed as far apart as the code allows. The result: Every time you walk across the kitchen, dishes rattle. Most model houses do not have any dishes in the kitchen cabinets, but you can make an inference if the model decorator has glued down chairs, tables, and table settings. In the unfurnished house, try jumping on the floor. A two-hundred-pound man will be able to tell if it is bouncy—the windows will rattle (if you try this in the model, the furniture will shake as well).

the builder

As mentioned in Chapter 2, experience and reputation are crucial in evaluating any builder, production or otherwise. The easiest way to check a production builder's reputation is to talk with recent customers. Spend a couple of weekend afternoons walking around the projects you're considering, and ask residents about their experiences with their builder. You'll get an earful if he's not delivering. If their comments are positive, ask more detailed questions about the builder's willingness to come back and fix things. Even a well-built house will have minor problems that require adjustment, and you don't want your first year in a new house marred by irritating noises or doors that won't shut properly. Also ask about the site superintendent—the person who will be managing the day-to-day construction.

Should the project be so new that no one is living there, visit another project by the same builder that has been recently completed. If you want to be really thorough, visit a few projects that are several years old to see how the houses are holding up. From the street, you can tell how the exterior finishes are weathering and if the builder used decent paint that is not flaking off. To see the inside, look for a for-sale sign and make an appointment to see the house.

If you encounter any of the original homeowners, ask about what problems if any emerged after the builder's initial warranty expired and how the builder responded. Though not obligated, did he repair or at least provide any guidance with such things as leaky windows or roofs? (Also see Chapter 11 for more on warranties.)

A builder's standing with his subcontractors and suppliers is just as important as his standing with former clients. Ask the two or three builders you are considering for the names of their key subcontractors and suppliers—the carpenter/framer, the lumber supplier, the plumber, the electrician, and the heating and air-conditioning man. The two key questions to ask each sub: Are you satisfied with this builder's payment performance? How long have you worked with him? If the sub and the builder have a long history, that's a good sign. Not only does this attest to the builder's reliability, it also speaks to the quality of his houses—no builder has a long-term relationship with a subcontractor who does bad work. Conversely, if the builder's relationship with his subcontractors and suppliers are all short-term, it may indicate that he's money driven, not quality or consumer driven.

In boom times when every builder in town is busy, it's almost impossible to maintain the same roster of subcontractors for every job. You may find that some of the subcontractors on your list do not have a long history with your proposed builder. But if two or three have worked on many houses with him and think well of him, that is a good sign of his reliability.

customer service

Customer service is the division or office of a production- or semi-custom-home-building firm that deals with buyers during the often stressful process of construction and the first twelve months of occupancy, when the house is under warranty. Large production builders often have a whole staff devoted to customer service; smaller ones may have only one or two people. Regardless of how big the department is, having someone who will respond quickly and answer your questions will make the process go more smoothly. You may give customer service short shrift—after all, it does sounds like glorified handholding—but if you observe a broken window on your house when you visit the job site or have a sudden panic attack that your kitchen will look horrible and want to reconsider the colors, you want to talk to someone from the builder's office *right away*.

Many builders tout their customer-service ratings. Pay some attention to these, but go to the source and ask the people living in the communities specifically about their experiences with the builder's customer service.

quality control

Quality control is just as important as customer service, but less common. This is a builder's systematic way of monitoring construction as the house goes up, to ensure that there are no unpleasant surprises or structural disasters down the road, several to many years after the owners move in.

The system generally comes down to "an extra pair of eyes"—an individual who follows on the heels of the site superintendent at critical points and takes a second, careful look. For example, if the nailing is done with a nail gun or a staple gun, the carpenter can't always tell if the nail or staple actually went into anything, and the site superintendent may miss something. The quality-control point man also checks to see that the foundation was built correctly; the walls and floors are plumb; the heating, cooling, and plumbing systems and the electrical wiring are properly installed; the dryer vent is in place and actually vents to the outside; and every other item affecting quality, right down to making sure that the front door can be locked securely.

After a firm has built the same house twenty or thirty times, a quality-control monitor might seem redundant. But every house is different. The color and finishes are never the same, and buyers often move doors and windows or add a bay window here or there. Though a builder can use the same subcontracting firms on every house, the chances of the same 175 or so people who actually installed the ducts and pounded the nails on one house ever working together again on another one are remote.

In some home-building firms, the quality-control monitor is on the payroll; others use an independent third party. When the quality monitor is on the payroll, the site superintendent's annual bonus often depends on his quality-control ratings, so he has a strong incentive to do his job well. Builder Lee Wetherington of Sarasota, Florida, has found that an outside party to monitor quality allows his buyers to feel freer in voicing their concerns. From time to time, Wetherington's inspector acts as an informal mediator, helping to sort out the anxieties ("I'm worried that what I picked will look terrible") from the genuine issues ("Some of the floor tiles are cracked").

Should you hire your own private home inspector when your builder has a quality-control monitor? Yet another pair of eyes to check things over might seem excessive. But "Home building is an intensive human business, not a manufacturing line," Wetherington says. As an exercise, he once calculated just how human it is. In tallying up all the parts and people involved, start to finish, for a 2,200-square-foot house, Wetherington counted 150 to 180 workers, as many as 90 different companies, and between 350,000 and 400,000 parts. With this many variables, he concluded, "You can't have too many pairs of eyes checking things."

Hiring your own private home inspector can also have deterrent-effect benefits, Wetherington said. "Just the act of having a private inspector out there has an effect. The subs know it, so they know they can't get away with anything."

Which options selected today will make a mid-market, single-family house more sellable when the time comes? When asked this question, real estate agents in California, Texas, Illinois, Virginia, and Florida were remarkably consistent in their responses.

tips**from**the**trade:**
what realtors say
about options

on the exterior:

◆ Upgrade the front. All the agents emphasized that the courting of potential buyers begins the moment the agent starts down your street with prospects in tow. First impressions count, so plan on upgrading the front elevation. The specifics depend on where you live—in many parts of the country, for example, this means a partial or full brick front. In every market, though, front porches seem to be a good bet. Even if you never use it, a front porch adds character and enhances curb appeal.

◆ A huge garage door on the front can be a turnoff. Front porches are a nostalgic plus, but large two-car garage doors that dominate the facade are not. A side-load garage (the garage is entered on the side of the house, not the front) solves the big-ugly-door problem, but as lots get narrower, this solution is only feasible on a more expensive corner lot. If you can't avoid the front-load garage, two single garage doors installed side by side will look better.

◆ Don't buy a cheap lot. Lot choice counts, and cheaper is not better. If a builder offers a discount on a lot, there's a good reason.

Typically it's at a busy intersection or has some other negative. It will always be worth less, and it will be harder to resell a house on it.

◆ Get the landscaping upgrade. If no upgrade is offered, plan on adding some landscaping yourself after you move in. As with the front porch, strategically placed shade trees and shrubs will add character and make your house stand out.

◆ On the interior, choose finishes for the entry that make a strong first impression. Hardwood, tile, or stone wear better than carpet, look better, and will delineate the entry in a house with an open floor plan. If you have the choice, a two-storied space here will make the house look bigger.

flooring advice:

◆ Carry the hardwood flooring through from the foyer to the kitchen, breakfast area, and family room. This is almost expected, and buyers will pay more for it. Plan on upgrading the kitchen floor in any event, because the standard one will be a utility-grade vinyl that will tear easily. A vinyl upgrade, even if it looks nice and costs nearly as much as the hardwood or tile, does not have the same cachet.

◆ In California and Florida, tile in the foyer, kitchen, and other heavily trafficked areas is on a par with hardwood, but the tiles should be the larger twelve-by-twelve-inch size. These are more resistant to cracking, and with fewer grout lines, they're easier to maintain. If you're leaning toward tile, though, avoid ones with a customized pattern, as these will immediately attract negative attention. The first thing a buyer will say is, "This tile doesn't go with a thing I have"; gaudy ones can be a deal breaker.

- Expensive carpet upgrades are not cost effective because the next buyer won't keep the carpet, no matter what it is.

kitchen tips:

- Upgrade the kitchen cabinets to get ones with raised-panel doors. Additional features such as forty-two-inch wall cabinets, a planning desk, and roll-out trays in the base cabinets also impress many house hunters.

- Upgrade the kitchen counters to get Corian or granite. Formica counters are definitely déclassé—"no way anyone will look at it," agree several agents. Unlike many options, however, a pricy granite or Corian countertop can easily be added later. Deferring its installation to some future date is a reasonable strategy if your budget is tight.

- A triple sink with one deep well for washing large pots, one normal-depth sink, and a third shallow one for a disposal is another upgrade that buyers will notice. If you frequently entertain, a second dishwasher and a stove with six burners instead of the usual four will be useful while you are in the house, and will also impress future buyers.

- Limit your kitchen palette to lighter colors for the countertops, floors, and cabinets; this will make the space appear larger.

bathroom tips:

- Upgrade the master bathroom, but what to get depends on where you live. In the Los Angeles area, whirlpool jets are not important, but a large soaking tub is a great upgrade. In the Chicago area, the jets would be a plus; Miami buyers want a bidet.

additional space:

- If you have any option dollars left, get extra space. Once past the foyer, kitchen, and master bath, the next thing midmarket buyers focus on is space, and most will choose square footage over other options. The extra space offered depends on the market. It doesn't necessarily have to be finished, but get plumbing rough-ins so that the next owners can add a full bathroom when they finish it off.

- Smaller, less costly additions that enhance individual rooms, such as a box bay window or a four-foot family-room extension are also plusses that will enhance resale.

- Most buyers do not have three cars, but a three-car garage when offered is "absolutely a better idea." The space for the third car will be used as storage, especially in Florida and California, where houses usually do not have basements.

the backyard:

- Get a rear deck. In benign climates, people spend a lot of time outside, and buyers expect a rear deck or patio and a built-in barbecue. Even in Chicago, where people can use outdoor areas only about half the year, decks are hot.

the custom-built house

The major appeal of a custom-built house is that you get to call all the shots and make all the decisions—you choose the builder, the lot, the floor plan, the detailing, the materials. In short, you get to put your personal stamp on everything. The mechanics of actually building such a house, however, are not quite that simple.

The first step toward realizing your dream house is deciding how you will get your design on paper. You may have been working it out in your head for years, but you have to get it fleshed out and put together all the documentation that will instruct a builder and his crews on how to build your house. This requires much more than a sketch on the back of an envelope. Do you want to hire an architect to design a house for you? How about choosing a design from the catalog of a home-plan design service, a company that designs and sells home plans? Or take the design/build approach and hire a builder who offers design services to design a house for you?

These different approaches differ by thousands of dollars, because the amount of design input differs in each one. The architect-created design is the most expensive by far, because the design will be the most carefully and elaborately developed. The architect will spend several weeks to several months creating a schematic design. This will then be detailed in very elaborate drawings and written specifications that tell the builder exactly what to do. Every surface, every point where one material meets another, every corner where two planes meet, will be carefully considered. The design will also be tailored to your site; topography, views, and orientation.

Purchasing a predrawn plan from a home-plan design service is the least expensive way to get a design. The smaller services may have a portfolio of about fifty designs; the larger ones have several hundred to several thousand. The largest such firms sell magazines showing their floor plans that you can find in newsstands or in the magazine racks at the checkout counter at your local grocery store. The smaller companies often have websites and advertise in magazines like *Fine Homebuilding*.

The level of detail provided by home-plan design services varies, but even the most elaborate plans will contain far less detail than an architect's, so much of the finished product will be left to the builder's discretion. The plans will very likely have to be modified to meet your local building-code requirements and to fit on your site, so their bargain-basement price may not be a great deal.

You may also discover that the custom builders in your area typically have a portfolio of plans that they build, as well as finished examples. The plans may have originally come from a service, or the builder may have had an architect design them. The obvious advantages here are that the builder will have already modified the plans to meet local requirements, and the builder will already know the construction cost. The builder may not charge you directly for the plans, but he will fold their cost into his overhead; one way or another, you will pay for them.

With design/build, you hire a home builder, who in turn hires an architect to design a house for you, based on your tastes, requirements, and budget. The design will be created just for you and tailored to your site, but it will be less elaborate than one provided by a traditional full-service architect, whom you engage directly. As with a home-plan design service, much here is left to the builder's discretion. The design will cost less than an architect's, but more than a home-plan service's.

Asking yourself some pointed questions about the house itself may help you sort out which way is best for you. For example, do you see your house as one with relatively simple lines and conventional detailing, but with exquisite finishes—Brazilian cherry hard-

If you veer toward the high end of the anxiety scale, hiring an architect to spell out everything to the builder beforehand may be the right move, even if your design tastes are simple. If you are uneasy about the bottom line, the design/build or the home-plan service approach in which the builder monitors costs from the start might be a better idea; at any point in the process, you will know what your design decisions are costing you.

temperament and design

With the traditional full-service architect approach, the architect designs the building and then puts it out for competitive bids; the total cost is known only when the bids are received. It is also possible, however, to hire an architect and a builder at the same time. Every detail will be documented, and the costs will be monitored at each step. (For more on this, see Chapter 3.)

wood floors throughout and granite countertops in the kitchen and all the bathrooms? Does your interest in detail extend to how the surface is articulated—authentic layered wainscoting that is site-built by a finish carpenter, for example? Do you want to create unique character with lots of nooks and crannies? Do you eschew a lot of furnishings and want the built-in look with lots of cabinetry?

If you want a straightforward floor plan, and you're more interested in the finish materials, design/build or the home-plan service may be more appropriate. If you want a unique character or plenty of intricately designed built-ins, you need a more developed design and should hire an architect.

Another important difference among these three approaches is that when you hire an architect, he will help you find a builder—the key player to making your project a success. If you buy a plan from a home-plan design service or opt for design/build, you will have to find the builder yourself.

Finding the right architect or the right builder will take time, so give yourself several weeks to several months. If you sign on with an architect, expect to spend at least four months working with him or her to develop the design and complete the construction documents. If you decide to work with a builder, you won't spend nearly as long developing a design or modifying a predrawn plan, but you will certainly spend two months or so finalizing details and making material selections.

Once the design is completed, building permits are in hand, and you're ready to break ground, don't expect to leave town for an extended vacation and return just as your new house is finished. During the six to nine months it will take to build your house, you need to visit the site frequently to keep abreast of developments. You will very likely find that as the house goes up, you want to make changes here and there—for example, adding a bay window or making a window opening larger or smaller. These decisions cannot be done long distance.

If you stay involved throughout the process, you will be more pleased with the results. More important, you will have far less chance of any misunderstandings and acrimony developing among you, your builder, and your architect.

Whichever design route you take, you will go back and forth many times on design features (the breakfast room bump-out in or out) and finishes (Corian counters in or out). You will have to make agonizing choices—bigger walk-in closets and smaller bedroom or vice versa, which shade of beige carpet, which cabinet door style for the kitchen.

can you afford a custom-built house?

Before you spend time exploring the various ways to get a design for a custom-built house and find a builder, crunch the money numbers to see if you can afford it. All the customizing comes at a price. On average, the construction costs for a custom-built house are about double those of a production-built one. And while a production builder sells both the lot and the house, a custom builder's price covers only the cost of construction. He builds on *your* land. If you don't already own a lot, you will have to purchase one, and this must be factored into your total budget.

why are custom-built housing costs higher?

Some of the higher construction costs for a custom house can be attributed to using a higher grade of finishes and materials and more labor-intensive detailing than a production builder typically uses. But much of the higher cost is intrinsic to the endeavor. Most custom builders take on ten or fewer houses a year. The builders may belong to a purchasing cooperative, but they won't get the same price breaks on materials that a large national production-home-building firm enjoys by purchasing items by the train load.

A custom builder might build as many as three houses at a time, but not on adjacent lots. The lots and job sites will be scattered, so he won't get the management and scheduling efficiencies that come with building ten to twenty production houses in a row. Moreover, a production builder buys lots from a land developer who may have moved thousands of cubic yards of dirt to create a flat building pad. In contrast, custom builders often work on more challenging lots. They may have eye-catching views, but construction may be harder and more expensive because of steep slopes, poor soils, or some other condition.

Equally important, a custom builder's houses may be very similar, but they are rarely identical, so the builder has to add in some margin to cover the unknowns. If you want something really different, this margin will be greater. A production builder builds the same house over and over. By the third or fourth time around, he will have calculated its cost practically to the penny.

cost per square foot

To get a range of cost-per-square-foot figures for custom-home building in your market, call your local home builders' association or ask several local custom builders. This is not a defining figure, but initially it can be quite helpful in determining the feasibility of a project (for more on this, see Chapter 3). If the figures range from $150 to $200 per square foot, the cost of a 2,400-square-foot house could range from $360,000 to $480,000. The higher figure allows for many built-in features and adventurous details such as stairs that morph into bookcases that in turn become the back of a built-in sofa, or the use of unusual woods such as walnut, red birch, or cherry. You might also get unusual flooring in the entry foyer and granite counters in all the bathrooms and the kitchen. The lower figure would afford a nice house but one with fewer details, fewer built-ins, and granite counters only in the kitchen, for example. If these numbers are too high, you might be able to push the cost down to $130 a square foot (which would bring the total for a house down to $312,000), but you would have a very simple house with modest detailing.

strategies to lower costs

You could reduce your cost by building a smaller house. But if you go below 2,400 square feet, you will be eliminating rooms that most people want, such as a den/study, and you will have smaller walk-in closets for the master suite. Below a certain point, there are so many fixed costs—foundation work, framing, plumbing, electrical work, and so forth—that you won't save that much by shrinking the living area.

Another strategy to lower costs is eliminating the basement or cutting out some conveniences such as a two-car attached garage, but this could affect your resale prospects if these are expected amenities in your area.

financing a custom-built house

Unless you have the cash in hand, you will have to find a lender. Most lenders offer a two-part construction–permanent mortgage loan with only one closing (so you pay all the fees related to borrowing the money and sign all the legal documents only once). During the construction phase, you will be charged interest only; after the house is finished, the loan will roll over into the permanent mortgage, and you will start paying principal as well as interest.

The size of the down payment, which most lenders require to be paid in cash, depends on the specific loan program and the lender. If you already own the land and have owned it for six months to a year, you may be able to apply the equity (the difference between what you paid and what it's worth today) to your down payment. It's unlikely, however, that you would accrue sufficient equity to cover your entire down payment unless you have owned the land for years, by which point it may have appreciated enough that the equity will cover a good portion if not all of your down payment.

If you have to buy the land and borrow the entire amount to purchase it, this will affect how much money you can borrow for building the house. For example, if the lot cost is $75 thousand, and the total cost of the project that you can afford is $440 thousand, your construction budget cannot exceed $365 thousand. In some cases, you can get a loan for as much as $400 thousand with only 5 percent down. But most lenders require a 10 percent down payment for loans above $300 thousand, and some lenders require a 10 percent down payment for all residential construction loans. As the total loan amount increases, so does the down-payment requirement. At the $500 thousand point, it will likely increase to 20 percent or $100 thousand. If you are planning to finance your new house with the equity you've accrued on your present one, you will have to convert your equity into cash by taking out a home equity loan (for more on this, see Chapter 4).

There is some good news here, however. At the end of the project, the appraised value of your new house and lot is often more than your total cost, because the bank makes the construction loan based on your construction drawings and specifications. When a bank appraiser sees the finished house on your lot your $400 thousand project might be appraised for $450 thousand, in which case you will have a hefty chunk of equity before you move in.

so,youwanttohireanarchitect?

If you've concluded that the only way to get the house you've always dreamed of is to hire an architect, how do you find the right one? Though designing a house may seem straightforward—especially when compared to a technically complex building type like a hospital—to do it well requires at least five years of experience in residential work. Architects with this background will have taken a design from a quick sketch to a finished house many times and will be familiar with local construction costs and building-code intricacies. Even more important, they will know qualified home-building contractors in your area.

You might well ask: What does the architect do and why does it cost so much to hire one?

The biggest part of the architect's traditional full-service package is not the creation of a design concept but its elaboration, called design development, and the preparation of extremely detailed construction documents. These instruct a builder how to build what the architect has designed. They specify the materials to be used and form the basis for competitive bidding to get a firm construction price. After the contract is awarded and construction has begun, the construction documents serve as an outside check on the builder's performance. The full-service architect also supervises the bidding process, helps the homeowners select a builder, and, on the homeowners' behalf, monitors construction. If there is a dispute with the builder, the architect acts as the owner's advocate in resolving it.

In addition, an architect may spend many hours developing a design expressly tailored to both the client and the site. During the initial design phase, the architect may meet frequently with the clients to explore different design options. To help clients visualize the project, the architect may build a scale model or transfer the design to a computer-aided design program (CAD) that provides a three-dimensional rendering of the design from many different vantages.

why do architects cost so much?

The design development phase, during which the architect refines and customizes the initial concept and prepares construction documents, is even more labor intensive. Supervising the bidding, helping to select a builder, and monitoring construction also demand time.

To keep design fees down, some architects offer a more limited service. For example, the architect may carry the project through the bidding process but won't monitor it during construction. If your design tastes are simple and the design is relatively easy to build, this may be a sensible course. But if you want anything unusual, you're better served by having the architect onboard for the entire project.

The traditional full-service architect will often get cost estimates from builders on his bid list as he or she is designing it, but the actual cost will not be known until the project is competitively bid. If it comes in overbid—that is, the cost is higher than you want to pay or can afford—portions of the project will have to be redesigned.

Rather than design the entire project and then bid it, you can hire a builder at the same time that you hire the architect. While the architect is designing your project, the builder is monitoring its cost (for more on this, see Chapter 3).

Since no two architects work in exactly the same way or charge exactly the same fees, be prepared to shop around and talk with several to find the one who's right for you. You should get the names of at least three residential architects, either from friends or from your local chapter of the American Institute of Architects.

On your first phone call to each architect, don't hesitate to ask about fees. The architect won't bring it up, but you should ask. You'll quickly learn how differently every architect calculates this. For residential work, many architects charge an hourly rate, but will estimate their fee as a percentage of the total construction cost. The fees can vary anywhere from 5 to 15 percent, depending on the complexity of the design you want and the total cost of the project. For the same job, some firms charge more than others. Well-known, prestigious firms generally charge more. Within a given market, the architects based in the outlying suburbs often charge less than those whose offices are located in the higher-rent, central business district.

Some architects charge an hourly fee but will cap it at a specified percentage of the estimated construction cost. For example, if your construction budget is $300 thousand and the architect charges 15 percent, his fee would not exceed $45 thousand. However the architect computes his fee, *it will be in addition to the construction cost.* If the design charge is $45,000, the total cost of getting your $300,000 house designed and built will be $345,000. If you have to buy a lot, add at least $50,000 to $75,000 for a total of $395,000 to $445,000.

Be sure that you also ask about liability insurance. Some architects "go bare" and don't have it because the premiums can be very expensive. But even the most experienced architects can make mistakes, and you are engaging one to design a never-before-built house. You should make sure that your architect has both liability and errors-and-omissions coverage (and you should stipulate in your contract that the insurance policy be maintained for the duration of your project). In addition, ask the architect if all designs are routinely reviewed by a structural engineer, another safety check that protects both the client and the architect (you should also stipulate this in your contract).

In this initial call, tell the architect what your approximate budget is and what sort of house you want to build. If you're not sure stylistically what you want, that is fine; but you certainly will know if you want something more traditional or more contemporary. Some architects will tell you flat out that your budget is too small or that they don't do "traditionally styled center-hall colonials." It is much better to be up front on these matters, so don't be put off. Secretly thank him or her for being so frank, and call the next person on your list.

If anyone seems promising after your phone conversations, the next step is meeting face to face. While you're talking, assess the personality mix. You will be working together closely for at least a year, so it's important that you get along. The architect who did a great job for your best friend or your neighbors might not be the one for you. Consider the following:

- Does the architect seem interested in your project? Assessing this is completely subjective, but you want someone who is enthusiastic.

- How soon can he start? If he says six months, you should keep looking.

- If the firm has a lot of work, will they be able to devote enough time to the kind of residential project you want to do? Ask how many jobs the firm has in progress and how many personnel. If the firm has only three or four people and fifteen jobs, they may not be able to give you much attention.

- When you see the architect's portfolio of completed work, check it for both style and substance. Does the architect seem versatile and comfortable with any number of styles? If you want Spanish mission or Tudor and the architect has never done it, do you think he or she can handle it? If the portfolio shows that the architect is versatile, he can very likely work in a style he hasn't done before.

- Some architects have a marked preference for one or two styles. Do you feel that you are being shoehorned into a style the architect prefers rather than one you prefer? You want to be open to new possibilities, but you are going to live in the house, so follow your gut instincts.

- Has the architect worked with a variety of site conditions? This is especially important if you're considering a site that has a funny shape, a steep slope, or problematic soils.

- If you want something really unusual such as steel post-and-beam construction, curving walls, or walls made of straw bales, look for an architect with experience in these specialties.

- As the architect develops the design for your house, what will he do to help you understand and visualize what he's creating? For example, does he make scale models or use a computer to create exterior sketches and interior perspective drawings?

- What time frame does the architect propose for designing your house? You should anticipate at least four months and likely more than that if you want a large house with many details.

- How long will it take to build the house? Six to nine months is about average.

The attraction of building a custom-designed house is getting exactly what you want. But if you're too single-minded about it, your dream house can end up costing more than you expect. If you have to drop the price substantially to attract buyers when you eventually sell it, those flyaway rooflines were not just an expensive tour de force of engineering, but they also ate up a good chunk of your equity.

"Unusual" in houses is not just a look, it also applies to a floor plan. You may hate to cook, but having a closet-sized kitchen and a cavernous master suite is not the choice that most future buyers will make. Likewise, separating the master suite from the other bedrooms may provide more privacy, but most buyers, especially those with young children, want the bedrooms close together.

Planning for the eventual sale of a dream house is not how most people approach such a project. Nonetheless, Norman Smith, an architect in Washington D.C., a community where people can move on a moment's notice and resale is a big issue with all buyers, addresses the resale issue early on.

Though Smith loves to design the unusual, he wants his clients to be very clear at the outset about the potential cost of their design decisions. Smith periodically readdresses the resale issue because he has found that most people get carried away as the design work progresses. He says, "I tell my clients, 'Someone out there will appreciate this, but you won't get Joe Smith off the street to buy it right away.' I try to make them aware of the cost of their money if they can't sell their house right away, and to weigh the cost of their lifestyle and aesthetic against financial gain."

In many cases, Smith has found the client can achieve the "something different" with a more traditional floor plan and very unusual treatment of surfaces—walls, floors, cabinetry, and countertops. "This can give a lot more bang for the buck than clients

If things still seem promising, go look at several of the architect's completed jobs and talk with the owners. Although the architect may want to accompany you, the owners will be more candid if you go by yourself. Don't worry about intrusive questions—most people are eager to talk about their home-building adventures and will be forthcoming. Questions to ask:

- How well did they get along with the architect?

- Were there any cost overruns? (This is always a risk when you are building a never-before-built house.)

- Did they feel that they got what they paid for?

realize. Even more importantly, from a resale perspective, these touches can be easily removed and replaced by a future buyer."

Another pitfall in custom housing that can affect resale is trendy details that eventually become dated, and in some cases ridiculous, observed architect Carl Hunter of Chicago. When Hunter worked in Los Angeles in the late eighties, owners wanted as tall an entrance door as possible, and houses had fourteen- to sixteen-foot-high doors, or panels above the doors to make them appear that high. These doors opened onto an entry foyer that would have a ceiling that was the same height as the doors, but the floor area was often as small as six by eight feet. "Even then it looked silly, and today it looks like a Hollywood set stuck onto a conventional living room with eight-foot ceilings," Hunter said.

Another resale issue with very unusual custom houses is the ability of future buyers to get financing. John Colby, an architect, developer, and bank board member in Great Falls, Virginia, pointed out that even if you have buyers willing to pay your price when you eventually sell, the amount of financing they can get depends on how much a lending institution thinks your property is worth. Most banks do this by sending out an appraiser to compare your house to similar ones sold recently, then come up with a dollar amount of what he thinks your house is worth. Colby said the problem comes when your house is so unusual there's nothing to compare it to. "In that case the appraiser is likely to fall back on standard criteria such as lot size, number of bedrooms, and total square footage. You can't assume that he will be able to evaluate exotic architecture, unusual detailing, and expensive craftsmanship. And on the basis of the appraiser's report, the bank may conclude that your house is worth only five hundred thousand dollars, not six hundred and fifty, and approve a loan amount accordingly. If your buyer can't come up with the other hundred and fifty thousand, he can't buy your house."

- How well did the architect handle disputes between the builder and the owners? The architect is supposed to be the owner's advocate for such disputes. Since you and your builder are bound to have a disagreement at some point, the architect's ability to resolve any disputes quickly and evenhandedly is important.

- Does the house include any unusual details that you might want the architect to replicate in your house?

Next, talk to the builders whom the architect has worked with, especially the ones who built the houses that you saw:

- How many houses has he built with this architect? If they've done a number of jobs together and know each other's working style, there's less chance for miscommunication and errors.

- Were the architect's drawings and written specifications useful and informative, useless and confusing, or somewhere in between? The clearer the construction documents, the easier and more smoothly the job will run. If these documents are confusing, errors, misunderstandings, and disputes are more likely to occur.

- During construction, was the architect responsive to field questions? If it's urgent, the architect should be available to answer questions right away. Most of the time, field questions are not that urgent and getting a response within a day is fine.

- How often did the architect visit the site and was this a problem? The frequency depends on the stage of construction. At some points, he or she needs to be there two or three times a week. At other times, once a week is adequate.

- How well did the builder think that the architect handled client-builder disputes? If the builder also thinks the architect resolved disputes quickly and evenhandedly, it's a sure sign that the builder likes working with him.

homeplanservices

If you think you'll never get to first base on a custom house because finding the architect sounds too hard or too expensive, consider purchasing a predrawn plan from a home-plan design service. You can pick a design from a catalog, magazine, or website offering anything from fifty to several thousand plans. You will receive detailed floor plans, all the elevations, and a framing plan. You then engage a builder to add the other required drawings (generally this means plans for the heating and air conditioning, electrical wiring, and plumbing), to get a building permit, and to build it for you.

Although this sounds simple, you will spend as much time searching for the right builder as you would for the right architect. You will save the architect's fees, of course, but the house will not necessarily be any less expensive to build. Those embellishments that you want to include—varying ceiling heights, fireplaces, a multi-gabled, multi-hipped roofline, a meandering footprint with room extensions, bay windows, and recesses and those granite countertops will quickly drive up the cost.

The plan services charge anywhere from four hundred to several thousand dollars for a design, but you will have to pay additional charges. The builder won't supply the systems drawings for free. And the plans will very likely require modifications for local climates and soil conditions. For example, if you live in a part of Texas where it rains a lot and order a plan from a service in Arizona where it doesn't rain much, your builder may have to alter the roof framing and the overhangs. If you live where expansive clay soils necessitate foundation modifications (frequently the case in Colorado and Texas), the builder will have to get the foundation design from your plan service re-engineered. And then there are the specifics of your own lot—the plans are designed as if the site were perfectly flat, but in reality that's rarely the case.

There are at least a hundred home-plan services. Some are small and local, others are large and market their designs nationally. If there is a service in your area, using it can be advantageous because the designs will already conform to your local climate, building conventions, and building codes. With a local service you may also be able to get the designer to meet with you at your site and discuss changes that would incorporate the view and address the lot orientation and the sun exposures.

For an additional charge, the services will make the needed changes for you. But unless the service is a local one, you're better off ordering the more expensive repro-ducibles and having your builder modify them ("reproducibles" are plans that are printed on a special paper so that a draftsman can erase and redraw the parts that need to be changed). Your builder will also charge to make such changes, but having him do it ensures that they will be correctly done to meet the local building-code requirements and your site conditions. Depending on how many changes are required, the added costs could be twenty-five hundred dollars or more. If you have to get the plans re-engineered for your soils, for example, this can drive up the cost further.

The home-plan design services do not usually supply a list specifying the required amount of material for each component of the house in their basic package. This essen-tial piece of information usually costs another fifty to a hundred dollars and specifies only quantity, not quality. An architect's services include detailed specifications and address quality. If you opt for the plan service, you'll have to sort out the materials requirements with a builder yourself.

finding a builder

Who will bring all the pieces together and how will you find this person? DesignBasics, a home-plan service based in Omaha, Nebraska, has a national registry of builders who have used their plans (listed on their website, DesignBasics.com). This is a real advantage because a builder who has worked with DesignBasics plans already knows how they must be modified to meet the specific climate and code requirements in your area. Should you choose a plan that the builder has already built, there won't be any guesswork on the price.

HomeStyles.com, another plan service based in Minneapolis, does not have such a registry, but their website is linked to Improvenet.com, an online service that matches homeowners with builders, and is free regardless of whether you buy a HomeStyles.com plan or not. Using electronic databases, Improvenet screens builders, architects, and designers nationwide for legal and credit problems. Whenever possible, Improvenet also checks licenses, liability insurance, and references. If you choose a professional from Improvenet's list, he or she pays a finder's fee. If a contractor or architect is not on its list, Improvenet will screen the firm for a twenty-nine-dollar charge. Though most of Improvenet's website is devoted to remodeling, they will match up new home seekers with builders.

You can also ask friends, Realtors, or your local home builder's association for the names of custom builders in your area. Whatever route you take to get the names, though, you still have to go through a winnowing process, similar to finding an architect.

In your initial phone call, ask the builder what kind of houses he usually builds and what size budget he typically works with. If he says a million dollars and you can spend only a third of that, ask him if he's comfortable working at a smaller scale. You're not giving away the ranch, at this stage, by giving him a ballpark figure of what you can afford and what size house you want. If your project is too modest, and he's not interested, you're saving everyone's time by learning this at the outset.

When you meet the builder face to face, size up the personality mix. You will be working very closely with the person for a year or more, and the project will be very stressful at times, so you need to get along.

The builder will have a portfolio of finished projects, similar to the architect's. You should look it over carefully for both style and substance, and consider these questions:

- Does the builder have a variety of styles? If he has only one or two, it may be that he's not comfortable building anything else. If you want something substantially different, he may be unable to deliver it. If he has worked with a variety of styles, he may be comfortable tackling anything and be willing to build what you want. As with the architect, this is your judgment call.

- What size house does he routinely build? If he's used to building houses that are twenty-five hundred square feet or less and you want one that's thirty-five hundred square feet, the detailing and logistics will be different. Ask him how he would handle a difference of this magnitude.

- Be sure to ask if he's ever built a house using a plan from a home-plan design service, and, in particular, the one that you are considering. If he has, this will be a plus, because he will already know what modifications, if any, will be required.

- When you look at the builder's portfolio, ask how much each house cost. You've already given him a ballpark figure of your budget in your first phone call; now ask whether or not he could build something similar for you. You may resist telling him what your true budget is, but if the builder doesn't know your constraints as well as your goals, he can't deliver a realistic price or product. It's a waste of everyone's time if the builder develops a project and works up a budget for a house you can't afford to build.

◆ Does the builder have a portfolio of plans? If so, ask to see them. Using the builder's own plans has advantages—he will know the costs and there will be far fewer unknowns (but every plan, including one designed by an architect, will have a few surprises as the house goes up). Can he modify a plan he knows well and has used before to get the house that you want?

◆ When the inevitable cost-per-square-foot question is posed, don't be surprised at the inevitable Delphic response, "It depends." The price *does* depend on what you put in that square foot. At this initial meeting, though, the builder should be able to give you some parameters so that you can correlate the house size and the finishes you want with your budget.

◆ How soon can he start on your job? If he says six months, give him credit for being candid, but keep looking if you want to start sooner.

◆ Does he carry liability insurance that includes errors-and-omission coverage? This is an important protection for both you and the builder, and you should stipulate that an insurance policy be maintained for the duration of your project.

◆ How many houses does he build at a time? If he says more than three, ask how big his operation is and how many people are working for him. A custom-home project requires keeping track of endless details and scheduling subcontractors and deliveries of materials (many more than with a production-built house). If the builder has only a skeleton office staff, building more than three houses at a time could mean the builder is stretching himself very thin. If the houses are nearly identical or very simple, he could do more with a small staff; but most people who go to a custom builder want a house with many extras.

◆ To get a true comparison among builders, ask each one for a standard specifications sheet. It should list brand names, model numbers, and other descriptive information for every material. Note that many items will be listed simply as "allowances," meaning that the builder allocates a specified dollar amount in the budget and you select the item yourself. Ask what kind of allowance items you can expect with your budget. Would the ceramic tile be a grade that goes for eighty cents a square foot or one that is twenty dollars a square foot? Would the kitchen cabinets be custom, semi-custom, or stock? Which cabinetmaker does he regularly specify?

- Many people find that going through the process of selecting everything can get overwhelming. Does the builder offer help in making the selections? Accompany you to the suppliers?

If you have any promising candidates after your initial meetings, get lists of their former clients, contact several, and arrange to see the builders' work. Seeing a portfolio is helpful, but seeing a completed house is much more informative. As with the architect, you will get more candid responses if you go by yourself. Ask the same questions that you would of an architect's clients:

- Did you like the builder?

- Did your house cost what you expected?

- Were his allowances adequate to get what you wanted?

- Did you feel that costs were adequately monitored? When you work with a builder directly, he should be monitoring costs at every step so that you will know how much your design decisions are costing you, whether you are at the initial phase and deciding on the shape of the house or further along and looking at bathroom fixtures.

- Did he answer questions promptly?

- Were you able to resolve disputes amicably?

- Was he there every day to check the job?

- Did he come back to fix things after you moved in? This is an important point because *every* house will require minor adjustments after completion.

When you narrow down the builder choices to one or two, engage a private home inspector who is familiar with new construction to help you make that final decision. For each builder, the home inspector can advise you on the quality of construction and on the specifications list. After you've hired one, keep the inspector on board to help you fine-tune the spec list and periodically inspect the construction as it goes up. (For more on home inspectors, see Chapter 11; for more on choosing a builder, see Chapter 2.)

Even if you have no interest in buying a design from a home-plan design service and building a custom house, perusing the home-plan websites is a valuable exercise. Since many production builders use plan services, you'll get a useful overview of what's out there as well as some practice in correlating house size with floor plans. For example, what do room layouts with twenty-four hundred square feet look like?

There are more than a hundred home-plan service websites. HomeStyles.com and DesignBasics.com both have a huge number of plans posted. HomeStyles.com sorts its designs by house size, number of stories, bedrooms, bathrooms, the car capacity of the garage, and architectural style (they have eleven different styles to choose from). DesignBasics.com sorts its plans by architectural series and total square footage. With both of these services, the plans shown on the web do not have a scale, and the scale of the floor plans for the first and second floors often varies (the first floor will appear larger than the second floor). But after clicking through a number of floor plans, you will begin to get an idea of the possibilities. Houses range from the very small—one-bedroom, one-bath honeymoon cottages of less than five hundred square feet—to the very large six-bedroom, seven-bath houses of palatial proportions with more than nine thousand square feet.

home-**plan**web **sites** provide **useful** information **for** *all* **new**-home**buyers**

If you purchased the home plans before you hired the builder and bought a lot, be prepared for another essential truth: Not every plan will fit on every lot. Rather than shoehorning the plan onto the lot and changing it beyond recognition, you may be better served by starting over with another plan, selected with the advice of your builder.

design/build:**the**middle**path**

If you want a design that's created for you, tailored to your tastes, budget, and site, but you don't want to hire an architect on a full-service basis, the design/build option could be your ticket. With this approach you hire a custom-home builder who offers design services. After you and the builder have nailed down a construction budget and he gets a fix on your stylistic preferences, he hires a designer for your project. The design fees will be much less than with a full-service architect, but so will the design input.

The builder's designer may actually be a licensed, registered architect or someone with an architectural degree who is very experienced with residential design but not licensed. The designer may be in-house or hired for just your job. You will meet with him several times, but not nearly as many times as you would if you hired an architect yourself on a full-service basis.

The builder and the architect work together as a team—as the architect develops the design, the builder monitors it for cost, ensuring that it can be built within your budget. The designer will produce only a preliminary, schematic design—enough to get a building permit and to build with, but not the full set of construction documents required for competitive bidding. The job will not be competitively bid—you have already hired a builder—and an experienced builder will already have his own set of details for framing, foundations, and so forth.

Such a stripped-down approach drastically reduces the architect's fees. Instead of the additional 5 to 15 percent of the construction budget that you would pay to get a full-service package, you may pay only 1 to 5 percent, depending on the region of the country and the size of the house. As a house gets bigger, more design is required, because bigger rooms with higher ceilings require more detailing, or they will look naked. A 2,500-square-foot, $300-thousand house might have a design fee of only $3,000 to $15,000, whereas a 3,500-square-foot, $600-thousand house could have a design fee as high as $20,000 to $30,000—high, but still less than the $30,000 to $60,000 you would pay for an architect's full-service package.

Most design/build firms require payment of design fees up front. If you go forward with the project, they may credit it to your construction cost.

the design/build team

Since the builder's architect or designer will not be producing a detailed set of construction documents, you need to have a designer who has worked with the builder on other projects and knows his modus operandi. This will vastly reduce the chance for miscommunication and errors. And much of what the final product will look like is left to the builder's discretion, so the builder needs to have strong design sensibilities as well as a good sense of scale and detail. In fact, many of the builders who offer design/build services get into it because they are very design oriented. As you talk to different builders who offer design/build, be wary of those who characterize themselves as "bricks and sticks guys" and who regard architects and their "formal training in aesthetics" as unnecessary.

Within the custom-home building arena, there are builders who specialize in the design/build approach. To find the right one for you, you have to go through the same winnowing process that you would if you were buying a plan from a service. Get the names of several design/builders from friends or the local home building association. Ask the same questions that you would of any custom builder (see p. 110), but also ask them about their design fees:

- What size house does he usually build? If it's significantly larger or smaller than what you want, is he comfortable downsizing or upsizing?

- What size budget does he usually work with? Would he be comfortable working with your budget? Remember, you're not giving away the store by giving him a ballpark figure.

- Does he have stylistic preferences?

If things look promising after that first call, meet face to face and ask to see a portfolio of completed work to review, just as you would if you were hiring an architect. At the same time, you also have to ask the same questions you would ask any builder:

- Does the builder seem to prefer one style? Some design builders are comfortable working in a wide range of styles, and they may work with as many as ten architects. Others have a more limited stylistic repertoire and work with only one or two. If you don't see a variety, ask the builder if he has a strong preference for some styles over others.

- As you look at the portfolio, ask how much each house cost. Could he build the same thing for you with your budget?

- Can you meet the architect whom you would be working with before signing a contract? Since the builder hires the designer, you will have to rely on the builder's judgment that the person is up to your job. But you still want to feel comfortable working with that person. Unless the builder always works with the same designer, he or she is not likely to be at this initial meeting, because the builder will not know your stylistic preferences in advance.

- Is he enthusiastic about your project?

- When can he start?

- How many houses does he build at a time? How big is his staff?

- Will he give you his standard specification list?

- What kind of allowances could you expect with your budget and size of house?

- Will he help you select materials?

If you want to build your dream house in an old, established neighborhood with good schools and an easier commute to your job, the only vacant lots you're likely to find are either unbuildable for some reason or have been tied up in a probate court for years while heirs battle it out.

the **tear**-down **solution**

In most metropolitan areas now, the only way to build a new house in a close-in location is to buy an old one, tear it down, and start over. This tear-down solution isn't as crazy as it sounds—if the house is old enough, but not so old that it has historic value, most of its value is actually in the land under it. If you tear down the house, you haven't thrown away much. Before you get very far on a tear-down, though, you have to make sure that the money numbers work and that you will be comfortable with the values that you're ending up with.

Ted Visnic, a Rockville, Maryland, home builder who has constructed several tear-down projects in the Washington, D.C., area, said that in his market the general rule of thumb is that the value of the old house and lot should be about thirty to forty percent of the value of the new house and lot. If the old house and lot was worth $120 thousand, the new house and lot should be between $360 thousand and $400 thousand. If you want to add so many things to your house that the total cost comes to $450 thousand, you have to know the breadth of the market for this price range in your area. Will you take a bath at resale if you sell in two or three years? Five or six years?

If the numbers work, the next step is checking current and pending zoning regulations for building heights, lot setbacks, and floor/area ratios. The lot setbacks determine the dimensions for the maximum allowable "footprint"—the outline of the house at ground level. Floor/area ratios define the maximum size in terms of square feet. Since the house you may want to tear down was built, the zoning rules may have changed many times, in some instances in response to the tear-down phenomenon itself.

In many suburbs where tear-downs have become common, long-term residents resent the imposing nature of a large house next to a modest bungalow or one-story ranch. Glencoe, a suburb north of Chicago, now has a "daylight plane rule" to prevent

Should any of the builders whom you interview seem promising, the next step is to look at the builders' houses and talk with their former clients. The portfolio will be helpful, but a site visit to the finished work is always much more informative.

While you're evaluating the work, note the level of design and the presence or absence of any unusual features. If there aren't any, it may be that the builder does not feel comfortable building anything that strays far from the ordinary, and he might constrain the architect from designing anything unusual. If you want something more adventurous, that builder may not be able to deliver it.

new houses from putting existing ones in shadow. Highland Park, another Chicago suburb, has increased the minimum size of side yards to maintain visual continuity along the street and prevent a new and much larger house from overwhelming the neighbors and looking like a cowbird in a nest of wrens.

While the money numbers and the zoning restrictions are fairly straightforward calculations, the design of the actual house is not. You will need to hire an architect who is experienced in tear-downs and factor his design fees into your costs, because the special conditions that are in the nature of a tear-down project call for unique and inventive solutions.

If your chosen location has passed a "daylight plane rule" similar to Glencoe's, for example, your house may have to step back at each story. If your lot has mature trees that you want to save, you will have to build around their root systems, which could mean an unusual footprint for your house (for more on saving trees, see Chapter 10).

In addition to the building constraints imposed on your own lot, you have to look at the adjacent lots and ask yourself, "What is the worst thing that could happen?" Assume that it will. Your side yard may face the neighbor's garden now, but a new house built as close to the lot line as yours is may be less than twenty-five feet from yours. Given this possibility, the optimal room arrangement for your new house is to put the secondary spaces (laundry room, den, bathrooms, secondary bedrooms) on the sides and the primary living spaces (kitchen, family room, living and dining rooms, and master bedroom suite) at the front and rear.

Chicago architect Carl Hunter, who has designed a number of tear-downs, says, "You can't rely on the neighbors' open space as part of yours, so this type of house has to be more 'introspective.' Within the property lines, I design the house as if the side walls are solid with openings to provide privacy, light, and air but no views."

As the design develops, you may have to jettison some cherished ideas or conveniences such as a two-car attached garage because there's not enough room on the lot. On the plus side, however, you will be rewarded with some very interesting results. As Hunter observed, "There can be advantages from adversity. The blandest, most mundane architecture occurs on the blandest, most mundane lots."

Go by yourself to get more candid responses, and ask the same questions that you would if you had purchased a design from a home-plan service and were looking for a builder.

- Did you like the builder?

- Did your house cost what you expected?

- Were his allowances adequate to get what you wanted?

- Did he answer questions promptly?

- Were you able to resolve disputes amicably? When an architect is on board for the entire project, he resolves disputes. With design/build, you yourself will have to resolve any disputes that arise with the builder. You are certain to have at least one disagreement before the job is done, so this is important to know.

- Was he there every day to check the job?

- Did he come back to fix all the things that required adjustment after you moved in?

- Did you feel that costs were adequately monitored? An important advantage of the design/build approach is that the builder closely monitors costs at every step. You will know how much your design decisions are costing you at every stage. With the traditional full-service architect, he will often get cost estimates from builders on his bid list as he is designing it, but the actual cost will not be known until the project is competitively bid. If it comes in overbid—that is, the cost is higher than you want to pay—portions of the project will have to be redesigned.

As with the predrawn home-plan design service, engage a private home inspector who is familiar with new construction in your area to help you make the final decision when you narrow down the design/builder choices. The inspector can advise you on construction and specifications, and inspect the job as it progresses.

With a custom-built house, you get to choose everything down to the last, nth detail. How far you want to carry the decision making and the fine-tuning—those innumerable small details that make a telling difference—is up to you. Here are some examples:

tips**from**the**trade:** fine-tuning your custom-built house

- **doors and doorways.** If the ceilings in your new house will be nine feet, a higher and wider doorway—thirty-six inches wide and eight feet high, instead of the standard thirty inches width and six-feet, eight-inches height—makes you feel like you're walking through something.

Then there's the door itself. In old houses, the act of opening and closing doors is a more deliberate gesture and somehow feels grander because the doors are solid wood. To re-create the same sensation, but at a much reduced cost, you can use a solid-core door made of medium-density fiberboard, instead of the hollow-core Masonite doors favored by most production builders. It will have as much weight as a solid wood door, but it won't warp. When it's painted, only a professional painter will know the difference. The heavier doors also provide sound-proofing benefits.

Going a step further, there's the front door handle. Most home builders provide a plated, polished-brass handle that looks good. A solid brass handle also feels good. When you open the door with it, the handle feels more solid, subtly reinforcing the fact that in entering the house you're going from "out there" to "in here." And if your front door handle has a lifetime finish, it won't tarnish no matter how much weather it's exposed to.

◆ **foyer.** A natural stone flooring like mar-ble or granite is definitely a grand gesture. Or you can add a more subtle and elegant look with honed limestone or tumbled marble. With either of these, the tiles are put into a machine that rotates them so that the final product looks hundreds of years old.

Some of the small details that make the difference are really small. If stone flooring in the foyer is a budget buster, Turko Semmes, a custom home builder in San Luis Obispo, California, suggests dressing up a standard oak hardwood floor with a narrow border inlay made up of a two-inch strip of dark brown walnut and a quarter-inch strip of reddish padauk. If you're using hardwood in other rooms, add the inlay there and this tiny detail will pull the whole house together.

Some small details add both elegance and ease. If the foyer is large enough for a longer stair run, Arlington, Virginia, builder Chip Gruver advises his clients to modify the stair geometry and install a longer twelve-inch tread and a lower six-inch riser. Not only will this make going up and down easier; you'll also feel more dignified.

◆ **walls.** When clients decide not to cover up the walls in the formal areas with wall-paper, Gruver avoids unsightly drywall seams and nail pops by "skim coating" the drywall. This involves adding a thin coat of drywall "mud" to the entire wall surface to create a more uniform look.

Noting that "some wall textures are damn near eatable they feel so nice," Semmes occasionally turns the drywaller loose to come up with something. "I tell the drywaller, 'I don't want dead smooth, I want some texture and irregularities, so play with it.' We do test samples in a closet." Semmes added that in his experi-ence, "Most tradespeople want to do stuff better. Give them another 5 to 10 percent of their bill and they'll do some great stuff."

◆ **trim.** For details that add panache but are not excessively expensive, Semmes likes faux finishes that mimic stone. "For columns, you can make a piece of wood look so much like stone that you must feel it to know the difference. The real thing, such as granite or travertine, costs a lot of money." Adding that faux finishes look best when used in small amounts, Semmes also noted that finding a qualified person to do the work is essential.

- **paint.** When it comes to paint, every manufacturer has many different grades. The labor costs in application are generally the same, regardless of which quality you select, but Gruver has found that a higher and more expensive grade will generally last longer. An eggshell finish really does look different up close and, compared to the semi-gloss used by most production builders, it is much easier to clean.

- **faucets.** In the kitchen, architect and builder Leon Goldenberg of Tampa, Florida, recommends the old-fashioned wall-mounted fixtures with separate hot and cold knobs and the faucet placed well above the sink. This imparts a certain look, but it's also practical. Placing the faucet above the sink makes it easier to fill large pots. This combined with a single large and deeper sink compartment also makes it easier to clean big pots and pans.

- **cabinets.** Semmes' houses often include a lot of built-in case work—shelving and cabinetry. To give the wood a luster and depth that nearly everyone notices, he adds a coat of paste wax and machine buffs it after applying a stain and a protective sealer like lacquer, varnish, or urethane.

Cabinet knobs are not an item that most buyers think about, but very plain cabinets "sing with good hardware," Semmes said. An extra five hundred to a thousand dollars will get you onyx, malachite, copper, and aluminum combinations and unusual woods such as ebony and rosewood.

If such exotic fare is not in your budget or to your taste, try to get a modest cabinet knob upgrade. The standard knobs don't hold up well. At the very least, get a simple solid-brass knob.

part two

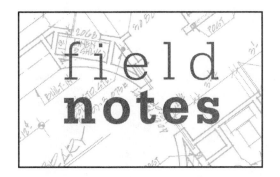

field
notes

chapter seven the kitchen

When you start to think about the kitchen for your new house, visit cabinet dealers, and tour furnished models, you'll find that it's easy to get seduced by a look—great cabinets! gorgeous floor tiles! love that granite!—and hard to stay on terra firma and pay attention to the details. In the end, though, the details will matter much more than the look. If the kitchen in your new house is not well laid-out and there's not enough counterspace or cabinets, you will hate it every day you live there, even if everything looks terrific.

How do you get the right kitchen layout for you? With a custom-built house, you can design it yourself or work with the kitchen designer at the builder's cabinet dealer. The latter course is advisable because certified kitchen designers know more about kitchen design, cabinets, countertops, and flooring than anyone else in the home-building business—in fact, many architects turn over some or all of the kitchen design to a kitchen designer. Their services will not cost any extra (their design fees are included in the cost of the cabinets), and with their input you will get a kitchen that is tailored to your cooking needs and your aesthetic preferences.

With a production-built house, a kitchen designer who works for the builder's cabinet supplier will have laid out the kitchen. But it may not suit your needs, and the builder is unlikely to change anything. This means that you must look very carefully when touring model homes, and keep looking until you find a kitchen that works for you.

In either case, the more closely you evaluate your current kitchen and what you like and hate about it, the more likely you will know what you want in your new one. For example, do you have enough counterspace? Is your food prep area by the sink too small? Are you constantly criss-crossing your kitchen to load and unload your dishwasher or to get food from the refrigerator to prepare dinner by the sink?

Moving from the big picture of layout to the smaller one of details such as cabinets, countertops, appliances, and flooring, more functional considerations emerge. For example, do you cook on the run and dispense with a cutting board half the time? A countertop material like granite that won't scratch might be in order. Is your current kitchen overflowing with cooking equipment? Base cabinets with roll-out trays and a large storage capacity could be your ticket. Do you stand for long periods cutting and chopping or stirring slow-cooking sauces over a stove? A more resilient flooring like wood or sheet vinyl will be easier on your feet than tile or slate.

Of course, looks do count, and you will spend plenty of time canvassing, comparing, obsessing about, and ultimately selecting cabinets, countertops, and flooring.

isitfunctional?

Whether you are building a custom house or buying one from a production builder, the best way to get an idea of how various layouts look and how you would work in them is to visit model homes. Kitchen cabinet dealers will have displays, but very few have complete kitchens. Visiting even two or three models will help you interpret the layouts and sketches drawn by the dealer's kitchen designer.

When you start touring models, you find yourself drawn to the kitchen like a magnet. Home builders know that a gorgeous kitchen will sell a house, so it will be eye-catching. But, to reiterate: If there isn't enough counterspace for food preparation or enough cabinets to store your things, you won't be happy. So take off those rose-colored glasses and give the kitchen a hard look.

First, check out surface area. Is the food-preparation space adequate? If more than one person will be cooking at the same time, is there enough room for two people to work together comfortably? If you hand-wash some items and leave them out to air-dry, is there room on the counter for a dish rack? Or will you have to put away the rack before you can fix a meal?

The best way to answer these questions is to act out in pantomime how you will use the space. If you and your spouse pretend to prepare a meal and find that you keep bumping into each other, the kitchen is clearly too small. Though you may feel ridiculous as you go through this Marcel Marceau routine, the hands-on information you'll collect will be invaluable.

As you field test the kitchen, make sure your imagined meal preparation includes all the appliances. A kitchen that is awkwardly arranged can be just as irritating as one that's too small. The stove, sink, refrigerator, and adjacent work areas should be in reasonable proximity to one another so you don't have to spend a lot of time criss-crossing the room to get a meal together.

A wall oven can be off to one side because you won't spend much time at it, but a microwave should be convenient to the work area because the cook may be heating, defrosting, or otherwise using it for preparing the meal. The dishwasher should be close to the cabinet where dishes and glasses are kept, which should, in turn, be close to the daily eating area. The refrigerator should be close to both the food-prep area and the cabinet where dishes and glasses are kept. Because of its size, the refrigerator is frequently put in a far corner, causing endless unnecessary trips back and forth across the kitchen.

storage

Storage needs vary with lifestyle, but this will be another sore point if there isn't enough. If the base-cabinet storage is inadequate, can you hang some pots and pans on the wall? If there isn't enough wall-cabinet storage for dishes and plates, can you store the special-occasion plates in a dining-room buffet?

Adequate food storage depends on both your shopping and eating habits. Do you go food shopping once a week or every few days? Are your food preferences simple, or do you prepare meals with many pantry ingredients? If the kitchen has a pantry closet, the shelves must be at least twelve inches deep and twelve inches high to accommodate cereal boxes, but a twenty-four-inch depth will be more useful. If you buy cereal in bulk quantities, the shelf height should be eighteen inches.

lighting

Lighting is often overlooked because most buyers visit the model during broad daylight, when windows can flood the room with light. At night, however, you still need to see what you're doing. Even if there is adequate general lighting, the counter areas can be dark and hard to work in. Under-cabinet lighting will eliminate this problem. If the builder doesn't install these (and very few do), ask if he will install the wiring so you can add the lights yourself after you move in. A "slim line" type of fixture that fits in the recess under the cabinet box is more expensive, but it gives a kitchen a more finished look that makes the added cost worth it.

counter layout

There are many different types of counter arrangements, but most kitchen designers consider the galley-type to be the most efficient. With a single aisle and counters to either side, you only have to turn around to go from sink to cooking range.

As lifestyles have evolved and become more informal, however, more and more people want a kitchen with an eat-in area. In small houses, the galley-type kitchen has given way to the L-shaped counter. In this configuration, the appliance arrangement may be satisfactory. But make sure that the counter area is adequate for food preparation, especially if two people will be preparing food at the same time. Packing a sink, dishwasher, stove, and refrigerator into one L-shaped counter can also compromise base-cabinet storage, so check this too.

In larger houses, kitchens frequently have island counters. For an island to add function as well as style, it should be no more than forty-two inches from the main counters. If the island is too far away, it becomes awkward to reach, especially if the island has a cooktop. Buyers who want an island cooktop should make sure that the island is at least sixty inches long. With this length, you can get a fifteen-inch counter on each side of a standard thirty-inch range and have space for pot handles to overhang as well as a place to put bowls and utensils.

Staggering an island cooktop rather than placing it directly opposite the sink makes it easier for two people to work in the kitchen at the same time. Turning the island 45 degrees to create a triangle-shaped floor area between it and the adjoining counter also gives more space for two people to work, and is especially convenient when children are underfoot.

yourcooking**style**

The functionality test addresses the big picture. The second test, "does this kitchen mesh with my cooking style?" addresses the smaller issues that must be factored in so that you end up with exactly the right kitchen for you. What is your "cooking style"? The way you organize yourself when working in a kitchen (*not* the style of cuisine that you prefer).

After observing hundreds of clients work in their existing kitchens before designing them a new one, certified kitchen designer Jim Bingnear of McLean, Virginia, has concluded that there are basically two kinds of cooking styles: Type A and Type B. Type A tends to be more slapdash and cooks on the run, preparing an entire meal at one time—cutting up vegetables for a salad while stir-frying chicken while steaming rice and keeping an eye on dessert in the oven—and cleaning up afterward. The more fastidious Type B, in contrast, works at a slower pace, fixes dishes sequentially, and cleans as she goes, wiping up spills as they happen. The Galloping Gourmet is a classic example of Type A; Martha Stewart is clearly Type B.

Since Type A puts out all the food items, utensils, pots, and pans before she starts and does several things at once, she will require more counter area than Type B. But, Bingnear cautions, Type A will not be happy with ten-foot-long counters—her space needs to be constricted in some way so cleanup will not be odious. Since Type B cleans up as she goes, any kitchen will work, even one with a small food-prep area.

When assessing yourself, it's important to be honest, even if it means admitting neatness is not your highest priority. Once you've determined your cooking style, factor it into your consideration of kitchen layout and your choices for materials, colors, and finishes—depending on your style, some will be more prudent choices than others.

With countertops, anything will work for Type B because she tends to be neater. A scratch-resistant material is not a must because she will reliably pull out a cutting board every time. Staining is not a problem because she cleans up every spill. A heat- and scorch-resistant material is not required either because she doesn't put hot pots on a countertop.

Type A, however, should be more judicious in her choice of countertops. She is much more likely to put hot pans on the counter and to cut up food directly on the surface. And since she cleans up at the end, commonly used and frequently spilled household foods like mustard, grape juice, and tomato sauce will have already dried and stained.

Type A's kitchen will look better over the long haul if her counters are made of a harder, more durable material such as Corian or granite. If these are not in the budget—and they can add several thousand dollars to a kitchen price—Type A should opt for a scratch- and stain-resistant plastic laminate such as Wilsonart's Premium 90 or Pionite's Crystal. The laminate should be a medium dark color with some pattern variation to camouflage scratches and smudges, Bingnear advises. Type A should ask the kitchen installer to rout out a sizable rectangle in the counter and insert a piece of Corian to use as a cutting surface.

Ceramic-tile countertops and backsplashes look nice, but the grout stains easily, no matter how quickly you mop up spills. To keep the stain problem under control, Bingnear advises using a bigger tile and a dark grout.

Cooking style should also be factored in when you select cabinet finishes and colors. White cabinets will suit neat and fastidious Type B, but the more impatient and messier Type A will not be happy because "the ketchup stains and the place where the tea bag splashed when you threw it toward the trash will show," Bingnear says. In fact, one of the ways that he distinguishes neat from messy cooks is by their reaction to white cabinets. "When people come to my show room and say 'white cabinets—I hate them, they show everything,' I know they are Type A cooks." Oak, maple, or cherry cabinets with a medium to dark stain are a wiser choice because these won't show dirt and stains.

The right floor finish depends on both neatness and how many hours you spend over a hot stove. If you're not going to clean up right away, get something in a medium color with a pattern, Bingnear suggested. If you spend a long time preparing meals, you need a soft flooring material such as wood or vinyl, rather than a hard one such as tile or slate. What's the difference? Hard materials have less capacity to absorb any impact. Your back and leg muscles will get sore more easily because the floor won't absorb much impact from normal body movements; also, things dropped are more likely to break. If you like to spend a long time preparing gourmet meals, think twice about that gorgeous Sautillo Mexican tile.

cabinets

When you start to zero in on the details, the first will certainly be the cabinets—the biggest-ticket item in any kitchen, and the one that will have the most impact on its appearance.

cabinet grades

In your initial discussions with cabinet dealers and builders, you will often hear the terms *stock, semi-custom,* and *custom,* the three main divisions or grades of cabinets. There is much overlap between them; the only hard-and-fast distinction is price. Custom cabinets are the most expensive, stock are the least expensive, and semi-custom are in between.

With custom cabinets, the cabinet boxes are made with higher grade materials, the finishes are hand applied, there is a greater choice of wood species and stains, and the detailing is more refined. Most of the higher cost, however, is due to the custom factor— custom cabinets are made to order in any size requested.

With stock cabinets, there are fewer choices of wood species for the doors (but they can be stained to mimic other woods), fewer coats of finish, the finishes are machine applied, and less expensive materials are used for the boxes. But some stock cabinet lines now include features that were once the hallmark of custom cabinet makers, such as base cabinets with roll-out trays and solid-wood drawers with dovetail joints and under-mounted drawer glides (these are stronger drawers with a tonier look).

The critical distinction between stock and custom cabinets, however, is the sizing. Stock cabinets come only in fixed sizes, so there is less flexibility in designing a kitchen with them.

Semi-custom cabinets occupy an ill-defined gray area between the other grades. If the semi-custom cabinet is made by a stock cabinet maker, the semi-custom line will offer more wood species and finishes and more sizes. If the maker is a custom cabinet maker, its semi-custom line will have fewer features and finishes and there will be some limitation on the sizing.

Nearly all production-home builders use stock cabinets. Price is certainly a factor, but almost as important is the easy availability of stock cabinets. They can be delivered within one to three weeks of placing an order, whereas a custom or a semi-custom order generally takes eight to twelve weeks, at a minimum. For a home builder on a very tight schedule, as all production builders are, this is critical. If the wrong size or style is of a stock cabinet inadvertently ordered or delivered, the problem can be quickly rectified.

If you end up with stock cabinets, either because you are working with a production builder or because your budget dictates it, don't feel that you are unduly compromising. Over the last fifteen years, the quality of stock cabinets has vastly improved in appearance, detailing, and durability. In fact, stock cabinets may be the most sensible choice for anybody regardless of budget. Do you really care about the costlier hand-applied finishes or ball-bearing drawer glides that are standard issue with any custom line?

doors

Once you've dealt with the preliminaries, you can jump into the fun part: looking at specific lines and door styles. Custom and semi-custom lines offer the most choices in the doors, but stock lines also offer enough to keep you lying awake at night.

Broadly speaking, there are two door styles: completely flat, which is a contemporary look, or with a panel that can be raised or flat, which is a traditional look. In either style, most doors are wood. With stock cabinets, the least expensive wood door will have a single flat panel of veneered plywood; this is the standard door for many production builders. A medium-priced stock door will have a raised panel that is veneered wood over particleboard. The most expensive stock door will have a solid wood panel; these look and wear the same as the others, but you will still know the difference.

With semi-custom and custom cabinets, the wood doors will be *solid* wood. Their flat-paneled doors can have more panels on the front as well as more refinements that give it particular style.

The flat-paneled door is fine for a bathroom, but in a high-use area such as a kitchen, you should upgrade to a raised panel if possible. The increased thickness of the door gives it more strength and rigidity, a plus for households with small children who often hang on the base cabinet doors.

The size of the cabinet doors will affect both price and appearance. Larger doors and drawers that cover the front of the cabinet box when they're closed are more expensive. The difference is subtle, but it can give a traditional look a more contemporary feel. With standard door and drawer sizes, the front of the cabinet box is partially exposed when the doors are closed.

Nearly all stock cabinet lines offer oak, maple, hickory, cherry, and vinyl-wrapped white doors. At the semi-custom level, birch and poplar doors are also available, and white doors are lacquered, an expensive process that gives a more refined look; the number of stains, which can affect appearance dramatically, also increases. At the custom level, tropical hardwoods such as teak and mahogany are also possible. Nearly all cabinet lines offer wall cabinets with glass doors, which will add an upscale look if your dishes, cups, and glassware match.

Though rarely shown in model homes or offered by production-home builders, most stock cabinet lines offer accessories such as dental molding that give a stock cabinet a more customized look. You can get these when you order the cabinet or install them yourself after you move in. To check the possibilities, look at the cabinet maker's website.

Before you make your final decision on the doors, try to see an entire kitchen with the ones you have selected, even if this requires some effort: Ask the cabinet dealer if you can see a completed job of a former client, or ask the builder if you can see the finished house of someone who got them. This is especially important if you want a dark wood or stain, because dark cabinets will make a kitchen appear darker and smaller than you expect. (See Resources for websites of major stock and semi-custom cabinet makers.)

storageandfunctionality

When most people talk about choosing a cabinet, what they are really talking about is choosing a cabinet *door* style. But the storage capacity behind the doors—and often within the drawers—will matter more in the long run than what the doors look like.

A trip to a cabinet dealer's showroom will be helpful. You will see a tempting array of gizmos, including a drawer that pulls out to an ironing board, or a door that swings open to reveal a tea cart on wheels. These options mainly serve to liven up the display, since few people ever buy them. Nestled in among the various options, however, you will find some truly useful ones. For example, narrow pull-out cabinets designed to fit in the gaps between cabinets. As you look, check out the drawers and the base cabinets, the areas that deliver the most utility of any kitchen storage element, with recent refinements that make these basics even easier to use.

A drawer is still a drawer, but mounting the glides underneath instead of on the sides can add as much as one inch to the interior width. Multiplied across an entire kitchen, it's a significant increase in storage capacity. Besides the added utility, many designers think a drawer with the concealed glides looks better. When drawer glide extensions are added to large drawers, they can be pulled out all the way, so large items in the back can be easily accessed.

Base cabinets with vastly increased storage capacity are much easier to use, thanks to roll-out trays that function like pullout shelves. Instead of having to take out everything at the front to get the pot at the back, you just pull out the tray and grab the item. The storage capacity is greater because each tray is the full depth of the cabinet; in a traditional base cabinet with fixed shelves, the upper one is only half the depth of the cabinet.

The roll-out trays have proved to be so useful and flexible that tall cabinets with roll outs have all but replaced that quintessential eighties gizmo—the swing-out chef's pantry. The swing-out units had shelves that could be loaded on either side, plus shelves mounted in the rear of the cabinet and on the doors. Though it looked like a great addition to any kitchen, in fact many homeowners (including me) complained that the shelving system wasn't flexible enough for the varied sizes of goods being stored. We wanted to be able to see things at a glance instead of having to swing out one or two units to find that errant can of tomato sauce, and items stored on the doors often flew off whenever the cabinet was opened. Not only do the roll-out trays solve all these problems, they're also much less expensive than the swing-out chef's pantry.

The sides of the roll-out trays are usually only two or three inches high, so that everything on a shelf can be seen easily. When ordering custom cabinets that can be made to any size, however, certified kitchen designer Ronda Royalty of McLean, Virginia, watches her clients prepare a meal before finalizing this dimension. "If they tend to yank things, I make the trays deeper to keep things from flying off. And if liquor and wine bottles are being stored in the cabinet, I make a much deeper tray with dividers to keep bottles from clanging against each other."

Trash compactors, another hot gizmo in the seventies and eighties, are close to being history now. "They get smelly and disgusting and we observed a high breakdown rate," noted certified kitchen designer Jeff Adler of Los Angeles. His low-tech solution for trash and recycled items: a base cabinet with two hampers on glides. A second recycling cabinet with a newspaper collector can be added, but Adler said he rarely specifies it because it's not a good use of the space. Most kitchens do not have any base-cabinet storage to spare, and newspaper collecting is one recycling activity that does not need to be near a food-preparation area.

blind corners

There is one place in a kitchen where a souped-up gizmo-laden cabinet is appropriate: a blind-corner condition. This is the area under the counter where the two legs of an L-shaped counter intersect; a blind corner cannot be accessed unless a special cabinet is used. The oldest and cheapest solution is a cabinet with a fixed shelf and a door at one end. In many cases, the only way to retrieve the pots in the back is to crawl in with a flashlight.

A better solution is a lazy Susan cabinet with two shelves that rotate around a metal pole. This type of cabinet is comparatively large and limits the other types of cabinets that can be used with it. Some designers think the pole itself takes up too much space. Functionally, the lazy Susan is better suited to heavier objects such as casserole dishes and mixing bowls. When light objects such as cereal boxes and Tupperware are stored in it, they can easily fall off and get caught in the back of the cabinet box.

In some situations, especially small kitchens, a newer type of lazy Susan with half-moon-shaped shelves will work. These are rotated out and then pulled forward, so that everything on the shelf is easy to reach. This type of cabinet is also more compact, giving a designer more flexibility in choosing the other cabinets and drawers to go with it.

Adler's choice of a blind-corner cabinet could have been designed by Rube Goldberg. When the cabinet door is pulled straight out, two large wire trays attached to it are accessible. Swinging the door with trays to the side pulls forward two more shelves that were hidden in the corner. Referred to by many in the cabinet business as "the miracle corner," the swinging-tray mechanism is made by Häfele, a German company, and used by a number of custom cabinet makers in the United States.

Kraftmaid, a semi-custom cabinet line, makes a less expensive and less sophisticated "base blind with swing out" version of the miracle corner. A wood pantry unit pulls out and swings to the side. To access the two shelves in the blind corner, the user has to reach in and pull them forward. (See Resources for information on blind-corner cabinets.)

very narrow pullout cabinets

For narrow gaps between cabinets that would otherwise have been covered over with a fixed filler strip, a number of cabinet lines now offer three- and six-inch-wide pull-outs. Though an intriguing concept, designers generally give these mixed reviews. The three-inch wide pullouts with narrower one-and-a-half-inch-wide shelves are meant for spice storage, but most people prefer to keep spices in a tiered drawer or in a wider ten-inch pullout that will also hold larger items frequently used in a cooking area such as cooking oil, flour, sugar, and even paper towels.

appliance garages

Appliance garages for small appliances are still popular, but further refinements will make these more useful. By installing outlets in the rear of the garage compartment, the chef only has to pull the appliance out to use it. Closing it with two doors that swing open instead of a slatted, sliding tambour door means that no space inside the compartment is lost to the opening mechanism, and thus larger items can be stored.

Despite the many advances in cabinetry, however, kitchen clutter continues to bedevil designers as much as it does homeowners. The unfortunate truth is that no matter how many catch-all drawers you add, there's always more stuff to store.

drawer bases only

In nearly all kitchens, most of the storage units below the counters are base cabinets. But this is not fixed in stone. In fact, many kitchen designers now recommend a storage system below the counters that consists almost entirely of drawers. The reasons: A drawers-only storage system can be more precisely tailored to individual needs and it is easier to use than base cabinets.

The biggest plus is the convenience. When you pull out a drawer, you can see everything in it at a glance, and you can easily reach the items at the back. With base cabinets, even the ones with roll-out shelving, you need to move things around to get what you want, then rearrange things before you can push the shelf back in. If you don't push the shelf in all the way, the cabinet door can crack when you try to shut it. Another advantage is the drawers are easier to open and close than base cabinets, which require you to open both doors before you can pull out the shelves.

Though some clients are initially skeptical that the drawers will meet their needs, certified kitchen designer Debby Saling of Beltsville, Maryland, said they become convinced when she demonstrates that a full set of frying pans and saucepans will fit in the bottom two drawers of an eighteen-inch drawer base. Because drawers have so much capacity, she always recommends them for small kitchens.

Another benefit is that the design can be customized to a degree that is impossible with base cabinets, even in a very large kitchen. For example, one drawer can be allocated to Tupperware, one to saucepans, one to frying and omelette pans, and one to casserole dishes. This can be further fine-tuned by adding dividers to individual drawers, creating smaller compartments. For example, adding a divider to a twenty-four-inch-wide drawer can create an eighteen-inch-wide compartment for saucepans or Tupperware and a six-inch-wide compartment for tops or lids. This system is especially useful for casserole lids, often the hardest items to store. For the occasional client who wants a kitchen with no wall cabinets, kitchen designer Jim Bingnear has used dividers in drawers to create square compartments for stacking plates or slots for vertically storing them and smaller "stalls" for mugs and cups.

Even when clients see the increased utility of using the drawer system, some of them worry that the weight of their pots and pans will break the drawer, Saling noted. The affected part would not be the drawer, but the drawer glide and almost all drawer glides are designed to hold seventy-five pounds. A whole set of pots and pans—even a set heavy-duty cast-iron ones—wouldn't weigh that much.

drawer widths

Though it's possible to get drawer bases as narrow as twelve inches, they're not very useful. The inside width of the drawer itself will be less than eight inches, so what you end up with is essentially a stack of cubby-hole drawers for tchotchkes. If the counter width for a drawer base goes to less than fifteen inches, most designers specify a tray-divider base cabinet. Even a fifteen-inch-wide drawer base is not that useful, so most designers try to keep the drawer widths to at least eighteen inches. The upper bound for drawer width is thirty-six inches; if a drawer was wider than that, it could be loaded with more than seventy-five pounds, which could break the glides.

Even with all the utility of the drawers, however, it's still a good idea to include a base cabinet in your kitchen to accommodate the awkward-sized pot or the one or two pieces of large cookware that you will inevitably accumulate.

Although Saling usually works with custom and semi-custom cabinetry, she has also designed drawer-bases-only kitchens with the same stock cabinet lines that many production builders use. Most production builders have not yet caught up with this trend, but an adventurous few may be willing to consider it, especially if they sense that other buyers may also want it and you are willing to be the guinea pig. If your production builder gives it a green light, you will have to work with the kitchen designer at his cabinet supplier to redesign the kitchen. Your new design will slow down the builder's installers, because when they install the same or very similar kitchens over and over they can do it quickly. So you may have to pay an additional charge to cover the longer installation time; you will also have to pay a surcharge for the drawer bases, which cost more than base cabinets.

If you can work through all the logistics with your builder so that you get the drawer-bases-only kitchen in your new house, you'll be happier with the end result, Saling predicted. In her experience, the planning of a kitchen with drawers forces clients to think through exactly what's needed. With base cabinets, storage specifics do not have to be spelled out so precisely, and something can be overlooked.

countertops

If the cabinets are the first thing you notice when you walk into a kitchen, the countertops are the second. So, naturally, you want ones that look good. There are also practical considerations such as durability and price to consider. But as you wade into this subject, you will find that for each material the number of choices is huge, and each one has its pluses and minuses. If you're already losing sleep over the cabinets, this could worsen your insomnia.

You can get real stone such as granite or marble. Or the hot new thing—a stone-synthetic composite that is mostly quartz particles mixed with a binder. Or you can get a

Many new kitchens these days have open wine racks. But unless you plan to drink the wine right away or you want the bottles just for looks, you're better off getting another cabinet for general storage in place of this rack, and relocating your wine somewhere else in your house. The quickest way to ruin a good bottle of wine is to expose it to heat for any period of time. This accelerates the chemical reactions within the bottle and causes the wine to age prematurely. The dishwasher and stove put out heat when they're turned on; a frost-free refrigerator belches it continuously; the sunlight streaming through big kitchen windows to create a cheery atmosphere—another thing you probably want in your new home—also affects wine adversely, hence the dark bottles. Too much heat will make wine undrinkable, in extreme cases turning it into vinegar.

openwineracks

If the kitchen is not a place to keep your wine, where should you put it? Basically the darkest, coolest place in your house. Wine keeps best when stored at a constant temperature of 55 degrees and a constant humidity of about 70 percent. It's not for nothing that those French châteaux with dank, dark depths produced some of the world's best wines. With those storage conditions, the naturally occurring chemical reactions in the bottle happen very slowly, and the taste noticeably improves over time.

Without building a wine cellar, few homeowners can approach the château ideal, but most people can find some place that will work. If you live in an area of the country where basements are common, put your wine there. Just make sure that you put it next to the earth and away from the furnace, water heater, or sun-exposed wall, advised

100 percent synthetic solid surfacing material such as Corian. There are more than a hundred different granite stones to choose from, at least fifty marbles, and Corian is available in more colors and textures than ever—eighty-three at last count. So far, the manufacturers of the stone-synthetic mix offer a modest selection that numbers about forty.

All of these products could look terrific in a kitchen. Price might seem the easiest basis for a decision, but within each category, the majority of the choices fall roughly within the same price range, about $100 to $150 per linear foot of counter, installed (some materials are less than this, and some are considerably more). The least expensive countertop material, by a significant margin, is plastic laminate, but that won't make the choices any easier. The four major manufacturers—Wilsonart, Formica, Nevamar, and Pionite—each offer more than a hundred colors and patterns.

Practicality might be a reason to pick one material over another, but none of these products is trouble-free. Some of them scratch easily, some require periodic resealing, and all of them will stain if food spills—especially such common staining agents as mus-

wine storage specialist Jim Mackey of San Francisco, who stores his own wine in his basement.

If you live in a part of the country where virtually no one has basements, such as Florida or Southern California, an interior closet will do, as long as it's not next to a heating duct, a hot-water heater, or a washer and dryer. Since the temperature at the floor level is always cooler, you should put the wine on the floor of the closet rather than on an upper shelf.

To keep the corks from drying out, the bottles should be stored on their sides. The easiest way to store them this way is to repack them into the type of wooden cases they were originally shipped in. You can get these for free at most wine stores, especially during the holidays.

While wine can be kept in a wine cellar for years, how long can you leave it in the basement or closet without ill effect? For a basement, two or three years is certainly reasonable. For a closet, though, the time horizon is considerably shorter. The general consensus is about a year; after that you're tempting fate.

Wine-storage specialist Gene Walder of San Marcos, California, used to keep a couple of cases of wine in a dark interior closet. This worked well, but he didn't let it sit more than six months. He now keeps it in a small wine cooler with consistent temperature and humidity control that he installed when he renovated his kitchen. The unit, which is about the size of a trash compactor, fits under his kitchen counter and holds twenty-four bottles. Larger units that hold as many as forty-eight bottles and are about the size of a dishwasher are also available. If you have a case or two of wine in your closet now, you already have a strong interest in wine. So Walder's solution to the storage issue might be appropriate for your new kitchen.

For further information on wine-storage options, ask your local wine merchant or local wine-storage specialists. (See Resources for website addresses.)

---

tard, red wine, or strawberries—are left to dry for any period of time. With effort, though, you can usually get the stains out. The only fool-proof countertop material that absolutely won't stain, whose scratches are inconsequential, and that's a cinch to maintain is stainless steel. But then your kitchen will look like a hospital lab.

If you don't want the laboratory look and you're not the fastidious type who will clean up spills right away or dependably pull out a cutting board every time, practicality dictates that you pick a darker color with a mottled surface so that stains, scratches, and general wear and tear won't show as much, whatever countertop material you get.

granite

The number of granite choices available to you will depend on where you buy it. Home-center stores such as Home Depot sell only about fifteen stones. Many production builders now offer granite countertops as an upgrade, but they need to keep things simple when building ten or twenty houses at a time, so they offer at most four or five choices.

The granite fabricators who cut the large stone slabs into kitchen-counter-sized pieces usually sell forty or more different stones, with a wide range of textures and subtleties that increase with price. For example, Luna Pearl, which is offered by many production builders, is a light-colored stone with large black, white, and gray flecks. It looks the same when seen from near or far or under different lighting conditions, and it is among the least expensive granites; the installed price of a countertop is about $75 a linear foot (on a par with a base-grade Corian). At the other end of the granite price scale is Blue Pearl, a smoldering dark gray stone with large translucent chips that give it depth; different lighting conditions affect its appearance. Blue Pearl runs about $175 to $200 a linear foot, installed.

The color range with granites is wide, but it is a natural material, and there can be marked irregularities within one countertop. The degree of variation will not be evident on a small four-by-four-inch sample, but even the most homogenous-looking granites can have large, dark, amorphous areas of discoloration. To avoid any unpleasant surprises, you should visit the fabricator and pick out your slab yourself. If possible, bring along samples of the flooring and cabinetry you're considering to make sure that all three work together. You may find that you still like the countertop, but want to rethink the other two. Or you may serendipitously discover a granite among the fabricator's stock which was not included on your builder's sample board that you like better, and you may decide to rethink your whole kitchen.

Although granite is regarded by many as simply an upscale look, it is surprisingly practical. It is nearly impossible to scratch or damage the surface with a hot pan. As the literature says, you need to use a cutting board to protect your cutlery, not the granite. Granite is a porous stone, however, and it will stain if not sealed regularly. Even with the sealing, it will still stain if spills are not cleaned up promptly; but the sealing makes the stains easier to remove. The initial sealing will be done by the fabricator who cuts the slab to your specifications. Thereafter, you will need to reseal it about once a year, though in heavy-use areas, around the sink and cooktop, you may need to reseal it more often. The telltale sign it's time for this is when water stops beading on the surface and leaves a darker spot if you let it sit for a minute or so.

marble and limestone

Marble is softer than granite. It scratches easily, so a cutting board is a must. And certain food spills will affect the finish. A polished-marble surface has a rich look, but common acidic foods such as lemon juice, red wine, and tomatoes will eat through the polish and leave dull patches if they're not wiped up right away. A honed-marble surface with a matte finish may not look quite as rich, but it will not be affected by acidic food spills. With either type of finish, though, the marble will stain if foods are left on it, and this will show more with a lighter stone color. As with granite, marble must be regularly resealed.

If you're after an Old World look, another possibility is honed limestone. But it has all the problems of marble: It is a soft stone, it scratches easily, it will stain if food spills are left to dry on, and because it is a light cream color, the stains will show more. Limestone must also be periodically resealed.

Because marble and limestone can be problematic in a kitchen, many stone fabricators discourage their use, and some insist that you sign a waiver before they will install it. Marble countertop prices range from about $50 to $200 per linear foot, installed; the honed limestone runs about $100 to $150 per linear foot, installed.

the stone-synthetic composites

The stone-synthetic composite—Corian's Zodiac, Formica's Crystalite, and Cosentino's Silestone—are all made of about 90 percent quartz particles and 10 percent acrylic or epoxy binder. Some of the composites look like natural stone, but not one that you could identify. Others are so close to real granite that you're left asking, "Is it real or is it Memorex?" And then there are the composites that you might describe as "improvements on mother nature": If you've longed for the brilliance of quartz and the rich blue of lapis lazuli, Zodiac's Celestial Blue or Silestone's Cobalt Blue could be your ticket.

Since the composites are man-made materials, they do not have the unexpected variation of granite or marble. Nonetheless, you should still try to see a large piece at a countertop fabricator's, because making a selection from a small, four-by-four-inch sample is difficult. When you go, try to bring along the flooring and cabinet samples as well.

The composites do not need to be sealed, and fabricators who work with them say they're as scratch-resistant as granite. But they can stain if food spills are not cleaned up promptly, says Fred Hueston, director of the National Training Center for Stone and Masonry Trades.

Cystalite and Silestone countertops are similarly priced at about $110 to $160 per linear foot, installed. Zodiac prices are higher, ranging from about $120 to $250 a linear foot, installed. Since all three of these products are fairly recent market entries, their availability varies.

corian and the solid surfacing materials

The most widely available and widely known 100 percent synthetic countertop material is Corian, made by Dupont; but other manufacturers including Wilson Art, Formica, and

Avenite also make it. Known in the building and remodeling industry as solid surfacing materials, these are either a pure acrylic product or a polyester-acrylic mix.

Some of the solid surfacing materials are solid colors, but most have flecks that give it a textured look. In some cases the look approaches real stone; in others, especially with the greens and reds, liberties have clearly been taken with nature.

When a solid surfacing material such as Corian is installed, no seams are visible; as a result, the counters look as if they were created just for your kitchen. If you get a Corian sink as well, you get a continuous unbroken surface as you go from counter to sink, and this adds to the "made just for me" look. All the solid surface materials feel like silk, and this adds to their cachet.

The solid surfacing materials are scratch-resistant; if you do get a scratch, you can sand it out. Should you get deep scratches or gouges, the damaged area can be removed and a new piece installed. If the new patch is made from the cut-out for your sink (the fabricator will give it to you), the repair will be invisible. Otherwise, the new piece will be from a different die lot, and the repair may show.

As a practical matter, it is difficult for the average homeowner to sand out scratches so that they don't show, because most people lack the right sanding techniques and experience. Rather than trying to get out every scratch, you're better off accepting the scratches as part of the patina, observed countertop fabricator John Murray of Washington, D.C. And Hueston has found that the solid surfacing materials will also stain if heavy staining agents such as mustard or strawberries are left to dry.

As with the other countertop materials, you should go to the fabricator who makes the countertops to see a large piece before making your final selection, and bring your cabinet and flooring samples along.

The price for solid-surfacing materials ranges from about $75 to $150 per linear foot of counter, installed.

plastic laminate

If the lower-priced granites, marble, or solid surfacing materials still exceed your budget, Formica, Nevamar, Pionite, and Wilsonart, the major manufacturers of plastic laminates, offer a very wide variety of colors, patterns, and finishes. Some, such as Pionite's polished Olive Organix, look like polished granite. When an Olive Organix countertop is edged with wood, "no one can tell," said one high-end builder in Florida who uses it when clients get in a budget crunch.

No plastic laminate is scratch-proof, but some—including Wilsonart's Premium-90, Formica's Sparkle, Pionite's Crystal, and Nevamar's Crystal—have subtly textured surfaces that are more scratch-resistant than a standard laminate matte finish. These are well suited for kitchen use, but they can also stain if you don't clean up food spills promptly.

appliances

If you haven't bought any of these in the last ten years, you're in for a very pleasant surprise. Appliances today are easier to use, easier to clean, more energy efficient, quieter, and, to top it off, they look better.

electric ranges

The electric range has undergone the greatest transformation. You can still buy a range with electric coils, but now you also have the option of a glass-top one with radiant elements below the surface. Most glass-tops have at least one variable burner: Depending on how you turn the dial, a burner can accommodate a small pot or a large one (this is particularly advantageous if your spouse is forever putting small pots on the closest, large burner). Some models also have a "bridge burner": a small burner wedged between two regular-sized ones, handy if you want to steam fish in an oblong pot. With the low-heat simmer feature for melting butter or making slow-cooking puddings or sauces, you can kiss that pain-in-the-neck double boiler good-bye forever.

When you turn off the glass-top, all models have a "hot surface warning light" that remains on until the surface cools. Another important plus with the glass-tops is cleaning them—you just wipe off the surface with a sponge or dishrag. If food cooks on, you remove it with a special cleaner.

Some of the coil ranges heat up faster than the glass-tops, but this type does not have a simmer feature or variable burner sizes. The coil-tops are not as easy to clean as the glass-tops, but modifications have made them easier to clean than the old ones. Instead of having to clean spillovers by removing the coil and drip pan and then reaching in and feeling your way around with a sponge, you lift up the stove top and support it with rods (just like lifting the hood of your car) while you clean underneath. More expensive coil ranges have porcelain drip bowls that are easier to clean—you can use a scouring pad without damaging the surface. They look better longer, so you won't eventually be wrapping aluminum foil around them every week. Even better, one manufacturer makes a solid drip bowl without a hole at the bottom, so the spills are contained. As you compare different coil-top ranges, note the number of coils per burner. The lower-priced ones have fewer coils for each burner and they won't heat up or cook as fast.

The thermostats in electric ovens are now much more accurate, so you'll have to recalibrate your cooking times. The old ovens were "fast" or "slow" because the thermostats often varied by as much as 25 degrees.

Besides more accuracy in temperature, the major change in ovens is the convection option. A fan distributes heat equally around the food, allowing you to cook more things at once, to cook them more evenly, and to cook them a little faster. If you like to bake up

If you are working with a custom builder, you will be picking out the appliances yourself, and you can specify exactly what you want. If you are working with a production builder, the kitchen appliances will already be specified. If you stay with the same manufacturer that the builder is already using, but want to upgrade it, the builder should be able to get it from his distributor and credit you for the unit he would have ordinarily installed. For example, if the standard dishwasher is a GE Potscrubber (about $250), but you want a GE Profile to get the better cleaning features (about $400 to $500), he should charge you only the $150 to $250 difference. If you want to upgrade the builder's standard refrigerator, which is likely to be a top-freezer model, to a side-by-side type, make sure that it will fit, as the side-by-sides tend to be wider.

a storm, you can cook several pies and cakes at a time. As yet, there's no industry standard for what constitutes a convection oven. Some manufacturers provide only the fan but others have a third, concealed element that helps maintain a consistent temperature.

Cited and actual oven capacity in new ranges can differ because the broiler element in some models can hang down. This could affect your ability to cook a twenty-pound turkey at Thanksgiving, so before you buy the stove, check carefully to see if your big bird will fit.

gas ranges

Gas cooktops have also changed, but not as radically as the electric ones. Almost all of them now have sealed burners that make clean-up easier because there's no space for spills to seep below. You can adjust the cooking temperature with more precision on a gas burner than on an electric range, so many chefs prefer them. On the higher-priced gas cooktops, you can adjust the cooking temperature with even more precision, because the dials rotate 180 degrees instead of only 90.

The burners on a gas stove are all the same size, but they can vary in the amount of heat or BTUs that each one puts out. A lower-priced gas range may have burners with a maximum BTU output of only 9,600; the food won't cook as fast, and stir-frying and sautéeing will take longer. Higher-priced ranges will have at least one burner that goes as high as 12,000 BTUs, and some professional ranges have burners that will go to 15,000 BTUs; but many of these do not have sealed burners or the self-cleaning ovens that are now common on residential ranges.

If you're a chef who wants gas burners and an electric oven, dual ranges are available, but they are expensive. A residential dual range is about three times the price of a residential range that is either all-gas or all-electric. A commercial-grade dual range is about five times as much.

dishwashers

In the past, most dishwashers functioned as "final rinse and dry machines," because you had to make sure *all* the food particles were removed before loading the dishes. Low-end dishwashers still have a limited cleaning ability, but at the mid-price level and up, dishwashers remove food, wash, rinse, and dry. The machines have an internal heater that gets the water hotter (it boosts the temperature to 135 degrees Fahrenheit; to prevent scalding, your hot-water heater should be set at 120 degrees) and a hard-food disposer. With this combination, you can take the dishes straight from the table and load them.

The mechanisms of these better-cleaning dishwashers include filters that catch food particles. American machines dissolve the food particles during the cleaning, but with European models, you must manually clean out the filter. If you scrape off the biggest food particles before loading the dishes, you need to clean the filter about once a month. By scraping off the biggest food particles before loading, you will also use less water and energy to clean the dishes (this is also true with American dishwashers). To conserve water even further, some machines have a soil sensor that detects how dirty the dishes are and adjusts the timer and amount of water accordingly.

Another difference between low- and mid-priced dishwashers is the quality of the racks. The ones in low-priced machines are clad with vinyl, a soft material that can chip or tear, causing the metal underneath to rust and break off. More expensive machines have racks made of nylon, a more durable material that is unlikely to break or tear.

Another plus with the mid-priced machines is that they have more insulation, so the machine is quieter while in operation.

refrigerators

The most significant changes to refrigerators are not ones that you will notice. They're quieter and better insulated, and changes to the motor and compressor have greatly increased their energy efficiency. As of July 2001, as per federal mandate, they will be 30 percent more energy efficient than they were the year before, and 50 percent more efficient than they were in 1991. New refrigerators are also more environmentally friendly. The old chlorofluorocarbon refrigerants (CFCs) that were shown to be harmful to the ozone layer have not been installed in refrigerators since 1993. The hydrochlorofluorocarbon refrigerants (HCFCs) used today are a significant improvement. The hydrofluorocarbons (HFCs) that will be phased in by the end of 2003 are even more environmentally benign.

The changes to refrigerators that you may notice are their larger size and increased storage capacity, better lit interiors, and in many models the shelves pull out so you can find the food more easily. One manufacturer even has a crank so you can raise or lower a shelf without having to remove everything first. Nearly all models now have glass shelves, but make sure that the ones on the refrigerator that you purchase are sealed at the edges. Otherwise you can have a small gap at the edge and spills will drip through.

energy star appliances

Another point to consider when choosing appliances is their energy efficiency. The Energy Star Program, jointly sponsored by the U.S. Department of Energy and the Environmental Protection Agency, rates both dishwashers and refrigerators. A refrigerator with the Energy Star sticker exceeds the federal standards for energy efficiency in refrigerators by at least 20 percent; a dishwasher with the sticker exceeds the federal standard by at least 13 percent.

Every major appliance manufacturer has a website listing all the appliances that they sell and "suggested retail prices." However, the appliance business is very competitive, sales are frequent, and most dealers will match the price of a competitor.

The cabinets-countertop-flooring combination that you pick will make your kitchen uniquely your own. The opportunity to put a personal stamp on things, however, can be daunting. Are there any secrets to insuring a good result? You can get exactly what is in the builder's furnished model, but so will half the other buyers. Or you can trust your instincts. Or take some expert advice. Two award-winning interior designers, Lita Dirks of Englewood, Colorado, and Susan Gulick of Herndon, Virginia, offer these tips:

tips**from**the**trade:**
choosing colors and
finishes for your
new kitchen

♦ **choosing colors:** start with the cabinets. With white, both designers would pick contrasting colors for the rest of the kitchen. The actual materials will depend on your budget. If it is generous, try combining white cabinets, black-speckled Corian counters, and a medium-tone hardwood floor with a white and random black tile backsplash. If your budget is more limited, a similar effect can be achieved with white cabinets, black-speckled plastic-laminate counters, and a sheet-vinyl flooring with a warm faux-tile pattern. The tile backsplashes can add color and texture; they're also practical. Though rarely standard, many production builders offer them as an upgrade.

- **wood cabinets:** You can have a light or dark wood that can be further refined with a stain. Most stains retain the look of natural wood. The ones that don't—for example, bluish "indigo" or greenish "cypress"—will soon look dated. If resale is an important issue for you, go with a perennial favorite species and stain such as mid-toned red oak. Many people want wood cabinets and a hardwood floor to match, but both designers caution that this can be overwhelming. Moreover, with oak, it's very hard to get a match between the cabinets and the floor that looks right because there is so much natural variation in the grain and color. If you just have to have that seamless wood look, maple cabinets and flooring are a better bet because maple has less grain and it's easier to match. If your heart says it has to be an all-oak kitchen, stain the cabinets and floor different colors so that each enhances the other. For example, use a mid-tone oak that is slightly reddish for the cabinets, and then go darker on the floor. That way you will get enough differentiation that it won't look like a mistake.

- **countertop color:** As with the white cabinets, the color of the countertops and flooring should contrast with the wood cabinets. If you pick a darker wood, go with a lighter counter and floor, or vice versa. If you get a darker-colored plastic-laminate counter, get one with speckles to hide fingerprints and scratches.

- **countertop texture:** When choosing countertop material, try to select something that will add another texture. With tile floors, get plastic laminate—generally a production builder's standard countertop finish—or Corian. With wood floors, do the reverse and get tile counters. With a sheet-vinyl floor, any type of counter finish will add variety.

- **cabinet color:** A darker color will make the space feel smaller—a dark cabinet and a dark floor can make it positively claustrophobic. Conversely, a light cabinet and a light floor will make the kitchen feel larger.

- **floor color:** If you really love dark wood and hanker for blue floor tiles, this can work if the kitchen has a large window or two that floods the room with natural light, and you can add extra lights to brighten up the kitchen at night. Even with this, though, the space will still feel smaller than it will with the lighter cabinets and flooring.

- **an all-white kitchen:** White will make the space feel bigger, but you can easily end up with a sterile laboratory look. If you really want white, soften it by including almond or bisque, a near almond color currently favored by appliance manufacturers. For example, mix white cabinets and appliances with almond or bisque counters, and a ceramic tile checkerboard pattern with alternating white and almond squares for the floor.

- **inexpensive color:** To add a dash of color on a low budget, get a different color for an island counter—for example, the same color as some of your furnishings or one that is found within the design of the vinyl floor. Since the counter area of the island is small, you can afford to change it more often than you would an entire kitchen. An even simpler way to add color to a kitchen is replacing the cabinet knobs. Most standard knobs are white or brass, but home-center stores offer them in many bright colors.

- **color cohesion:** If you're using sheet vinyl for the floor, take advantage of the color highlights in the material to unify the kitchen. For example, you can tie white cabinets and black counters together with a white vinyl that has a black diamond pattern, a classic look that never gets old. A vinyl pattern with the same color base as the carpet will make for a smooth transition from the carpeted area to the kitchen.

chapter eight other rooms

Whether you're building a custom, semi-custom, or production-built house, the kitchen is likely to get the lion's share of your attention. And for obvious reasons—you have to make more decisions about the kitchen than you do for any other room. But every room, including the garage, deserves a close look. If the garage is too narrow to get both your cars in or too short for your Suburban, you'll be unhappy even if the kitchen is fabulous.

Attention is especially important for rooms that you may not have in your present house, such as a home office. Just because an office or den/study has been included on a floor plan or is in the furnished model doesn't mean it's workable for you. Most floor plans are geared to that elusive "average family," but every family is different. In some instances, minor modifications such as moving a window or a door will make a room more functional. But in others, especially a home office, you may find that another room is a better fit than the builder's designated spot. A spa-sized master bathroom can be a real kick, especially if the one you have now is the size of a closet. But you'll be frustrated if there isn't a place to put your toiletries or enough counterspace to go with that double sink.

As with planning the kitchen, the more precisely you can nail down exactly how you would use each space and act this out in the builder's model, the more accurately you can assess how well the space will work for you. Make a list of what you like and hate about each room in your present house. If you have unusually large or oddly shaped pieces of furniture, measure them and take the dimensions with you when you visit models.

the family room

This is the modern version of the Victorian era's back parlor—the inner sanctum where family members congregate. In the old days, the family gathered around the fireplace, but today they're more likely to gather around the television. Unfortunately, many builders and floor plans still follow the Victorian model and put the fireplace front stage center—when you look at the family room in most models, the fireplace is the focal point and the television is nowhere in sight.

Since you will put one there if you buy the house, try to see how you would fit it in. More than likely, you'll find that the only way to get a comfortable furniture arrangement is to move the fireplace to the side or a corner, and make the television the focal point. Easing such a potent symbol off to the side may seem unnatural—after all, every homeowner sums up his dream with the phrase "hearth and home," and no one ever says "television and home." But the truth is that you look at the fireplace only when there's a fire going, and even then only from time to time. A fireplace has a comforting presence, but it can be anywhere in the room. On the other hand, you do *watch* the television, so making the television the starting point in planning the family room and organizing the seating is more sensible. Moving the fireplace is not that difficult structurally, because many builders now use a direct-vent gas fireplace that does not have a chimney; it vents directly outside through the wall.

When the fireplace and television are in some proximity to each other and even on the same wall, the furniture placement is easier. Many production-builders already do this, but often in a way that is still problematic—they put a viewing niche for the television above the fireplace. This *looks* good, but in a small room you will be craning your neck to see the television and you may feel like you're in the front row at a movie theater.

A better alternative is to move the television to one side of the fireplace, and to put it in a cabinet with a swivel base and pocket doors. The television will be closer to eye level, so you'll be much more comfortable when you are watching; when you aren't, it will be neatly out of sight. Another plus to this arrangement is you can get additional cabinetry for a handy place to put the rest of your entertainment paraphernalia—a VCR and video tapes, a CD player and CDs, a turntable and all those old record albums you can't bear to get rid of.

Televisions and fireplaces are not the only points of contention in planning a family room. There's also the view outside: When you incorporate it into the room, you will not only enjoy the space more, but also feel you are in a bigger space. The view to the backyard will be obstructed, however, if the fireplace or a built-in entertainment center are centered on the rear wall. You may also have a view to the side of your house. In either case, you don't want to cover it up, so move the fireplace and television to another wall in the room.

While the television should be an important factor in the planning of your family room, it's only one of many activities that occur there. In most floor plans, the family room shares the same space with an adjacent eat-in kitchen. How well a family room works for you can also depend on how these functions are merged together as well as the makeup of your household. For example, if you have young children who must be constantly supervised, you need an arrangement that allows you to keep a watchful eye while you're fixing meals. You also need this area to be a "contained space" that can be closed off from the rest of the house. If a house has a very open plan with all the main living areas opening onto one another, supervising very young children becomes a very daunting task.

Conflicting activities in the family room can be a problem when children reach school age. They still want to be in the bosom of the family, but they now have homework and need quiet to concentrate. If another family member wants to watch television while they're struggling with algebra at the breakfast table, no one is happy. A floor plan with a den/study adjacent to both the kitchen and the family room—not uncommon in many production-built houses today—will solve this problem. With French doors for the den/study, the child doing homework will still be connected visually to the rest of the household, but will have the quiet needed to concentrate.

When children become teenagers, their needs change again. They don't want to be in the bosom of the family, but most parents want them to stay in the family orbit rather than sequestering themselves somewhere else in the house. This is more likely to happen if the kitchen–family room is separate from the rest of the first floor, so that the teenagers can "have their own space" without retreating to their bedrooms. On the other hand, a very open floor plan with all the living spaces opening onto each other will not accommodate their need for privacy.

When the teenagers have taken over the family room, you'll need some space for yourself. One solution is to convert the potentially under-utilized living room into an adult refuge where you can watch television or read quietly while your teenagers hold forth in the family room.

thehomeoffice

If you plan to work at home in the evenings and occasionally on the weekend, your home-office needs are modest. You'll have many choices for a place to hunker over your laptop: the rarely used dining-room table, a corner of your bedroom, or even the builder's designated den/study, to name a few. But if you plan to make a home office your primary work space, be prepared to set up shop in a second-floor bedroom or the basement, because the builder's den/study most likely won't be big enough.

The den/study will certainly be bigger than the cubicle you have at corporate headquarters. But to meet your needs at home, it has to be a lot bigger. First, there's your office furniture. If you spread out papers or drawings while you work, a desk or a computer work station won't be enough. You'll also need a table or counter. And you'll have those other essential items that were "just down the hall"—a fax machine, a copier, file cabinets and bookcases with reference materials. Some of the file cabinets can go in a basement or a garage, and some of the reference materials you need may be available on CD-ROM, but you'll still need to allow for some storage. Your equipment won't take up too much floor area if you get a combination printer-fax-copier.

You'll also need some breathing room. "Only a cave dweller could be happy in a room that's less than ten by ten feet. And to feel really comfortable, most people need a space that's at least twelve by twelve feet," explained architect Ivar Viehe-Naess of Washington, D.C., who specializes in commercial interiors and office design.

Noise may also be an issue with the builder's den/study, even if the size works. The favored location in many floor plans is next to the family room, usually the busiest and noisiest room in the house. This is fine for children doing homework, but most adults find the hubbub distracting.

If you can't decamp to a quieter room, you can reduce the noise significantly by installing a solid-core door (most builders install hollow-core ones) and batt insulation in the walls and ceiling (which is the same material that is put in exterior walls to reduce heat loss in winter). Some manufacturers now make an "acoustical batt insulation" specifically for sound-deadening purposes.

If these modifications do not eliminate the irritating noises, you can get a white-noise machine that masks them. Even if you've solved the noise problem, you may still want the white-noise machine to provide innocuous background sound, because most people find that an office space that is too quiet is also uncomfortable (for more on this, see Chapter 14).

Then there's the daylight issue. Most people want plenty of daylight in their home office, especially if they worked in a windowless office; and no one wants to shut out the view. But too much daylight can be a problem if you work with a computer, because daylight can be five times as bright as the monitor screen, observed architect Murray Milne of Los Angeles, whose home office overlooks the Pacific Ocean. His suggestion: Purchase drapes or blinds. If the room exposure is southern, you can use horizontal blinds. If it's eastern or western, you'll need vertical blinds that you can adjust as the sun moves across the sky.

Since home-office workers will inevitably become more technically sophisticated in the future, you should install multiple phone lines and high-speed Internet access in your home office for their resale value, if not for your own use (for more on this, see Chapter 14).

When you are down to selecting furniture, flooring, and paint, some interior designers suggest that you strongly differentiate these from the style and color scheme in the rest of your house. A home office offers endless opportunities for diversion and procrastination. Changing the look and the style helps to underscore the idea that it's a room for serious endeavors, not paper-clip basketball.

bathrooms

Over the last twenty-five years, no room has changed more than the master bathroom. Not only has it ballooned in size, appurtenances have been added as well. The separate stall shower, large soaking tub, double sinks, and vanities that once were found only in high-end houses have become the norm for nearly all price ranges.

All this razzle-dazzle, however, tends to distract most people from any functional considerations beyond the basic idea of a bathroom as a place for personal hygiene. The large soaking tub inevitably commands the most attention, but the sink area is where design and detailing make a telling difference. Before you buy the house or approve a floor plan, give it a careful look.

In many households, both people who use the master bath get ready for work at the same time, so the second sink does have practical value. But to be really useful, each sink needs some adjacent counterspace and a place to put, for example, the mousse, hair drier, and comb and brush when fixing your hair. Since a second sink provides only so much utility, a single sink with sizable his-and-her counters to either side is more useful if the total counter length is less than sixty-eight inches. This arrangement will also provide each person with a set of drawers for storing all those products and appliances when not in use.

Besides the drawer storage, a medicine cabinet for makeup and medicine bottles is a must. Otherwise, you have to burrow through the drawers to find the small items. Many home builders provide either the medicine cabinet or the drawers; you should insist on both.

If you're honest enough to admit at the outset that you're a shower taker who will never use the soaking tub, and want to put those option dollars somewhere else, how about a big, jazzy shower with two showerheads and dual controls? Or a single, large, six-to-ten-inch-diameter shower head that produces much more water? Or you can re-create the sensation of being in a car wash with multiple body sprays.

bathrooms 201

Certified bathroom designer Carolyn Thomas of Bethesda, Maryland, often gets such requests from clients who are eager to convert the large soaking tub or a standard-sized bathtub into something they will use and enjoy every day. With the body sprays, Thomas usually installs two sets of three sprays each. Each set has its own controls and, if desired, variable sprays. When installed, each set should be positioned according to the height of the user, with the highest spray head directed at the top of the shoulder, and the middle and lower ones at the user's mid- and lower-back regions. If two people use the shower and they are not of similar height, adjustable sprays are required. Thomas has found that these showers appeal to men more than women.

The size of the pipes supplying the water to your jazzed-up shower will have to be increased from the standard one-half-inch size to at least a ¾-inch or even larger, depending on the size and number of fixtures that you want. Also, with all that water, the size of the drain may need to be larger. Before you buy the fixtures, have your plumber check the output of each fixture and the local codes on the drain sizes. The maximum size mandated by some jurisdictions may be insufficient to drain the water output of all

Then there is the sink height. Despite increasing public awareness of ergonomics, most home builders still install bathroom sinks that are thirty-one inches high, which is awkward for most adults. A thirty-six-inch height, which is standard for kitchen counters, is more comfortable because you don't have to lean over so far; higher counter height in the bathroom also increases the storage area below. Since most cabinet manufacturers now make a thirty-six-inch-high vanity, your builder can very likely get one as an optional upgrade. If you're over six feet tall, you should not only consider getting the thirty-six-inch-high vanity, but also raising it another six inches.

Separate vanities on opposite sides of the room can be an added plus when neatness between spouses is an issue. The source of irritation is usually the sink area, and separate vanities will defuse it. If this isn't possible, raising one vanity and sink to a thirty-six-inch height will clearly demarcate his and hers.

Lighting can also be an issue in the sink area. The easiest, cheapest solution is a ceiling-mounted fixture above the sink. To make this look more upscale, many production

these fixtures. If the drain is too small, you'll be standing ankle deep in water every time you turn all the fixtures on full blast.

For the truly self-indulgent with an extra twenty-five hundred to forty-five hundred dollars to spend, the shower can also have a steam-bath feature. The shower must be completely enclosed, with walls going up to the ceiling and a hinged door with a transom overhead. The boiler unit that generates the steam can be housed in an adjacent space, even another room or in an insulated attic. To get enough steam for a steam bath usually takes about fifteen to twenty minutes, but many units are programmable and can be preset so that the steam bath is ready to go when you get home from a stressful day at work.

The steam itself comes out of a small cylindrical pipe that is plated to coordinate with the other shower fixtures. The temperature of the steam bath ranges from 100 to 120 degrees Fahrenheit. The units have auto-matic turn-off timers that can be set anywhere from five to thirty minutes. If you opt for the steam bath, a seat is a must, because standing up in steam for any period of time is uncomfortable.

To get all these features, the shower must be at least three by four feet, but four by five feet is optimal, Thomas said. When showers get larger, different possibilities arise for enclosing them, the most intriguing of which is glass block: The translucent material makes the shower area much brighter and more pleasant. A glass-block wall can also be curved to create an enclosure and eliminate the need for a door or shower curtain. If you like the look of block, Thomas suggests you checkout the European styles as well as the American ones. The glass-block enclosure is more expensive, but once installed less maintenance is required. Since the shower area is bigger, the glass block hardly gets wet, and there are no droplets to clean off.

builders put a recessed fixture above the sink. But overhead lighting is uneven and creates shadows, making it nearly impossible to put on makeup. If you wear it, a row of strip lighting above the mirror is essential.

Another place where the details make a difference is the shower. The separate stall shower is certainly convenient, but make sure that's it's big enough to eliminate the showering-in-a-phone-booth sensation. Thirty-two by thirty-two inches is a minimal dimension; forty-two by thirty-four inches will be more comfortable. You also need a place to put soap, shampoo, and conditioner. A twelve-by-twelve-inch niche in the wall of the shower should be adequate. This may sound excessively large, but in many households spouses use different products.

Though the niche will likely be an extra, it can easily be added when the shower walls are framed in, and the niche can be finished with the same ceramic tiles used to cover the shower walls. Another shower convenience is a built-in seat, also covered with ceramic tiles. This can be a handy place to rest your foot while washing it or, for women, shaving your legs.

If you get a stacked washer and dryer to free up floor area and get a laundry tub, you will have to get a front-loading washer to get a full-sized one. Ten years ago, a front-loading washer was a pain in the neck, but modifications have made them much more user-friendly. For example, if you start the cycle and find a sock on the floor, you can open the door of the machine and toss it in without water pouring out. Other pluses with the front loaders: The agitating action of the machine is less wearing on clothes than the agitation in top loaders, so your clothes may last longer. With no central agitator taking up space, the washing drum can hold more clothes. This means fewer loads per week to get the household laundry done. During the spin cycle, the front loader removes more water, so the clothes require less time in the dryer. The front-loading washers are also more environmentally benign and energy efficient. They use less water and, in most cases, less heated water, thus less energy.

Technological developments in recent years have also produced more energy-efficient and user-friendly top-loaders. For example, some of the new top-loaders have no central agitator, so they can hold more clothes. Some include a sensor that matches the amount of water to the amount of wash.

Whether loaded from the top or front, the high-efficiency washers use up to 50 percent less energy and up to one-third less water than conventional washers, explained Howard Newman of the Consortium for Energy Efficiency (CEE) in Boston, which has been promoting high-efficiency washers and rating them since 1993. The most efficient model on the CEE qualifying list is actually a top-loader

The clear-glass shower stalls shown in models always look terrific, but the glass spots easily and looks grimy if you don't wipe it off quickly after each use. A less expensive, translucent type of obscure glass is not as attractive, but requires less maintenance.

The soaking tub with whirlpool jets adds the quintessential Hollywood touch. But once the novelty has worn off, most people use these tubs only a few times a year. You should think twice about the whirlpool jet upgrade, which can cost two thousand dollars or more. If you're troubled by resale issues, leave a cavity for the motor so that future owners can install the jets if they wish. With some builders, the larger soaking tub itself is a "garden-bath upgrade," and the standard master bath has a standard-sized tub. You should pass on this upgrade as well, unless there is also some other benefit such as a bigger bathroom or the inclusion of a sizable linen closet or a second vanity. If the size of the bathroom will remain the same, the bigger soaking tub could eliminate a linen closet, which would be more useful in the long run.

Some builders offer a large soaking tub made of fiberglass; once the shiny surface

made by Fisher & Paykel, a New Zealand manufacturer.

U.S. Department of Energy and the Environmental Protection Agency's jointly sponsored Energy Star Program also rates washers. The ones that carry the Energy Star endorsement use one-third less water and up to two-thirds less hot water than standard machines. Many Energy Star washers also have a high-speed spin cycle that removes more water, saving up to 25 percent of the energy required to dry them in a dryer as well as shortening the time to air-dry them. (See Resources for more information on washers.)

The changes in dryer design over the last ten years have not been as dramatic as those in washers. The biggest difference is moisture sensors, which prevent the dryer from over-drying clothes, potentially shrinking or excessively wrinkling them.

The installation of the dryer vent is critical. You need to make sure that it's properly vented to the outside, and the shorter the length of the vent, the better, explained Alex Wilson, executive editor of *Environmental Building News*.

If the dryer is located in the center of the house, the vent should be made of smooth metal, rather than flexible vinyl or flexible metal, because the longer the venting duct, the more likely lint will collect if it's not smooth. Even with smooth sides, lint can still clog the vent, and Wilson advised homeowners to clean it out periodically by sticking a vacuum cleaner hose down it.

During the construction of your house, make sure that the dryer vent really does go to the outside. If it is vented into a crawl space underneath your house or, as occasionally happens, into a wall cavity by mistake, you will eventually get mold problems (for more on this, see Chapter 14).

material wears off, the tub acquires a dull gray color. Acrylic tubs hold up well and will look fine for many years, though they scratch easily, and should not, for example, be used to wash a dog.

The large window that most builders routinely put next to the large soaking tub looks great in the model, but privacy will be an issue once you move in. The simplest solution is to install a window shade that pulls up from the bottom. A classier but more expensive solution is to install translucent glass or acrylic block in the window frame itself instead of standard window glass. A number of manufacturers now make windows with acrylic block that are specifically intended for master bathrooms.

If you have small children, giving them a bath in the larger soaking tub will probably be easier than doing this in a smaller hall bathtub; it will also be more fun. But be forewarned: Once other family members start using the capacious master bathroom, they'll never want to go back to the other one. You may find yourself in the same situation you face in your current house—five people using one bathroom, just one that's bigger.

thelaundry**room**

Without a doubt, the laundry is the Rodney Dangerfield room of most floor plans. Tucked into a leftover corner, it is almost never big enough to accommodate its designated function. This chore is not just a matter of tossing clothes into a washer and dryer. You need enough floor area to sort out loads, and a place to hang wet clothes that can't go into the dryer. If your household includes a teenaged daughter who frets that the dryer will shrink or otherwise damage everything, there will be a lot of wet clothes to air-dry. A flat surface, such as a table, that can be used when folding clean clothes is also handy.

An inadequate laundry room is not just a minor inconvenience; it's a major one in a household of any size, because laundry is not a once-a-week task. It's an ongoing one that may be done every day if there are small children or newborns. When the laundry room has been reduced to an oversized closet off a kitchen or in an upstairs hallway, loads of wash will be underfoot constantly, and there's no place to hang wet clothes.

Another laundry room gripe is its location. Most of the dirty clothes, towels, and bed linens are generated in the bedroom areas. When the laundry is one or two floors below, you'll be making a lot of extra trips up and down stairs hauling loads of wash. The inconvenience may be worth it, however, if it allows a sizable laundry room or one next to the kitchen so you can do the wash while preparing meals.

There's also the matter of a laundry tub, which many builders do not provide. Not only is this convenient for dumping dirty wash water when washing floors, it's also a place to work on stained garments and baby clothes before putting them into the washing machine, and to hand-wash delicate items that can't go into the washer. If the washer and dryer must go into a closet, get a stacked set so you can still have the laundry tub.

thegarage

In theory, a garage is a place to keep your car. In fact, it's the modern version of Fibber McGee's closet—a big room that's filled to the rafters with all the stuff that you can't put somewhere else, plus recycling bins, garbage cans, sports equipment, bicycles, a lawn mower, gardening equipment, and, if there's any room left, your cars. Since a move provides a great opportunity to prune belongings and reduce inventory, by the time you move into your new house you may have pared down your garage contents to the essentials. But even that will be more than just a couple of cars.

When you scope out a production builder's furnished model, it is nearly always impossible to tell if the garage will accommodate either your present or your anticipated trimmed-down requirements, because the builder has converted the garage into a temporary sales office.

You should ask for the dimensions of the garage and then look at one in a nearly completed house. To accommodate a modest assortment—the cars plus the garbage cans, recycling bins, and maybe a bike or two—the garage must be at least nineteen feet wide and twenty-one feet long, or four hundred square feet. If you want to be able to open a car door and not hit the other car, *and* get your lawn and gardening equipment in, the garage needs to be wider, longer, and bigger: twenty-four feet wide by twenty-four feet long, or six hundred square feet. Since most production-built houses tend to have garages that are narrower than twenty-four feet, ask if you can "test park" your cars when you go to look at the garage in another house.

Other garage dimensions will be important if one of your vehicles is unusually high or long. For example, if you own a Ford Expedition, clearance when the garage door is open must be at least seven feet; otherwise you will hit it when you try to drive in. If you own a Chevy Suburban, the garage must be at least twenty-three feet long, just to accommodate the car.

And then there's the issue of how the garage is attached to the house. This connection will invariably be awkward, whether the garage is at the front, back, or side, and whether the house is production-built or custom-designed for you by an architect. All owners want to go directly from their car into their house to avoid any contact with the elements. The invariable result is that owners are funneled into the kitchen through the laundry room. The actual entry foyer in the front of the house, whether modest or voluminous, is rarely used.

Finding the aesthetics of this arrangement distasteful as well as impractical—there's no place to put anything in a laundry room—architect Randy Creaser of Gaithersburg, Maryland, adds a "garage foyer" whenever possible. He includes a countertop to drop a briefcase and sort mail, and a closet. If the space is large enough, he designs a row of large cubbies for family members to put backpacks, coats, and sports equipment.

Perhaps one reason that the garage confounds designers is that unlike other rooms that have been added to houses over the last hundred years, it didn't grow out of another function. As another architect, Sami Kirkdil of Bethesda, Maryland, put it, "All the images of old houses we know and love, there is no car."

At the turn of the century, when the rambling Victorian, colonial, and Tudor houses that we cherish today were built, car ownership was unusual. The few households that owned one kept it in a separate storage shed behind the house, and brought it out only for special occasions, said architect Barry Berkus of Santa Barbara, California, who has studied the history of car storage in American houses. In the following decades, car ownership became more common, but most households still owned only one car. Two-car households and two-car garages became the norm, and gardening and sports burgeoned, only in the late sixties and seventies. Today, as buyers press for three- and four-car garages, Berkus and many others observe that the car and the garage "seem to be possessing the house."

The perfect garage solution remains elusive. But given the ingenuity of architects and builders to bend historical forms to current functional needs or to design something entirely new, this dilemma will eventually be solved.

Architect and author Sarah Susanka, who is known for designing wonderfully livable houses, has spent many hours helping clients sort out the television-fireplace dilemma in the family room, a debate that often becomes contentious. "The husband and wife will argue about what's more important, the television, the fireplace, or the view. The husband usually wants a big-screen television, the wife doesn't watch television much and wants a view. Both want the fireplace, but they're not sure where to put it."

You *can* keep everybody happy, Susanka says, by housing the television in a cabinet with pocket doors, so that it can be out of sight when not in use. How about the VCR, CD player, video tapes, and so forth? The simplest solution is to build in a bank of cabinets to hold everything. This can start to sound pricey, but certified kitchen designer Debby Saling of Beltville, Maryland, says that creatively combining kitchen cabinets can make this surprisingly affordable. With a more expensive semi-custom cabinet line, you can get a base cabinet specifically designed for a television, with folding pocket doors and a swivel base, and additional base cabinets with customized roll-out trays to hold everything else.

If your budget or your builder limit you to a stock cabinet line, you may still be able to get cabinets with these features because the major stock cabinet makers, including Merrilat, are starting to offer them. Should your builder use a stock cabinet line that doesn't yet include any entertainment-center features, Saling says you can combine stock

tips**from**the**trade:**
television and home

base cabinets with open shelving above for the television, books, photographs, plants, and anything else you might want to display. The CDs, VCR, and other less sightly items can be stored in the base cabinets, but you will have to modify them yourself. The builder's cabinet distributor should have a kitchen designer on staff who can help you figure this out.

If the television ends up on a wall with windows, you may have glare problems if you watch it during the day, because the light coming in will be brighter than the screen. Even when the television is on a wall with no windows, you can still have glare problems if the windows on an adjacent wall face south (this will bother you all day), east (glare will be a problem in the morning), or west (glare will be a problem in the afternoon). The only solution is to install shades or curtains.

Another family-room television issue is the size of the television. The twenty-seven-inch television will work well, but if you're like many people building a new house, you're flirting with the idea of a super-sized forty-five- or fifty-inch television.

But a super-sized television requires a large viewing space. As a general rule of thumb, you need to sit back a distance at least twice the diagonal dimension of the television screen. If the screen is fifty inches, you need to sit back at least a hundred inches, or about eight and a half feet. But consultant David Wogsland of Pelen, Minnesota, cautions that this distance will only be comfortable if you want to feel like you're very close to the screen in a theater. If you're more of a spectator type who sits farther back in theaters, you may want to sit ten to twelve feet from your giant television.

If you conclude that you have the space in your family room to accommodate the large-screen television, Wogsland suggests getting a surround-sound speaker system installed when your house is built. But, he noted, this will not work well in every space. If the ceiling of your family room is two stories high, for example, the surround sound will not deliver the best audial quality. (You should also note that a large-screen television can look ridiculous next to a normal-sized fireplace. If you want the two in close proximity, you should explore the possibility of housing the big television in a cabinet with pocket doors that will camouflage its bulk when not in use.)

Certain exposures can also effect your enjoyment of a large screen, Wogsland noted. When a family room has many south-facing windows, the daylight level will be too high to see the big screen well, and window treatments will be necessary. To see the large screen easily, the ambient light needs to be lower than it does with a smaller television, just as the light level must be very low in a movie theater to see the screen well. If the family room of your new house will have a high ceiling and lots of glass and sunlight, Wogsland suggested moving the television and sound system to another room. His favorite spot is the basement, away from the general hubbub of family activities, where sunlight is not a problem.

The kitchen is another favored spot for television viewing. If you want to watch it while you prepare a meal, you'll be listening more than you'll be watching, so you don't need a very large screen. Susanka's solution is a tiny television with a five-by-five-inch screen that is hung under a wall cabinet with a rotating bracket. Just make sure that you have wall and cable outlets close to where you want to mount the television.

Many households watch television in the kitchen while eating a meal as well as while preparing one. In this case, Susanka recommends a larger screen—about nineteen inches—and she likes to put it on a pull-out swivel base in a cabinet with pocket doors above a double oven. With this arrangement, the television can be watched from different places in the room and hidden behind cabinet doors when not in use.

A television in the bathroom is another common request. Most people want to be able to see it from a large soaking tub, but this can be tricky because most building codes require that the television be at least five feet from the tub. When the wall at one end of the tub is next to a closet, Wogsland has installed a television on a shelf in the closet behind one-way mirror glass. He made small holes in the glass to let the sound pass through, and the homeowner operates it in the bathroom with a remote. When the set is on, you can see it through the glass; when it's off, you see just mirror.

Some bathtub viewing calls for ingenious solutions. In some cases, the only way to make this possible is to place the set so that it is reflected in a mirror that can be seen from the tub. Just make sure that you have a good technician who can reverse the scan on a television so that you can read the words on the screen. Otherwise the printing will appear in reverse.

chapter nine flooring

When you imagine yourself sitting by a cozy fire in the family room of your new house or cooking in the kitchen, you'll have some kind of flooring in this picture. But if you're like most people, it won't be a major element. Your mind's eye is more likely to be focused on the cabinets, the food you're preparing, or how you actually would roast those chestnuts in an open fire.

The truth is that beyond choosing a material and a color, most people don't think much about the floor. They should, though, because it's the element that ties all the spaces together, especially when a house has a very open floor plan. Similar colors, if not the same material throughout, will also make a smaller house feel bigger. If your furnishings stylistically differ from one room to the next, the right floor will produce a smooth visual segue.

The flooring products that you select are likely to be man-made, because the natural ones, such as wood, cork, and wool, are usually top-dollar. But the quality of man-made flooring is excellent and the choices, broad. Because carpet is the most cost-effective way to finish a floor, you may select it for most of your house. For bathrooms and your kitchen, floor tile, a man-made material that has been around for millennia, is always an option, but an expensive one. If your budget is tight, a sheet vinyl for rooms that need a waterproof floor may be your best option, though the higher grades of vinyl can be as pricy as tile or the natural materials.

If you want to create an outdoor room by building a deck, you may decide to avoid the natural look altogether because wood is high maintenance flooring when in the great outdoors. Man-made composite decking materials that mix sawdust with recycled plastics have the look and feel of wood but require less maintenance. Recycled plastic and virgin-vinyl decking are nearly maintenance free aside from hosing them down once a month or so to clean off the dirt that will collect there.

Flooring is also one of those options, like countertop materials, that can be upgraded after you move in. You won't be able to fold that hardwood floor into your mortgage as you will if you get it when you buy the house, but getting a hardwood floor later and the four-foot extension to the family room now could be the more sensible choice. You may also find that an outside vendor such as your local flooring store can offer you the same flooring that the builder does for a lower price (this flooring would also not be included in your mortgage). The flooring salesman may even be able to take measurements off the floor plan shown in the builder's sales brochure. If not, he would have to come and measure the model.

As for the deck, it is one option that many homeowners add one or two years after they move in. If you do this, however, you must insist that your installer check the framing underneath the siding to make sure that he can attach the deck properly. Some builders erect the framing one way if you are getting a deck and another way if you are not. The only way to verify what your builder did is to check it before you start. (See Resources for more information on the types of flooring discussed here.)

carpet

Carpet may be the sensible choice for most of your living space. Your builder will offer plenty of colors, but as you look around his sample room, you'll quickly realize that the number of choices increases with price. Indeed, that is part of the builder's marketing strategy. Only six to ten colors are usually offered in the lowest, base carpet grade that is included in the house's base price. The carpet supplier typically sells the base grade to the builder at or below cost, and invariably it is of minimal quality. But as many as twenty-four colors may be offered in the highest upgrade category, where the builder's (and his supplier's) profit margins are greatest. Beyond color and price, there are additional but more subtle differences between carpet grades that can make one choice prudent (you'll get more wear out of it) and another extravagant (it looks and feels luxurious but doesn't last appreciably longer).

When comparing the carpet samples, the first thing to note is the fiber type. Your builder will most likely offer nylon, polyester, or olefin. Of these, nylon is the most widely used and the strongest. A nylon carpet never becomes threadbare, and in this conventional sense it never wears out. But nylon will "ugly out" and look ratty if not properly maintained or installed with inferior padding. Nylon will also stain if the fibers are not treated with a stain-resistant product such as Dupont Stainmaster. Higher quality nylon fibers are "branded," and the carpet label will list the fibers as "100% nylon Monsanto" or "100% Dupont Masterlife." Lower quality, unbranded nylon fibers are listed simply as "100% nylon."

Polyester carpet fibers are less strong than nylon and tend to shed some, but they are more stain resistant and the colors are brighter. Polyester is also cheaper than nylon and more environmentally benign. Some or all of the polyester fiber material, depending on the manufacturer, is made from recycled plastic bottles. Image Polyester, a division of Mohawk Carpets, manufactures polyester carpet made of 100 percent recycled material. Phil Cavin, Image's national procurement officer, estimates that the firm's manufacturing activities consume about 5.5 million bottles a day. Before you buy a whole house full of polyester carpet, though, try to see a room with it. Some people find it sounds odd when they walk on it, and it has a different sheen because it is plastic.

Polypropylene, commonly called olefin, is the weakest of the three synthetic fibers, but this material works well when made into a looped berber-type carpet with a knobby weave. Its knobby berber texture conceals dirt, even in light colors. For this reason, olefin berber carpeting is often selected for high-use areas such as family rooms.

After you've noted the fiber type, check the twist level of the individual carpet fibers. All carpet yarns are twisted together to form lengths of yarn, but the degree of twisting varies. The higher or tighter the twist, the better and generally more expensive the carpet. A twist rating refers to the number of times the fiber is twisted together in a one-inch length. With a loop-pile carpet such as a berber, the twist level is less critical because the fibers are looped in and can't unravel.

Now check the density, a measure of how tightly the fibers are attached to the carpet backing. The closer together the fibers are attached, the less wear to each individual fiber, and the longer the carpet will last. To test for density, see how easily you can move the carpet tufts to see the backing. The harder it is to see, the higher the carpet's density.

Face weight measures the number of ounces of fiber per square yard of carpet. It is a significant quality determinant, but harder to distinguish by visual inspection. The higher the face weight, the more yarn, and the better the carpet, with this caveat: A carpet with a longer fiber can have a higher face weight, because face weight simply measures the weight of all the fibers above the primary backing. But a longer-fiber, higher face-weight carpet can still have a low density, and it will not wear as well as a carpet of identical face weight but shorter, more numerous fibers and higher density.

To determine overall carpet quality, you need to look at both face weight and density as well as the twist level. As a general rule of thumb, carpet with a twist level of 4.0 or better, a density of 3,000 to 4,000, and a face weight of 35 to 40 ounces will hold up well. For production-built houses in the middle or lower price ranges, such a carpet may be two or three upgrades above the builder's standard. For production-built houses in the upper price ranges, some builders may offer carpets with face weights that can range from 45 to as high as 70 ounces.

Maintenance should be another consideration in selecting a carpet. A velvety plush can look and feel luxurious, but it will show every footprint and vacuum mark. A textured saxony weave may look more plebeian, but its footprint-hiding surfaces are more practical for busy households.

Durability is another important factor in selecting a carpet, but it is difficult to ascertain by visual inspection. Many carpet manufacturers assign a durability rating to each carpet style after testing it by simulating wear conditions over time. For example, Shaw Industries has a 20,000 Step Contract Walker Test facility at its headquarters in Dalton, Georgia. The 20,000 steps, the equivalent to about three years of normal residential use, are taken by six to eight people walking in shifts for eight hours a day over a five- to seven-day period.

The higher the durability rating of a carpet, the slower it will lose its like-new appearance. Shaw measures the durability of its carpets on a scale from 1 to 5, with 5 being the most durable. For a very active household with more than four adults or any household with toddlers, children, teens, household pets, or one that entertains frequently, a durability rating of 3.5 and above for heavily used areas is recommended. For other households, a durability of 2.5 for most rooms will be adequate.

While Shaw uses the sliding scale, other manufacturers describe their carpet's durability by rating its performance in individual rooms—bedroom, living and dining rooms, family room, hall, and steps. Still others rate their carpets by their suitability for light, normal, heavy, and extra-heavy foot traffic.

Besides helping home buyers evaluate an individual builder's carpet offerings, all of these factors enable buyers to compare one builder's carpet offerings to another's on an apples-to-apples basis. There is no industry-wide standard for disclosing this information, but many manufacturers voluntarily list it on the back of their samples. Manufacturers who do not will usually give out the figures when asked. If you don't see any ratings on your builder's samples, ask the sales agent to track it down from the builder's carpet supplier.

Yet another characteristic that distinguishes different grades of carpet and can serve as a quick test is the backing. An inexpensive, low-end carpet has big squares on the back. Better grades will have smaller, tighter squares; the best quality carpets have a woven backing.

A carpet manufacturer's warranty is also telling, especially the mat-and-crush clause that attests to the carpet fibers' "memory retention"—their ability to retain their twist level and return to their original upright shape after being walked on. A fifteen-year mat-and-crush warranty is offered on more expensive carpeting, and top-quality carpets offer a twenty-five-year warranty. A production-home builder is unlikely to offer this, but you should try to get carpeting with at least a ten-year warranty. If the warranty is shorter than this, the carpet will show wear in a few years. A production builder's base-grade carpet will likely have only a five-year warranty, but check the upgrades.

Carpet pricing has traditionally been given in square yards. After January 1, 2000, however, the federal government began requiring that all carpet prices be given in square feet instead, so that consumers can more easily compare carpeting prices with those of other flooring materials that are given in square feet.

carpet padding

Besides offering myriad carpet choices, most builders also offer several carpet-padding upgrades. Since a good pad will increase the life of the carpet substantially, you should upgrade the padding beyond the lightweight 3/8-inch foam pad that most builders offer as standard, even if you can't afford to upgrade the carpet itself. The padding upgrade is likely to be a 7/16-inch thick rebonded foam product; to be effective it should have a density of at least six pounds per cubic foot, but eight to ten is preferable. Most carpet manufacturers will not warrant their product if the padding is less than six pounds, so you should upgrade at least to this level. If you are getting a cut-pile-type carpet, a six- or seven-pound pad will be adequate. If you get a berber-type carpet with looped fibers for your family room, you should get a firmer, eight-pound pad. If you are concerned about volatile organic compounds (VOCs) off-gassing from your carpets, ask for a synthetic-fiber padding instead of the rebonded type, which the builder's carpet supplier can also get easily (for more on this, see Chapter 14).

hardwood

Considerably more expensive than carpeting, hardwood flooring is a perennial favorite. Some upper-end production builders now offer hardwood flooring made from such exotic species as Brazilian cherry (it looks fabulous but is expensive) and Australian Jarrah. The most readily available, least expensive hardwood, and what your builder will certainly offer, is oak. Most production builders offer two types—a 3/4-inch solid-oak hardwood and a 3/8-inch to 5/8-inch thick engineered oak laminate that can be glued to a concrete floor. Both types are plank-flooring, not parquet.

As far as durability goes, all the grades of solid-oak hardwood are similar and more than adequate for normal household use. The variant affecting price is appearance. Lower-priced, builder-grade oak flooring, usually offered in the middle to the lower end of the market, is a mixture of "select and better" and "number I common" grades of oak. It has more "character"—small knots, mineral marks, and pinholes. The more expensive "select or better" grade, more often found in higher-priced houses, will be a clearer wood. For many people, the visual difference in grades is inconsequential. If you find the "character" aspect of a builder-grade oak floor irritating, consider adding a darker stain to make the knot and stripes less visible (but see a sample and preferably an entire floor first), or get an upgraded, clearer grade.

Maple, long used for gymnasium floors, is a now a popular choice for houses, especially kitchens, because many buyers want to match their cabinets with the floors. Maple is clearer than oak, so it's easier to match cabinets and floors.

Plank hardwood floors are either prefinished or sanded and finished in place after installation. The latter, which gives a smoother surface, is considered "strictly custom," but it's actually less expensive. The prefinished floor, which will have small v-grooves between each plank, though more costly, is preferred by production builders because it's faster to install. The other one takes several days to finish, during which no other trades can be in the space.

Engineered laminate hardwood, which is close in price to the solid hardwood, can be glued rather than nailed into place, an obvious advantage if you want to install a hardwood floor over a concrete slab. The engineered laminate floor consists of a hardwood veneer that is glued to two to four layers of plywood. More layers of plywood costs more, but they make for a better floor that is more dimensionally stable.

Depending on how the hardwood veneer layer is cut off the log, an engineered laminate floor can have a grain pattern that looks like a solid hardwood floor or one that looks wavy. A floor made with the wavy type may be more of a visual feature than you want, so try to see one before you order it for yourself. Another significant distinction between different types of engineered laminate hardwood flooring is the thickness of the hardwood veneer on the topmost layer. More expensive ones have a $5/32$- to $1/6$-inch thick veneer layer that usually can be resanded and refinished twice. Some less expensive laminate floors have a thinner veneer layer that cannot be resanded. If you get scratches on it, the only way to get rid of them is to replace the flooring.

ceramictile

Four-by-four-inch ceramic tile has long been used for bathroom floors, but tiles as large as twelve by twelve inches are now a popular choice for bathrooms as well as kitchen or breakfast areas and entry foyers. The color possibilities are endless and largely a matter of taste and price. Two other tile characteristics to include in your calculus are durability and slip resistance.

Glazed tiles, the type most frequently offered by production builders, are rated for durability. Grade one is intended to be used only as a wall tile; grade two can be used in bathrooms; grade three can be used anywhere in the house; and grades four and five are considered commercial grades to be used in areas with heavy foot traffic. The durability rating is rarely listed on the back of builder's tile samples, but an on-site sales agent should be able to get this information from the tile supplier. Quarry tile, which has color all the way through it, is more durable than a glazed tile and can be used anywhere in the house.

Tiles are also measured for their degree of slipperiness—that is, their slip resistance or coefficient of friction (COF) when new. Though no tile is slip-proof, generally speaking a tile with a COF of .5 and above under dry conditions is considered to be slip resistant. For entry foyers, a tile with a .5 COF or better is recommended. For kitchens or bathrooms, a lower slip resistance is acceptable. As a general rule, textured tiles that look like stone have more slip resistance than smooth ones, and smaller two-by-two-inch tiles with more grout joints are less slippery than larger tiles, because any water runs into the joints.

Though a tiled floor has a great look, the tile grout can be a maintenance headache. If not sealed properly, mop water will seep into the porous grout, turning it dark. Even with a good sealer, some surface dirt will still collect on the grout lines. One solution is choosing a darker grout color to begin with.

Tiles may not be the best flooring choice in a temperate climate with large annual temperature fluctuations if you intend to put it over a wood subfloor. In these regions, the structural frame of the house expands during the summer and shrinks during the winter, and this movement can cause the tiles to crack. In warmer climates such as California and Florida, tile cracking is not a problem.

sheet-vinyl flooring

Tile can enhance the look of almost any kitchen or bathroom, but your budget may dictate sheet vinyl. Try to upgrade the builder's standard base-grade sheet vinyl, which will invariably have a shallow wear surface, will be susceptible to nicks and tears, and look worn after only a few years. More expensive sheet vinyls are thicker with a stronger wearing surface. They will hold the gloss longer than the cheaper ones, which tend to lose their luster and show traffic patterns.

Upgrading a sheet vinyl to the equivalent of a Mannington Silverado or an Armstrong Starsteps—usually a second or third upgrade—will significantly increase the wearability and durability of the flooring, and you will get more pattern choices. The higher grade of Armstrong sheet vinyl has inlaid color that goes all the way through the material, imparting a different look. With all other vinyls, the pattern is printed on the surface.

Some sheet vinyls have embossed designs, and the embossed surfaces provide more slip resistance when wet. These designs look appealing on the sample, but when installed, dirt can easily collect on the ridges of the patterns, making the floor harder to keep clean.

laminateflooring

Invented in Europe, laminate flooring has become increasingly popular since it was first marketed in the United States in 1994. This type of flooring has a wear surface and a look that is similar to the plastic laminate used in kitchen countertops—hence the name—but it is much harder and more durable. Most laminate flooring patterns mimic natural materials such as stone, ceramic tile, or hardwood. It makes for a nice-looking floor, but it does not look like the real thing—the almost eerie smoothness of the surface, and the subtle repetition of patterns, and joints at regular intervals are the giveaways.

Besides the difference in its manufacture, laminate flooring is installed differently than other types of flooring. It is neither glued nor nailed to the surface below. Instead, it floats: When properly glued together, laminate tongue-in-groove floor planks become a single unit, essentially a floor above a floor. This type of floor can be easily installed over a concrete slab, making it a favorite with apartment dwellers. It can also be installed over an existing floor, a great advantage in remodeling.

Laminate flooring was initially marketed as an alternative to sheet-vinyl flooring for kitchens and bathrooms. But with its distinct look, as well as its easy maintenance and resistance to stains and fading, it was soon regarded as a flooring alternative for the entire house.

In most cases, the laminate is fused to a core layer made of high- or medium-density fiberboard. The underside of each plank has a backing that provides dimensional stability, so that once installed the plank won't bow or "banana up," creating an uneven and unsightly surface.

Because laminate flooring was introduced to this country by Pergo, the European firm that invented it, many people use the terms *Pergo* and *laminate flooring* interchangeably; but now a number of American firms, including Wilsonart and Formica, make it. Another unusual characteristic of laminate flooring that you should note is the hollow sound made when anyone walks across the floor in a heeled shoe. The sound is not loud, just different; but many people find it disturbing. Some manufacturers offer underlayments that can dampen the sound. Before you make a final selection, try to find an installed laminate floor and give it a sound test. If your builder is offering it as an upgrade, there may be a finished house that you could look at.

Scratches are another issue with laminate floors. The surface is very hard, but it's only scratch resistant, not scratch-proof. If the floor becomes scratched, it cannot be sanded or buffed out. The only solution is to replace the plank. For this reason, Doug Carlson of Ann Arbor, Michigan, who has supervised the installation of hundreds of

As with every other type of flooring, laminate comes in different grades. Besides price, grades are distinguished by durability, water resistance, and warranty period. In general, "good" is warranted for

choosing a laminate
floorgrade

ten years; "better" for fifteen years; and "best" for twenty to twenty-five years. The "best" grade is usually installed in commercial installations with heavy foot traffic.

The first difference between grades that you will notice, is the number of pattern choices. The "good," or builder-grade, category has only six to ten, depending on the manufacturer, but the upgraded "better" category can have twenty-five or more.

From a use standpoint, the other differences between grades are more significant. With "good," the wear layer is less hard and more susceptible to dents, and many manufacturers do not warrant their low-end laminate flooring against water damage. If you want to install laminate flooring in a kitchen, laundry room, or bathroom, check the manufacturer's warranty first. With the "better" grade, the floor has a harder wear surface so it's more dent resistant. Most manufacturers claim that the better grade is

water resistant as well. Formica goes the farthest in its claims for water resistance, warranting its Formica against "ANY water damage" — the firm is so confident that it displays an overflowing bathtub with water continuously cascading down over several levels of flooring at trade shows.

The core material of laminate floors is made of wood fibers that will swell if they become saturated with water. In any room with water, the installation is critical, especially in bathrooms. Not only must each piece be glued correctly, the edges must be carefully sealed with a silicone sealant. Proper installation also prevents water from getting underneath the floor and causing mildew, which can eventually create indoor air problems. Buyers who like the idea of a laminate floor for their bathroom, but are concerned about water damage to its core, should consider Wilsonart's Performance ProFX, which has a core that is 100 percent plastic.

Because the installation is critical and laminate flooring is still a relatively new product, make sure that your installer has had the proper training.

laminate floors, urged buyers to consider their particular circumstances as well as how the space would be used. In his experience, laminates do not work for every household.

"Any of the laminates will hold up fine if you have clean foot traffic on it. But if you have a gravel driveway, for example, everyone in the household will track in grit, which is like having sandpaper on your shoes. It will mar the surface of a laminate floor in no time. In this situation, the homeowners will never be happy with a laminate and probably shouldn't use it."

outdoorflooring:thedeck

wood decking

If you're like many homeowners, you find yourself gravitating to the great outdoors and want a deck. But which material decking to get? If you have never owned a deck, wood might seem the obvious choice. If you have, it's not. You know only too well that wood decks weather, turning gray with exposure to the sun, darker gray in shade, and even black if not regularly maintained. Most species of wood used for decks will also warp, check, and crack if not resealed regularly. Tiny slivers that distress young children are always a potential hazard, and the surface eventually "corduroys"—it forms little ridges just like the cloth.

The least expensive decking material available, but also the one that requires the most upkeep, is pressure-treated southern pine. The pressure treatment protects the wood from decay and insect infestation but does not prevent the wood from swelling and shrinking as it is exposed to the elements. The swelling and shrinking cause the wood to check, crack, cup, pop up on ends, and even lift up nails; the resulting uneven surface can become a trip hazard. The rate of swelling and shrinking can be vastly reduced by sealing the deck regularly. Sealing will also lessen wood's discoloration.

You can get pressure-treated pine with an upgraded preservative that includes a sealer. This improves the performance of the wood initially, but after one or two years, washing and sealing must still be done on a regular basis. How often? On average, about once a year. But this varies with climate, and you should ask a local firm that installs or cleans decks. In many places, if you stretch out the intervals between cleaning and sealing too far, you end up with a black algae buildup that makes the cleaning and sealing even harder—and more expensive if you hire a cleaning firm to do it. You can spend a weekend washing and sealing your deck yourself, but after one or two years many homeowners elect to have it done by a professional service.

If you're intent on a real wood deck, but insist that it be maintenance free, Brazilian tabuia is a possibility. The hardwood, sold in the United States under the trade names Ipe, Ironwood, and Pau Lope, weathers to a light gray, and it does not require any sealing.

Cedar has long been a favorite decking material, but it is definitely not low maintenance. In many climates, it can turn gray, and a cedar deck that gets shade can turn black and icky if not regularly cleaned and sealed.

nonwood decking

If the maintenance is already beginning to sound like a headache or you've already been there, nonwood decking alternatives abound. You can choose among numerous brands of recycled plastic, virgin vinyl, and composite (a mixture of recycled sawdust and plastic that comes the closest to the real thing).

A composite decking product called Trex was one of the first nonwood alternatives to be widely marketed; it is so well known that consumers all over the country use the term *Trex* to refer to any composite decking product. But other manufacturers now also make it, including US Plastics, Inc., the manufacturer of SmartDeck, who has partnered up with Georgia-Pacific, one of the largest manufacturers of wood building products in the country; and Boardwalk is manufactured by CertainTeed, the largest manufacturer of vinyl building products in the United States.

All three of these composites are made with sawdust and recycled plastic—either milk jugs, plastic bags and pallet wrap, or vinyl building-product scrap. Much as the manufacturers emphasize their differences, the consensus of installers all over the country is that they are very similar. The only major difference that most buyers will notice is the colors offered. When installed, Boardwalk is gray-brown but it weathers to a light gray. SmartDeck starts as brown and weathers to a different tone of light gray. Trex now sells four colors: Natural weathers to a driftwood gray; Winchester Grey, to a darker, battleship gray; Woodland is dark brown and colorfast; and Madeira has a medium reddish brown color that weathers slightly. If a composite product sounds appealing, be sure to look at a weathered sample; if possible, see a deck installation that has been up a year or two and weathered a full seasonal cycle. All three manufacturers offer a ten-year warranty, although Trex claims that its accelerated testing shows that its product can last as long as thirty years.

The dimensions of the different brands vary slightly, but the installers say each is easy to work with. They did note, however, that the composite materials behave differently from wood. For example, with all three of these products, the material tends to form a slightly raised "mushroom" or "dimple" around nails or screws. The installers' advice on this point was to "whup it" with a hammer and the material would flatten out. In some areas with seasonal changes and a freeze-thaw cycle, the dimples can come back, but a whup with the hammer will flatten them out again.

When the wood fibers of some composite decks get wet, they pop up and the surface gets "grippy." In fact, Trex, Boardwalk, and SmartDeck all meet the ADA requirements (Americans with Disabilities Act) for a slip-resistant surface. Another plus is that the composite materials are flexible and the surface feels like it's padded when you walk on it.

Even the prices of these products are similar, though freight charges can affect the cost. The quotes given by installers around the country for the decking boards for a twelve-by-twenty-foot deck averaged at about one thousand dollars. By comparison, the cost of pressure-treated wood for the same-sized deck would range from three to four hundred dollars. When the cost to maintain the wood deck over time is added in, however, the wood is more expensive. The average cost, if the annual cleaning and sealing procedure is done professionally, runs about $1 per square foot or $240 a year for a twelve-by-twenty deck. Unless you elect to clean it yourself, the cost to maintain the deck for five years at current prices will be $1,280, and the annual cleaning cost will run onto into the future, as long the deck is owned.

Although composite products are often billed as no-maintenance, the installers emphasize that they are actually low-maintenance. Because they are partially wood, they do absorb grease, and owners need to clean greasy food spills promptly, using a degreasing agent if necessary. The composite materials may also get mold or mildew, which can appear as black spots or gray circles. A Chicago-area installer who specializes in nonwood decking materials cautions that this doesn't happen with all decks and it is more common if shade trees are present. Owners get understandably upset when the little black spots appear, but they can be removed by spraying with a fresh bleach solution, he said. To avoid the problem altogether, he recommends washing the deck about once a month during the warmer months of the year.

In hot and humid climates such as Florida's, the mildew is always an issue, and owners need to wash the deck at least every two months all year long. Boardwalk claims to be more mildew resistant than the competition because it is made with vinyl, but the company acknowledges that mildew can occur in hot and humid climates.

Some manufacturers of composite decking also make railings and posts. But railing systems do not generally take the same beating as the decking surface, so you may opt for a wood railing, considering the nonwood railings can cost two to four times as much as wood ones.

recycled-plastic decking

If you're not wedded to a wood look and detest even minimal maintenance, recycled plastic is a good bet. Carefree, which is made of recycled gallon milk jugs and detergent bottles, won't mildew or stain. It is close in price to the composites: for a twelve-by-twenty deck, the decking boards would cost about one thousand dollars. Carefree is sold in six colors and two finish surfaces, plain and knurled. The later, which is less slippery when wet, meets the ADA slip-resistance requirements. The only maintenance required is a monthly hose-down of the knurled surface to remove the dirt that collects there. The Carefree product line also includes a railing system.

virgin-vinyl decking

Virgin vinyl is another nearly no-maintenance decking product, but the grooves in the surface, which make the vinyl more slip-resistant, can be dirt collectors and need a monthly hose-down. Unlike the composite and the recycled-plastic decking materials, which are solid, vinyl deck pieces are hollow. They sound and feel different than a solid deck piece when walked on; some of the two-piece vinyl decking products even squeak or squish. Before purchasing any vinyl decking material, you need to find an installed deck of the same material and test it out.

Although cost and maintenance loom large in most buyers' minds, another consideration should be the temperature of the walking surface on a hot summer day. According to the installers, plastics, composites, and vinyl are no worse than wood, which itself can feel warm in bare feet. But this is a subjective judgment. When the sun is high in the sky, you need to test the different surfaces in bare feet for yourself.

how does it feel in bare feet on a hot day?

Vinyl decking tends to be more expensive than the composites and recycled plastics. For a twelve-by-twenty deck, EverNew deck boards, which are also manufactured by CertainTeed, can cost a thousand to thirteen hundred dollars. For the same-sized deck, Kroy deck boards would cost twelve hundred to twenty-two hundred, and Brock Deck Systems deckboards would be about seventeen hundred. Both of these manufacturers also sell railing systems that feature various railing and baluster styles.

glare

The color of the material should also be considered. White vinyl or plastic will always be the coolest color to walk on, but it shows the dirt the most and produces tremendous glare. The grays and tans show dirt less and are easier on the eyes. Because dark plastic colors will heat up in the noon-day sun, Carefree's Redwood is not sold in areas where this can be a potential problem. The darker Trex boards may also be hotter than the lighter ones.

building permits

Before purchasing any nonwood decking products or others that you may hear about, you should consult your local building department. Building codes for decking are based on all-wood construction, and most building departments require documentation that the synthetic product is structurally adequate before they will issue a building permit. Some may be willing to evaluate a manufacturer's own testing reports, but most require a National Evaluation Service (NES) report or an evaluation service report from one of the national code bodies: Building Officials and Code Administrators (BOCA), International Conference of Building Officials (ICBO), and Southern Building Code Congress International (SBCCI). The procedure for obtaining an evaluation service report is lengthy and expensive. Trex and Carefree have the NES report; Brock Deck has the BOCA evaluation report; Boardwalk, SmartDeck, Kroy, and EverNew are currently in the NES or BOCA evaluation process.

Some carpets look like new for years and others get ratty in no time. Vic Joffe and Bill Gordon, two carpet-cleaning professionals from Ann Arbor, Michigan, with forty-five years experience between them, have cleaned every type of

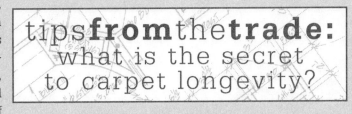

tips**from**the**trade:** what is the secret to carpet longevity?

carpet under every condition imaginable. Their advice: pick a fiber, texture, and color according to the use and amount of foot traffic you expect in each living area, catch spills promptly, vacuum frequently, and clean periodically.

To get yourself off to a good start, both experts said that a good installation and a good pad are essential. Some pads are so thin and insubstantial that they feel "wimpy" and you can tell they won't do the job, Gordon says. In areas with heavy foot traffic, such as a hallway, a lightweight pad will quickly collapse to the thickness of cardboard and lose its ability to cushion the impact of footsteps on the carpet. When this happens, every step will pound the carpet directly against the floor, causing the carpet fibers to lose their "memory retention," their ability to spring back after being crushed under a footstep. The carpet will quickly look ratty, and no amount of cleaning expertise can restore it.

But don't judge a pad by thickness alone, Joffe cautions. A thicker pad may look more substantial, but if it doesn't have enough density, the carpet will flex, stretching up and down like a trampoline when you walk on it. This will eventually break down the carpet backing, and cause it to delaminate. You

need at least a six-pound pad and preferably an eight-pound one with a thickness of ⅜ inch. Since a production builder's base-grade pad many be only a four-pound type, you should upgrade it even if you decide not to upgrade the base-grade carpet itself.

The key to a good installation is adequate stretching, which must be done with a power stretcher. If this is not done correctly, you won't notice anything amiss when you move in, but wrinkles can appear the first time the carpets are steam-cleaned because the hot water and heat relax the backing. The wrinkles may disappear as the carpet dries; if they don't, the only way to get rid of them is to restretch the carpeting. This can get expensive if the wrinkles appear in doorways or in areas where the carpet has seams.

You'll get the most value for your money when you match the fiber type, color, and texture to the use and amount of foot traffic in each area of your house. Wool wears well and dirt comes out easily with cleaning, but this natural fiber also stains easily. Moreover, the stains can be hard to remove and, Joffe notes, some do not come out at all. In a high-traffic area where you won't be eating such as a hallway or in a low-traffic area such as a formal living room, wool can be a good choice, but he urges you to think twice before putting it in your dining areas, especially if you have pets and small children who spill frequently.

Of the synthetic fibers—polyester, nylon, and olefin—polyester is the hardest to clean and olefin the easiest. It is also the most stain resistant because unlike wool, its fibers do not accept dyes and colors easily. Though not as strong a fiber as nylon, olefin wears well when used in a berber-style carpet with a looped fiber instead of a cut one. Another plus with a berber style—its knobby textured surface and flecks of color hide dirt.

A carpet with a light color will make a smaller space look larger, but you will see every spot. If you really want the lighter colors, Joffe suggests a carpet style that will hide the dirt and spots such as a berber or a sculpted type with a speckled color and a sculpted surface pattern created by mixing cut and looped pile. If neither of these types of carpeting appeal to you, consider the multi-colored pattern approach, a strategy long favored by decorators for heavy-traffic areas such as hotel lobbies and commercial dining rooms. The dirt-hiding subterfuge here: the dirt blends in because you can't focus on six different colors as once.

Even if you make prudent carpet choices, wear and tear will eventually show in the way that light reflects off the carpet fibers. When a carpet is new, the surface will be flawless because all the fibers are uniform and light reflects off them evenly. But as you walk around your house, the hundreds of thousands of dirt and sand particles that are on your shoes or your dog's paws will be ground into the carpet. The grinding action cuts the fibers, making thousands of microscopic scratches. As these accumulate, the light will reflect in a million different ways and the carpet will start to look worn.

You can reduce the grinding action with frequent vacuuming. For heavy-traffic areas, some manufacturers recommend doing this every other day. You probably won't be that vigilant, but you should vacuum at least twice a week in heavily used areas.

Frequent vacuuming won't remove all the abrasive particles that can accumulate, however. The only way to remove the dirt build-up is to steam-clean the carpets every six to eighteen months, depending on the number of people and pets in your household and the colors that you pick—lighter colors need cleaning more frequently than darker ones.

You can rent a machine and do the cleaning yourself, but an experienced, professional carpet cleaner will have a bigger, more efficient machine, and with it he can remove more abrasive dirt particles. This will help the carpet to look newer longer. If you get a high-density carpet with a face weight above 50 ounces, however, you should engage a professional and not try to do it yourself. The carpet fibers will be packed so closely together that only a professional's truck-mounted, hot-water extraction equipment will be powerful enough to penetrate all the way through to the backing and get out all the layers of dirt.

Between carpet cleanings, both cleaning experts emphasize vigilance in cleaning up spills—the faster you get them up, the better. Many people interpret "stain resistant" to mean "stain proof," but, Gordon explains, "The treatment only makes the carpet easier to clean and buys you time; you still must attend to the spill right away." Since a carpet disaster can always occur, even with the most conscientious care, Joffe suggests that you ask the installers to leave any remnants for future use as patches, should the need arise.

Scenario One: You're driving in the country and see a sign that says LOT FOR SALE—LAKE VIEWS. Suddenly, the country life becomes an idea whose time has come. Stop right there: Do not impulsively sign a contract before you have all the facts. If the farmer selling the lake-view property or the apple orchard is suggesting that he's got other suitors, put down a refundable deposit (typically about 5 percent of the purchase price) and ask for thirty days to make a feasibility study. Then check it out.

Scenario Two: You're looking at a new house in a planned community. You've looked at thirty-nine models and *this is the one.* You're getting pressure from the builder's sales agent because the lots are going fast. Stop right there: Do not take this gambit. Put down a small refundable deposit (typically about 1 or 2 percent of the purchase price) for a seven-day lot hold. Then scramble and do your homework.

You may have ten reasons why you want to buy a particular piece of property. Here are ten good reasons that you shouldn't:

1. Most sellers aren't hayseeds who are unsophisticated about land prices. If the price seems unusually low, there's probably a good reason. For example, the setting may be quiet and rural but the soils are unstable, so building on them will be expensive, or there are rocks lurking just below the surface. Before you close this deal, hire a geothermal engineer to take soil borings. In production-built subdivisions, as well, some lots will be cheaper than others. Some of the minuses that can lower the lot value: It is small or oddly shaped, it is adjacent to a noisy intersection, or it abuts the back of a shopping center or a busy highway.

2. The soils may be okay, but the logistics required to get equipment and materials onto the site are daunting, and these will jack up the construction cost. If the approach to your site is really steep, you could spend seventy thousand dollars just to construct a driveway and retaining walls. Get a builder to walk the site with you and assess the difficulty of building on it.

3. New regulations may have been enacted since the surrounding houses were built. Don't take the presence of other houses nearby as assurance that building there will be a cinch. Zoning regulations, minimum lot sizes for a septic field, and the building codes may have changed since the other houses were built, and these changes could make the construction of your house much more difficult and expensive. Check with the local zoning office, building department, and, in the case of a septic field, the health department.

4. The view that will cost you thousands is rarely guaranteed. You're buying the lot, not the view.

5. The spreading chestnut tree and other mature trees that make the lot so appealing may be diseased. Get an arborist's evaluation before signing anything.

6. You want to build a new house in the same school district where you live now, so your children's lives and the carpools won't be disrupted. There aren't any vacant lots so you want to buy one of those tiny fifties ranches, tear it down, and build a new house. Many residents who live in neighborhoods where this

has happened have protested mightily, and in response your jurisdiction may have passed rules that severely limit what you can build. Look up the zoning regulations and consult an architect first (for more on this, see Chapter 6).

7. You don't want a lake in your backyard with every downpour. In a production-built subdivision, all the lots may look the same, but some will be "collectors" of the runoff from five or six adjacent lots. To avoid this, engage a landscape architect to walk the subdivision with you and evaluate the drainage and grading of different lots.

8. Golf course communities are hot—all that greenery just outside your windows looks great. But you don't want a steady stream of errant golf balls or chagrined golfers in your backyard, so learn enough of the game to get a lot where weekend duffers won't spoil your home.

9. Don't overlook those prosaic considerations such as street layout and traffic patterns. Many buyers like cul-de-sacs because there's no through traffic. On the "feeder" streets that cul-de-sac owners use to reach their houses, however, you can have lots of traffic and speedy cars. And if you pick a lot directly across from a T intersection (a street dead-ends in front of your house), you will have a parade of headlights shining into your living room every night.

10. In the heat of a purchase, most buyers do not think about noise. And the source may not be very audible at the time you are looking. For example, Saturday afternoon and Sunday morning are low-traffic periods at many airports. If the lot is on the edge of a development and abuts a highway, the sound may be most apparent at night, when the ambient noise level is low. Verify the existence and location of any potential noise source, then make arrangements to visit the site when the sound is loudest. The noise will be less intrusive inside your house, but you also want to be able to enjoy sitting in your backyard (for more on this, see Chapter 14).

choosing a production-builder lot with a landscape architect's help

At the time you purchase a lot from a production builder, you're likely to be looking at streets, curb cuts, and acres of brown dirt. The landscape is a mess, and there's no way you can detect the subtle but important differences in drainage, grading, and soil types that distinguish one lot from another. Nonetheless, these subtleties can be critical, especially when the lot size is less than a quarter of an acre, as it is in most new-home subdivisions today.

drainage,grading,**and**soils

You need to check the drainage to avoid purchasing a surface-runoff collector lot that becomes a small pond after every summer cloud burst. You need proper grading to prevent rainwater from seriously damaging your foundation. And the grading is not just a matter of getting the right slope—some soil types drain less well than others, and this can affect the grading requirements. Soil type is also a major determinant for what kind of trees will grow on a given lot. If you've got your heart set on lilacs in your new front yard, you don't want to buy a lot where they won't thrive.

To assess these subtleties hire a landscape architect to walk the subdivision with you. Though landscape architects are generally regarded as "plant people," their training and expertise also includes soils engineering, building design, and hydrology.

Another issue with production-builder lots that a landscape architect can check is the amount of topsoil provided. For healthy plant material and a decent lawn, a six-inch layer of topsoil is a minimum, but many builders provide a topsoil layer of only one or two inches. You can't simply add another four or five inches of soil after you move in because this will disturb the developer's final grading plan. To get the right amount of topsoil and the proper slope at the end, the rough grade must be adjusted during construction.

lotorientation

Lifestyle, personality, and energy consumption all come into play in choosing lot orientation and a landscape architect can help you factor these in. If you're an early riser and always hit the ground running, east-facing bedrooms with the early-morning sun pouring in will be a good thing. On the other hand, if you're a night person who likes to sleep in, you'd probably prefer a lot in which the bedrooms face north. If you love gardening and envision a huge vegetable garden in your backyard, make sure the back of the house faces south so that your garden will get enough sun.

Lots with the back of the house and the main living areas—the eat-in kitchen/family room with big windows and large sliding glass doors—facing south are optimal from an energy-consumption perspective, observed Nadav Malin, editor of *Environmental Building News*. With this orientation, the rear-facing kitchen/family room will get little direct sun in summer when the sun is high overhead for most of the day, and the space won't heat up. This will make a significant difference in your cooling bill. In the winter, when the sun is much lower in the sky and its warmth welcome, the rooms will be warmer, and your heating bills less. Conversely, the worst lots from an energy perspective are those on which the main living areas will face east or west. In the summer these spaces will get direct sun, which will add to the air-conditioning load; in the winter they won't get much sun at all. Between east and west exposures, west is worse, especially in areas where the summer temperatures are particularly high.

If you can't pick a parcel that fulfills your orientation requirements, you can mitigate it with plant material. If your main living spaces face east or west, you can shade them from the summer sun with deciduous trees; judicious placement of deciduous trees will also shade south-facing rooms during the summer, but admit the sun's warmth in winter. To shield north-facing rooms from blistering winter winds, Gazso recommends evergreens.

Until the trees get big enough to have any effect, you will have to put up with some discomfort. If you want the benefits sooner and you can afford it, you can plant more mature (but more expensive) trees.

When selecting a lot, it is also important to find out what the future plans of the builder and developer are. The site plan in the sales brochure may include only Phase I, but in two or three years the woods that adjoin your lot may be cut as Phase II begins.

You should also check the setbacks and possible easements for the lot you are considering. These may restrict the area in which you can construct a deck or other outdoor structures and affect your ambitious plans to build the same large deck you saw on the back of the furnished model.

To ensure that you have an adequate level of expertise for inspecting lots, make sure that the landscape architect you hire is registered and licensed. Not all states require landscape architects to be licensed, but licensure ensures a certain level of competence, training, and experience.

Most landscape-architecture firms do large-scale regional planning or commercial design work, but almost every town will have a couple of small offices that do residential work and advise buyers of new tract houses. Usually they will do this on a hourly basis.

landscapingyournewyard

After you've covered the basics—drainage, grading, and soils—there's still the yard to deal with. If you're buying from a production builder, he's unlikely to provide much beyond what is required: "soil erosion measures," which usually means grass, one or two small trees, and a few shrubs along the front foundation line.

Embellishing the builder's meager efforts can create outside rooms that can be lived in some to most of the year, depending on where you live. Landscaping can also create views that will enhance the inside rooms and make them seem larger. There are also practical reasons for landscaping. Strategic placement of trees, hedges, and fences can provide privacy—increasingly an issue as lots become smaller and houses closer together. Trees also provide shade. If you can't avoid a lot orientation that has the main living areas facing east or west, the rooms will really heat up in the summer. Shade trees will make these spaces much more pleasant and significantly reduce your cooling bills.

Landscaping can also increase the value—or at least resale prospects—of your house. "Rules of thumb are dangerous when applied to investments," noted real estate appraiser William C. Harvey of Great Falls, Virginia. In his experience, landscaping is an "intangible" that can't be quantified in terms of adding dollar value, but it definitely enhances resale prospects.

"Hardscape" items such as decks or terraces, however, both add to the value and make a house easier to resell. They're aesthetic and functional, notes Martha Heric, an Urbanna, Virginia, real estate appraiser with a degree in landscape architecture. "They serve as a 'transition area' between the house and the yard; they're also a place to put a grill and to sit down."

If you're handy and enjoy yard work, you can do most of the landscaping work yourself. The trick is knowing what to plant and where to plant it while avoiding costly and classic Harry Homeowner mistakes such as splurging on an expensive tree and then having to remove it later because it over-matured and invaded gutters or blocked windows.

Engaging a landscape architect to design a master landscape plan might seem extravagant, but it will probably save you money in the long run. As you work with your landscape architect, you're likely to decide that some of your landscaping ideas are better left to the professionals. For example, you'll learn that a four-to-five-inch-diameter tree can weigh seven hundred to one thousand pounds.

A master landscape plan will be tailored to your personal tastes, budget, and most importantly to your maintenance capabilities, both time-wise and money-wise. The cost to design a plan can range from a few hundred to several thousand dollars, depending on your total landscape budget and how elaborate the design is.

Since minor changes to a floor plan can often make a dramatic improvement in a landscape plan, you need to develop a preliminary landscaping scheme before you sign a sales contract with your builder.

Modifying the builder's standard floor plan may involve only adding additional doors to the rear of the house, so that the rear spaces are accessible to the outside and not landlocked. Installing a door in the breakfast area could be especially important, because if the door to the rear is too far from the kitchen, an outdoor eating area will be underutilized. Other things to discuss with the builder before signing:

- Relocating the air-conditioning condenser so that it's not in front of a window.

- Widening the front walk. Most builder's provide one that is only thirty-six inches wide. Adding another twelve inches makes it easier for two people to walk side by side. If the front door has a wide stoop, a covered entryway, or embellishments such as columns or a large Palladian window, a wider walk also looks better.

- Adding a second walkway from the driveway to the house. Many visitors as well as owners pull up in the driveway and approach the front door from there rather than looping around to come up the front walk.

Although these details are important, the major portion of the master landscape planning will be designing the outdoor spaces around your house. Besides addressing your privacy concerns and shade needs, you also need to ask the same questions you posed to yourself when you looked for a house:

- Is your lifestyle formal or informal?

- Do you entertain a lot or a little?

- Do you have small children who still play in a sandbox?

- How much time do you want to spend maintaining your yard?

While the planting plan and outdoor hardscape items do not need to be finalized before you move in, you should have the master plan well worked out so that you can budget accordingly.

implementing a master landscape plan

If you take the plunge and engage a landscape architect to design a master landscape plan for you, the time to start implementing it depends on where you live. In the Midwest and on the East Coast, you can afford to wait until the houses around yours are built. Then you will know exactly where the views are and where to plant a tree to block a neighbor's garage wall or to keep you and the neighbor from staring at each other while doing the dishes. You may also find that your new neighbors are willing to share the expense of screening trees or a fence.

If you're buying in the coastal regions of California, or other areas where a naturally sloped topography has been drastically recontoured, you may need to start right away. In California, the lot will probably look great when you move in. But the first rainy-season squall could bring soil-erosion problems if you don't have adequate ground cover, advised landscape architect David Foote of San Luis Obispo. The erosion problems are caused in part by the way the slopes have been stabilized. The areas beneath and around the house have been filled and compacted to meet structural and seismic requirements, but this makes the ground hard as clay. Rainwater is not readily absorbed, so it runs down the slopes above and below your house, forming unsightly gullies. In addition, the same compacted soil may not drain well on the flat areas of the lot. These areas should be identified and corrected.

Compounding the problem is the poor soil that characterizes most recontoured slopes. Frequently the soil that ends up in the top layer was originally twenty feet below grade. Before anything in it can grow well, the soil needs enriching, but few builders include this in the development of the lot. To know how much of which kind of nutrient to add, you need to do a soil test. And even after you add nutrients, the soil may not be great, so you'll need a ground cover that is drought resistant and fast-growing in poor soil. Most people also want something that is low maintenance and colorful, Foote said.

After the ground cover is in, Foote would add shade trees, a must in the areas of California with hot summers. Since most lots in California are small, one shade tree in front and back should suffice, he said.

In the Midwest, soil erosion is rarely a problem. But summers can be long and hot, and you should start with shade trees, advises Ann Arbor, Michigan, landscape architect Barry Gazso. The bigger the tree you plant, the sooner you will benefit, but he says, "Speed costs money—how fast do you want to go? Most people can't afford mature trees. If you initially plant smaller but less expensive trees, you will be looking at a lot of mulch for three to four years. But you will have a lot of nice healthy plants that will eventually mature."

Deciduous trees that provide shade in the summer but shed leaves in the winter when the sun's warmth is welcome are ideal. However, recent studies have shown that a mature tree's trunk and branches still cut off about 50 percent of the sun. To get summer shade and winter sun on a southern exposure, you need to calculate where the tree shadows will fall in winter, then locate the tree so that sunlight can penetrate the windows, explains Nadav Malin. For eastern and western exposures, a shade tree is definitely a plus. But its placement is far less critical because the amount of direct winter sun that could hit the house is minimal anyway, Malin says.

At the same time you plant the shade trees, but before you've invested any time in yard maintenance, Gazso would install an outdoor sitting area. If mosquitoes are a problem, he suggests a wood deck with a roof and screens (similar to a screen porch but not as expensive) because an open wood deck cannot be used after sundown when the bugs come out. Gazso also points out that a roofed deck offers rain protection and shade.

Next on Gazso's list would be the understory, smaller trees that reach a height of only ten to twelve feet, compared to twenty to twenty-five feet for a shade tree; these are primarily for privacy. But even smaller trees take some time to grow, and many owners of new houses want privacy right away. The quickest solution is a fence, but many homeowner associations have height restrictions on these. However, Gazso says he has never seen any rules about the height of trees and hedges. A ten- to twelve-foot hedge in front of a five-foot-high fence will soften the look and add five or more feet of screening.

In California privacy is even more of an issue than in the Midwest because lots are smaller, the houses are closer together, and, if the site is sloped, the owners above you can look right into your backyard. There are many plant choices for privacy; the trick is selecting one that is fast growing but won't get too big. Foote recommends trees that reach a height of fifteen to twenty feet. They will provide privacy from owners above you, but they won't block the view or throw undesired shade into a neighbor's yard.

If you want a small outdoor sitting area, Foote advises identifying the sunny areas in the yard before building it. When the sitting area is complete, he would add some flower beds for color and fragrance.

Calling plants and shrubs the "frosting on the cake," Gazso would plant them last, and he offers a word of caution on what appears to be the easiest part of the landscaping effort. Many homeowners plant them by the doors to see them better, but in the Midwest "you fight a swarm a bees."

you're buying the lot, not the view

Every new home buyer wants an expansive and dramatic view out his or her windows, and some are willing to pay top dollar to get it. Unfortunately, these buyers don't realize that when they buy a lot, the view does not automatically come with it. If view protections are not in place before their purchase, they will be at the mercy of their neighbors or their builder/developer not to build or plant anything that will affect it.

View preservation may not be a priority for these other parties. The neighbors may want privacy, so plant trees. Or they may need more room in their house, so add a second story. Or the developer may decide to exercise his right to build on land that was to remain open.

How can you avoid such a headache, not to mention potential loss in property value? In legalese, "Perform due diligence." In laymanese, "Do your homework." This may cost you something in legal fees, but nothing approaching the thousands of additional dollars you may be spending just to get the view. First, you need to check zoning restrictions on building height, applicable view ordinances, view protections incorporated into property titles, or, if you're considering a purchase in a planned community, the Home Owner's Association documents.

As you check the zoning regulations, keep in mind that as a general rule these are written with the welfare of the citizenry in mind, not to further aesthetics and protect views. Building height can be restricted if a housing development is in the flight path of a nearby airport, but not because hillside lots overlook a harbor.

Next, check for municipal view ordinances. Though uncommon, they do exist in some areas. A number of communities in the San Francisco Bay area, for example, have ordinances that explicitly address tree growth. "Typically, the underlying presumption of such ordinances is that the view seeker pays for restoration and maintenance of the view, but the ordinances do not guarantee that views will be restored, " stresses Dennis

Yniguez of Berkeley, California, who is both an arborist and an attorney who has represented owners in view disputes.

You should also get a preliminary title report. The deed to the property may say something about view protection and restrictions on neighboring properties. An informal agreement with adjoining property owners about tree pruning, though assuring, is not binding and may not carry over to you after you purchase the property.

Should no view protections be uncovered, you might consider buying the neighbors' "view rights," suggests Miami attorney Dennis Haber. Similar in principle to selling mineral rights, some localities allow property owners to sell their right to go up. If such a last-ditch approach is not possible, you have to accept that you may at some time in the future lose your view—property owners in your view corridor own their air space, and they can put in it what they want.

If you are considering a purchase in a planned-community development with a Home Owner's Association, read the association's "Covenants, Conditions, and Restrictions" document. In most cases, when you buy the house, you agree both to accept the established conditions and to waive your right to dispute them in the future. The CC&R may or may not include specific view protections, a blanket height restriction for trees and houses, or a dispute resolution process. Since the CC&R can sometimes expire, be sure to note how long it will be enforced.

The mere fact that you are paying extra for a view in a planned community does not ensure its preservation. Buried in the fine print, the CC&R document can state words to the effect, "If we want to build something next door that could affect your view and we do so, you can't say we're depriving you."

Buyers considering a house in a golf-course community should read the CC&R with particular care. Assuming that the golf course will be a permanent feature is reasonable, but not always correct. In some golf-course communities, the Home Owner's Association assumes ownership and maintenance responsibilities for the golf course. But the CC&R can state that if the majority of homeowners don't want to continue doing this, the golf course can be sold off. Since the majority of homeowners in many golf-course communities don't play and may tire of paying for all the upkeep, this is not a hypothetical scenario.

In other golf-course communities, the developer/builder sells the lots and houses but retains ownership of the golf course. Should he decide to sell it in the future, what happens? He may not be obliged to sell it to another golf course operator. To find out if the developer has placed any restrictions on himself in this regard, you need to check the CC&R documents, the sales contract, the property deed, and the deed for the master plan of the community.

Should you uncover no view protections in a CC&R or otherwise, are you tempting fate to proceed with the deal anyway? If the only threat is vegetation, and if you can acknowledge that the other homeowners' desire for privacy is legitimate, you can probably work out a solution over the back fence. This will not only save you thousands in legal fees, it will also help create an air of cooperation over other potentially contentious issues such as barking dogs or noisy parties, attorney Yniguez says.

The back-fence solution can involve inexpensive pruning of a few shrubs and trees, but if large trees must be removed or replanted, it can cost thousands. As the view seeker, you may have to foot the bill, but Yniguez points out that when a number of neighbors are concerned about the view, the cost can be shared.

lotswithlotsoftrees

If you are considering a lot for its trees, bring in an arborist to assess them. Arborists specialize in the long-term care, disease, and insect-infestation problems of established, mature trees, whereas landscape architects are more concerned with tree selection and planting. An arborist can determine which trees are worth saving and where you can build without damaging them. Since these decisions will impact both the shape of your building envelope and how the builder organizes his equipment and supplies on the site, you should call in an arborist *before* you buy the lot. If many of the trees are diseased or the effort to save them will leave you with a minuscule building pad, you may want to keep looking.

If the arborist determines that the trees are healthy and there's sufficient area to build without damaging them, you should engage him to advise your builder on which trees to save and where to put his equipment. If you don't, you may regret it later. Most home builders, though well meaning, do not know much about the care and preservation of trees on a job site. And most trees that are damaged in this way die slowly. By the time the tree dies—from two to twelve years after the house is finished—most people don't make the causal connection.

You may be surprised at the arborist's evaluation of the trees on your lot that are worth saving. As a general rule, mid-sized trees are more likely to survive the stress of construction intact than older, larger ones, which may actually be entering a stage of decline and will die no matter how conscientious your builder is. "People design landscaping and even entire houses around declining trees when in some cases they would be better off to remove the tree and plant a new one after the house is built," observes arborist Yniguez. Even if it's the right decision, though, cutting down an old tree can still be heartbreaking.

Besides the infirmities of old age, trees can be diseased or hazardous. A diseased tree may or may not be treatable, but a hazardous one that has obvious signs of imminent structural failure should be taken down right away.

After an arborist has analyzed a site and designated the trees to be saved and how much of the surrounding ground must remain undisturbed during construction, the area left for building the house may be drastically reduced or oddly shaped. This is another reason to engage an arborist *before* you get very serious about a particular floor plan.

Most of the damage inflicted during construction affects trees' roots, which are much more extensive than most people realize. Some of the roots can be cut without harming the tree, but how much depends on both the tree species and the soils on your lot. Locating the utility trenches for gas, water, and sewer lines so as not to damage the roots can be especially tricky.

The roots have both structural and metabolic functions. When the structural function is compromised—usually by cutting roots too close to the trunk—the tree may eventually fall over. When the metabolic function is compromised, the tree may slowly starve. Most new-home construction causes the latter problem.

Even when roots are not disturbed, trees can be damaged during construction when heavy equipment, trucks, and stockpiled materials excessively compact the soil. This prevents roots from getting water and oxygen and will eventually kill a tree. The only way to prevent such severe soil compaction is to designate a staging area for vehicles and stockpiled materials.

Since most builders are not acutely aware of such protective procedures and prohibited areas of operation, you should have your arborist meet with your builder early on. When all the logistical concerns are addressed beforehand, the builder won't feel impossibly restricted during construction, and he's more likely to be supportive of your concerns.

Once the trees to be saved are identified, and a protective zone for each tree designated, your arborist should specify where materials can be stockpiled, and where machinery can or can't drive. *These stipulations should be included in your contract with the builder.* To ensure that trucks and equipment are kept away from the trees, fence off the area.

Even with all these measures in place, you still need to be vigilant, since some subcontractors may not be as careful as your builder. "The favorite place to change oil on a bulldozer is in the shade of the nicest tree," observed arborist James Biller of Arlington, Virginia.

Should you need to take out any trees before construction starts, an arborist can advise you on selection and siting of appropriate replacement trees to be replanted after the house is finished.

When engaging an arborist, what credentials should you look for? The first requisite is experience. The late Irving Humphrey, an arborist in Los Angeles, worked with trees for nearly sixty years, and, by his own account, "Looked at about a million trees." Few can match this, but you do need someone who has had extensive experience with trees in your area for at least four years.

In every state but New York, which has a licensing requirement, anyone can call him- or herself an arborist. However, the designation Registered Consulting Arborist indicates that the arborist belongs to the American Society of Consulting Arborists. Requirements for membership include extensive arboriculture education, experience, and rigorous peer review. A more widely held credential with fewer requirements is Certified Arborist, which is granted by the International Society of Arboriculture (ISA) in Savoy, Illinois. (See Resources for more information on how to find an arborist.)

golf-course communities

When you start to think about where you want to live in your new house, next to a golf course may not even be on your list. But looking out over the broad, green expanse of a golf course from the comfort of one's living room has proved to be such a sellable idea that golf-course communities are springing up all over the country. Chances are there's at least one in your market.

But bear in mind that golfers are part of the package. To have a pleasant time alongside their activities, avoid lots that adjoin a fairway in the "landing zone"—the area where the tee shots land. If your house is there, you will get lots of balls in your yard, golfers retrieving them, and the occasional broken window. Since most golfers can't hit the ball straight, and most are right-handed, most tee shots will veer to the right. This means that houses on the right side of the fairway will have more problems with errant golf balls. For this reason, some golf-courses communities are now designed with houses on the left side of the fairway only.

The landing zone will not be an issue on every fairway. A golf course will have par-3, par-4, and par-5 holes. The par-3 ones are shorter and easier, and most golfers can hit their tee shots relatively straight. The par-4 and par-5 holes are longer, and most tee shots will land about halfway down those fairways. Lots adjoining these fairways that are closer to the tee or to the green will have fewer golf-ball problems than in the landing zone. The lots with the fewest golf-ball problems and the best views are the ones around the greens.

In addition to balls landing in your backyard and golfers retrieving them, airborne golf balls can seriously limit your backyard activities. "Balls come from all crazy angles," golf-course architect William Newcomb of Ann Arbor, Michigan, says. "You could get hit by one. If you want to put a play structure for kids or you want to entertain in the backyard, this can be a problem with any lot adjoining the fairway. It will be worse if your lot is in the landing zone."

When a house is continually bombarded with golf balls, a netting will solve the problem. But to work, it must be a big net—about twenty-five feet high and stretched across the back of your lot. If the fairways were wider and the houses were set farther back from the lot line, nets would rarely, if ever, be needed, and home owners would get only the occasional ball in their backyard. Unfortunately, Newcomb says, the developer usually allocates more land for the residential parcels so he can sell more lots.

This being the case, what distances from fairways and lot lines are acceptable? The minimum distance from the midpoint of the fairway to your lot line should be 150 feet. From your lot line to your house is usually about 30 feet, for a total of 180 feet. If it's less than this, Newcomb says, "You're vulnerable to getting golf balls on your house, in your house, and on yourself."

Besides golf balls, another drawback to golf-course life is unwanted noise. The electric golf carts are not noisy, but the mowers and other equipment used by the maintenance crews are. Typically the crews start at daybreak, which in the summer in some places can be as early as 5:30 A.M.

Golfers can be noisy too. They chat at the tees, where golfers congregate waiting to play. And voices carry on golf courses, especially if someone yells when he makes a great putt. Golfers also play all day. During the height of the golf season, foursomes tee off from sunrise to sunset. In Florida, the high season is in winter and it's dark by 5 P.M., but in Michigan, high season is mid-summer and then players are on the course until 9:30 P.M., noted Larry Hirsh, a golf-course consultant in Harrisburg, Pennsylvania.

To get an idea of how many golfers will be passing by on a daily basis, ask the developer. Every golf course is different, but during high season, two to three hundred players on a busy day is not unusual, according to Hirsh.

All those golfers can make privacy an issue, but golf-course architect Cal Olson of San Juan Capistrano, California, said that golf-course design can ameliorate this. "If your house is relatively level with the course, you will have less privacy and less view. But if you're four to eight feet above the course, you can look down and the golfers can't see in your yard. If you're six feet above, you won't see the golf carts."

If you could engage him to help you pick a lot, Barry Gazso, a landscape architect in Ann Arbor, Michigan, would be ideal. He has designed site plans for production-built subdivisions all over the Midwest and has advised buyers on lot selections. He also speaks from personal experience—ten years ago he bought such a house himself.

tips**from**the**trade:**
how the experts
pick a lot

When inspecting a lot, Gazso generally starts with the drainage. He studies an entire block or section, not just the one lot a buyer is considering. Frequently, and legally, rainwater from several adjoining lots may collect in a drainage swale on one lot. In some jurisdictions, water from four or five houses can collect in a sixth yard. If this is your lot, you will have a small pond or even a flowing creek with every heavy downpour.

Since a swale—basically a ditch—can be very shallow, it is hard for most laymen to see it, but a swale's location can be critical. In some jurisdictions a swale can be as close as ten feet to the house, which can affect the feasibility and location of an outdoor deck or patio.

A swale cannot be eliminated from an otherwise satisfactory lot, because this will cause problems for the adjoining properties. However, you may be able to get the builder to relocate a swale or, as Gazso did himself, get the builder to install an underground drainage line that will carry the rainwater to the storm sewer in the street.

Next on Gazso's checklist is the drainage around the house. If the ground slopes away from it, the drainage is "positive." But, if the ground slopes toward the house, a condition that can severely damage the foundation if left unchecked, the drainage is "negative."

When a site is nearly flat, as it is in many new subdivisions today, the difference between having positive and negative drainage can be small. A 1 percent slope is inadequate, a 3 percent slope sufficient, and a 4 percent more than enough. Slope describes a vertical drop in feet per hundred horizontal feet; a 1 percent slope means the grade drops one foot over a distance of one hundred feet and looks basically flat; a 3 percent slope is discernible to the practiced eye. If the slope is less than 3 percent, Gazso advises adding a clause to the sales contract stating that closing (when the property is legally conveyed to you) is contingent on the builder's correction and a landscape architect's approval of the final grading of the lot.

The builder will have a set of engineered site plans that locate drainage swales and indicate the proposed slope around each house, but Gazso emphasizes that the actual conditions of a given lot can differ significantly from the plans, so buyers should always check them.

chapter eleven the purchase

You've visited fifteen master planned communities, seven stand-alone subdivisions, toured dozens of models, narrowed the list of possible builders and floor plans to three finalists, and made your considered decision. Now you're ready to sit down with a builder and discuss a sales contract.

At this juncture, you need to have the players on your team lined up, if you haven't done so already. If you didn't engage a buyer's agent to help you in your search, you can still benefit from his or her expertise at this final stage. An agent can fill you in on the building firm and the location, help you sort out what's an option and what's not so that you are very clear on what you are getting and which options will make a difference from a resale perspective. More important, a buyer's agent will help you negotiate both a sale price and financing details—for example, if you're not going to use the builder's lender and you want to apply his financing incentives to a flooring upgrade.

At this point you also need to engage the other players on your team—an attorney to review your sales contract, a landscape architect to help you choose a lot if you're buying a production-built house, an arborist if large, mature trees were the reason you are willing to spend thousands extra for a particular lot, and a private home inspector to check your house at critical construction points.

This is also the time to look down the road and prepare for a few what-if scenarios. What if your house isn't finished when the builder says it will be? You need a backup plan so that you have somewhere to live until your new house is ready. What if you are so freaked out that this project will flounder or are so afraid that you will hate it that you can't sleep for a week? What if you feel great about the whole enterprise, but the house really does fall down? Your builder may offer a ten-year limited warranty, but it may not provide as much comfort as you think. The only prudent and realistic way to protect yourself from such a disastrous outcome is to do your homework and check on the builder's reputation. If he has been building houses for fifteen years with 1,213 completed houses under his belt and legions of satisfied buyers, it's unlikely that you, as his 1,214th customer, would experience anything untoward. If the builder has been in business for only one year, has built only 37 houses and you're his 38th buyer, his track record is much shorter and you might be well advised to look at another builder who's been in business for at least three years, and preferably five.

negotiatingstrategies

When you're finally ready to get serious about a sales contract with a production builder, how negotiable is the price? When the economy is booming and there are lots of buyers out there, most home builders are not amenable to any protracted horse trading. When buyers are scarce, they will talk.

In good times and bad, however, you can always get the lowest price if you are the first or second buyer in a brand-new project. The builder is eager to gain credibility and wants to get some houses up in a hurry. He will intentionally undervalue the house to get a sale, and his lot costs at the beginning of a project are usually lower than they are at the end. Most land developers who sell finished lots to production builders have escalator clauses in their contracts with the builders that dictate a higher price for each successive parcel of lots purchased by a builder.

Being the first buyer, however, means buying off a floor plan, because the model hasn't been built yet. Unless you are very good at reading floor plans (surprisingly, even many builders can't read them well), you should wait until the model is built so that you can see what you are getting. However, if the home-building firm is fairly large, it may have already built the same model somewhere else that you can visit.

Similarly, at the end of a project, when a builder wants to close down operations and start up a new project, he may have a close-out sale. The last houses will be higher priced than the very first house was, but the builder may be willing to give you a price break.

You can also get a discount on an "inventory" house—a house that is finished or under construction but has not yet been sold. A builder can intentionally have a few inventory or spec houses to sell to buyers who want a house in 30 to 60 days instead of the 120 to 150 usually required to build one from scratch. A builder may also have inventory due to a deal falling through because of a sudden change in a buyer's circumstances, such as a job transfer or, less often, when interest rates go up. If a house is not finished on time, a buyer's lock-in on a specific mortgage interest rate may expire and he may not qualify for another loan at a higher rate.

The time of year can also affect a builder's desire to sell off inventory; getting unsold properties off their books will produce a better financial statement at the end of their fiscal year. Selling off inventory at the end of the fiscal year also increases their gross sales volume, which can affect their stock value. However, the fiscal year for a home-building firm may not necessarily coincide with the calendar year. After you narrow down your search to three or four home-building firms, ask each one when its fiscal year ends.

It's easy enough to learn if a builder has any inventory houses at a particular site— the sales rep there will always know. Inventory houses do have their downside, however. The floor plan, flooring finishes and colors, and cabinetry will already have been selected and you will have to live with someone else's taste—the very reason that many people decide to buy a brand-new house in the first place.

There is another situation where timing can affect the price. If you are buying a townhouse, being in the right place at the right time can mean a price break. A builder's lender may insist that he sell five in a row of nine to get his construction loan. If you are that fifth buyer, you are in luck.

Bear in mind, however, that a price break on the base price for a brand-new house does not mean big bucks, because the net profit for most production builders is not that great—nationally, according to the National Association of Home Builders, it averages about 6 to 7 percent. If you demand a price reduction of 5 percent, you're basically asking the builder to build for free. Pushing him to negotiate away most of his profit can be shooting yourself in the foot—if there is no profit, the builder won't be around to service your house after you move in. Beating him up to get the best price means he may not be around to service the warranty and all those niggling little problems that *every* new house will have in the first year.

Many production builders flat out refuse to negotiate the base price. When a builder does negotiate, it is often when he artificially pumped up the price in the first place. One way to find out if a builder deals on the base price is to ask the residents who are already living in the subdivision if they got a deal on the base price or if the sales agent said, "This is the price." When you're asking, try to talk with residents who worked with the same sales agent you are talking with.

When a builder deals, someone may actually get a deal, but you can't be certain that that person will be you. Besides the financial issues, dealing can poison relations among neighbors in a new community as some discover that they paid more than others.

In a stand-alone project, dealing is less likely. But in a planned community with four or five builders grouped at each price point, the competition can become fierce, and dealing can be common.

a price break on options

Negotiating on option prices is a different story from the base price. With options, a builder's markup can range anywhere from 25 to 50 percent, and sometimes even more. There is plenty of room for maneuvering, unless the market is very hot. If buyers are lining up to sign on the dotted line, most builders will say, "The price is the price" for everything, including options.

The high markup for options, however, explains why builders often use them as incentives when things are slow—they're actually not giving that much away when they offer ten thousand dollars worth of options "free to buyers who purchase before the end of the month." As a Virginia builder said, "If a buyer only takes two thousand dollars worth of options, no money is made. But if the buyer takes twenty-five thousand worth of options, I make more money so I have more leeway."

As you bargain for options, though, strike for prices that reward both sides—you get some price reduction but the builder gets some reward for the extra work and cost. If you want the fifteen-hundred-dollar upgraded kitchen cabinets shown in the model, offer the builder eight hundred to cover the extra work plus some extra profit.

Most options must be built into the house as it goes up. But flooring is one that can readily be changed after you take possession. Before you sign up for the builder's upgraded carpets or hardwood, price out what several flooring stores would charge. The dimensions given in the builder's brochure may be sufficient to get a price; otherwise the flooring salesman will have to measure the model. You may find that the flooring dealers offer a better price, even if they must move your furniture after you have moved in.

When the builder is ready to move on, he will be selling his furnished model. Purchasing it is rarely a good idea, however, because it will be loaded with options and it will be wildly overimproved compared to all the other houses in the neighborhood. Unless the builder is offering a *very* large price reduction, you're better off buying a house and improving it to a degree commensurate with the other houses in the subdivision.

When negotiating anything, you have the most leverage *before* the contract is signed. Some home builders want you to order the options after the initial contract is ratified and construction has begun. But by that time, you're too far into the deal to back out, and you will have to accept the builder's prices on optional upgrades.

a**buyer's**agent

Some people enjoy haggling over prices, whether it's carpets, cars, or houses. But you may dread it, and want an experienced negotiator on your side when you are finally ready to sit down with a builder's on-site sales agent and negotiate a sales contract. Enter the buyer's agent, the first person you should engage for your new-house team. A buyer's agent is a real estate agent or broker who offers advice as you go through the process of visiting models, comparing features, sorting out options, picking a floor plan and a lot, and ultimately agreeing on a price.

Unlike the builder's on-site sales agent, who can only discuss the product he or she is selling, a buyer's agent will point out the pros and cons of many builders and communities. Moreover, the buyer agent's services are usually costless—in most cases, the builder pays the agent a sales commission, even though the buyer agent's loyalties are with the buyer and not the seller. (In the past, a real estate agent's "fiduciary responsibility" was always to the person paying him or her the sales commission, which traditionally has been the seller. That meant that an agent was legally obliged to disclose to a seller any financial information that you disclosed even when you enlisted the agent to work with you. Today, however, an agent must disclose at the time you engage him or her who she is representing. If this is you, her fiduciary responsibility is to you and not to the seller, even if the seller is paying the commission.)

But there is a caveat here: Most production-home builders stipulate that a buyer's agent must accompany you the *very first time* you visit a model and sign a visitor card in order to receive a sales commission. Some are slightly flexible on this point, and will still honor a buyer's agent and pay the agent a commission if the agent faxes ahead or communicates with the builder's sales agent within a short time of your visit.

If you like to go off on the spur of the moment and cruise models, this will put a crimp in your style. But balanced against what an experienced buyer's agent can offer, the loss of spontaneity is worth it for most buyers. A major advantage is a much more efficient housing search. Rather than spend several weekends just getting a sense of what's out there, you can quickly narrow the field in only one or two hours at the agent's office. An experienced agent will be keeping tabs on all the new communities in his or her sales territory, which in some parts of the country can easily number thirty-five or more. She can readily match the appropriate ones with your location, price, size, and feature preferences. Moreover, the agent should have brochures from all the new communities in her sales territory. If you are just starting out and clueless about the market, the agent can outline what size house to expect in your price range, what to expect in closing costs, and how you should get started in obtaining financing. If you are relocating, buyers' agents offer another advantage: Some will regularly check on construction progress and even take pictures for their clients.

How about help with the price of the house? This is entirely dependent on the market. When it's booming, the builders won't budge on the price at all. Even the occasional incentives such as "$10,000 worth of options for $5,000" or "free upgrades on appliances" that are common in slow times will disappear. If the market is so hot that builders are holding lotteries, as has happened in Southern California, some builders won't cooperate with buyer's agents at all. If that's the case in your area and you still want to use an agent, you will have to pay the commission, which is usually 2 to 3 percent of the purchase price.

When the market is slow and buyers are scarce, there's some latitude in the price, and the experienced agent will know how to ask for it. Most builders will still hold fast on the base price, but they will knock a bit off extras. "The more extras you put in, the more you can negotiate. If you put in twenty thousand dollars of options, you may get the builder to knock off five thousand," explains buyer's agent and Realtor Sandra Kessler of Montgomery County, Maryland. When sales are slow, a buyer's agent can also look up the sales record for a project and gauge how hungry the seller is.

There are two exceptions to a no-price-breaks policy, even in the hottest markets, for which a buyer's agent can be especially helpful. If someone else's deal falls through and the builder has an inventory house sitting on the ground, he'll negotiate on the base price as well as the options. The other exception is in large planned communities with four or five builders competing at the same price point. One of the builders may be willing to adjust the price or amenity package or pay some of the closing costs—whatever it takes to get the buyer to sign a contract. An agent who sells frequently in the same planned community will know which buttons to push for each builder.

Whether the market is hot or cold, a builder will always offer lower prices at the very beginning of a project, when there's no model. Many buyers are hesitant when there's nothing to see, but an experienced and resourceful agent will know how to get around this. "Since builders tend to use very similar floor plans, I may know of another builder's model that is very close, or a resale house that is very similar, " explains Miami Realtor Dennis Hoffman.

At the end of a phase in a large development, a production builder may also give a price break to close out and get financing for the next phase. A well-connected buyer's agent in frequent communication with a builders' on-site sales agents will often know before the general public when a builder is at this point and what buyers should expect. "If a builder has three or four houses left in phase one that he must sell before beginning phase two, he will very likely give a concession. To get a deal, you must take the house and lot that's available, and these may not be the most attractive. You must also have a loan preapproved and no contingency or house to sell first," says Los Angeles, California, Realtor Meredith McKenzie.

Another important service that a buyer's agent provides is clarifying exactly what's included in the standard, base price and what's an upgrade. This can be essential in markets where the buyers are so numerous the builder's on-site sales agent may not be able to give you all the time you need. An agent's clarification is especially helpful when the options are unusual. Buyer broker Sally Kelley of Ann Arbor, Michigan, says that in her market, upgrades not only include the finishes such as flooring, but also structural items such as the size of floor joists. Even the material used for interior trim around doors and windows at the base of the wall can be an upgrade. The standard trim in mid-market houses in Ann Arbor is plastic; wood trim is an upgrade.

Agents can also offer advice on options that will enhance resale. These vary from market to market, but on one point, buyers' agents agree: Colors should be neutral—beige, taupe, or stone—and steer clear of blue, which is always hard to resell.

Most production-builders have a sample room in the model where buyers can pick flooring finishes, cabinet styles, and upgrade features such as polished brass faucets. In some markets, however, a few of the national builders have large, centrally located design centers with many more items. But, cautions McKenzie, "In either case, the builder's salespeople are there to sell the best and most expensive upgrades. Buyers can get carried away and throw all common sense out the window. In five years no one wants to buy a bathroom with fuchsia colored fixtures. Resale buyers will take one look and knock twenty-five thousand off the price to redo it. A good agent will accompany buyers to the design center, rein them in, and advise, 'Here's how you can make the house your own but keep it more neutral for resale.'"

In addition to the house itself, a buyer's agent can offer invaluable advice on choosing a lot. "If it's a bad lot, resale is tough," Realtor Dennis Hoffman points out. "If a builder offers an incentive on a lot, it's usually because it's harder to sell. And if it's hard to sell the first time, it may be hard to resell."

areal-estateattorney

The second player to draft for your new-house team is a real-estate attorney. You may regard spending a few hundred dollars for a review of your sales contract as unnecessary. But prudence dictates a thorough explanation of the terms of a contract for a purchase of this magnitude, with bankrupting potential if it goes awry.

Equally important, along with the buyer's agent, you need another person on your side of the table who will be protecting your interests. *Almost without exception, a contract is written to favor the writer, in this case the builder.* You need to insure that this favoritism is not at your expense.

The attorney you hire, however, must have the appropriate expertise. Within the area of real-estate law, there are a number of subspecialties such as commercial leasing, landlord-tenant relations, and title searches. You want someone who specializes in residential real estate and new-home construction and who is knowledgeable about production-builder sales contracts or custom-home-builder sales contracts, depending on which you need.

If you plan to buy a new house in the same jurisdiction where you live now, you can ask friends or a buyer's agent for attorneys' names. If you are buying a new house in a different location, you should ask the bar association in the new place for a referral. The lawyer you hire must be familiar with the law *in the jurisdiction where you are purchasing the house.* Contract law varies from state to state and even between jurisdictions within the same state.

When you get two or three names, you should contact each one by phone. Your first question should be, "Does your firm represent my builder?" If the answer is yes, then you have to call another attorney, since an attorney who represents both sides of a contract has a conflict of interest. Your next question should be, "Have you previously reviewed contracts from my builder?" If the answer to this is yes, you may have found your attorney.

"If the attorney has already reviewed contracts with your builder, he will have already gotten as good a compromise as he will get. The attorney must review the contract every time for any changes, but with prior negotiations he knows how much the builder will accept," says attorney Robert McNees of Carol Stream, Illinois.

Bear in mind, however, that the attorney's job is to come up with compromises that are acceptable to *both* sides. To do this, the attorney must know what the builder will or won't do. "The builder can just get upset if you try to give the nth degree of protection for the buyer. No builder will accept that," McNees says.

An experienced real-estate attorney should be able to review a sales contract with a production builder in about an hour, especially if he or she is already familiar with those written by your proposed builder. A custom-home-builder contract is much more complicated and requires more time to review. But since your risk is much greater, it's that much more important.

The time to have an attorney review your sales contract is *before* you sign it. If waiting means losing out on a builder's about-to-expire sales incentive such as the twelve-thousand-dollar finished-basement upgrade included in the base price, you need to write in this critical phrase: "This contract is subject to review and approval by purchaser's attorney for [X number of] days. If the purchasers' attorney disapproves of the contract, it will be canceled. If the attorney approves the contract, it will be enforced." You fill in the number of days—insist on at least five business days. This clause will enable you to get the special deal and still meet with an attorney to get his or her input.

the**private**home**inspector**

On that final walk-through before signing the papers and taking possession of their brand-new house, observant buyers will catch paint drips and scratches on a hardwood floor. Thorough buyers will know to check all the doors to make sure that they open and close tightly. Very thorough buyers will check all the windows to see if they open easily and if the tilt feature really works on the double-hung type that makes the outside surface easier to clean.

But only an experienced hand with years of construction under his belt would know to look up the chimney flue—a favorite place to stash scrap lumber—or take note of shortcuts that can compromise the structure or the owner's comfort—missing air seals, shortchanged insulation, or skimped nails for the vinyl siding (if there aren't enough nails, a strong wind will blow it off). Enter the private home inspector, another key player, whether you're purchasing a production or a custom-built house. Once a rarity on a residential construction site, private home inspectors are increasingly common.

Most buyers who engage a home inspector do it at the end of construction, when the house is finished. You would be better served hiring one *before construction begins.* A home inspector's expertise and experience can be invaluable as the house goes up. If a defect is found early on, it will be much easier and less costly to repair—fixing the foundation soon after its poured is a lot easier than after the roof is on.

If you are working with a custom or semi-custom builder, bring an inspector on board when the house is still in the planning stage and there's an opportunity to modify the design or specification list. While you may be well versed in cabinetry and flooring finishes, how knowledgeable are you about product reliability when it comes to framing materials, roofing, windows, and all those other items that are critical to structural integrity and comfort? A home inspector can also review the building plans for those prosaic details that can be overlooked, such as flashing, on-site runoff, and a good airflow in the house. Your custom builder's design and specs may require only minor modifications or none at all, but having an outside review can have a calming effect.

If you're working with an architect, he or she will have ironed out the construction details, specified all the materials, and made the call on quality issues. However, if you are not paying the architect to monitor construction or if you want more frequent monitoring than the architect can provide, you should hire a home inspector to make regular on-site visits.

If you are buying a production-built house, once the house begins to go up you should have a home inspector review the construction at four critical points:

♦ The first review should be done after the footings, foundation walls, and drain tiles are in, but before the dirt is backfilled against the basement foundation walls, which will cover all this up.

- The second review, generally referred to as the "pre-drywall" visit, should be done after the framing is up, the windows are in, and the electrical, plumbing, and heating and cooling systems have been installed but are still exposed. The exterior grading should also be checked at this time because a builder will be a lot more willing to fix it before any sod or landscaping have been planted.

- The third review is an insulation check; some inspectors do this and others instruct the home owners on what to look for.

- The fourth review is the final walk-through.

In the course of checking the construction, home inspectors may pick up building-code infractions that a building official may miss, especially since they work at a slower pace than most municipal building officials, who frequently perform as many as thirty inspections in a single day.

An experienced home inspector can also help buyers in negotiating repairs with the builder. A code violation must be fixed, but in many cases the things that an inspector finds are workmanship issues that a builder may or may not agree to address. Knowing this, a good home inspector will help a buyer prioritize and decide "what is worth going to war over," said home inspector J. D. Grewell of Silver Spring, Maryland.

Many home inspectors have had hands-on experience in construction, and buyers should insist on it. Some have college degrees in fields related to construction such as engineering and architecture. A few have passed the same code-certification examinations that the building-code officials are required to pass. After fifteen years in construction and fifteen in home inspecting, Joseph C. Walker, a home inspector in the Maryland suburbs of Washington, D.C., observes that it also helps to have strong diplomatic skills, a thick skin, and an eye for the telling detail.

"A good home inspector needs the skill of a diplomat to deal with the site superintendent's frequent hostility, the skin of a rhinoceros—you can't be afraid to look stupid if you encounter a new product, and you have to be able to take the heat if a superintendent vigorously disagrees with you—and the eye of a detective. A subtle clue often belies a significant problem, and one clue often leads to another. Since you don't have time to check all of the million and one details in a new house, you have to look for clues to tell you where to focus your attention. For example, a visible, basic mistake in a furnace installation probably means the installer didn't know what he was doing, and the whole system needs a closer look," Walker says.

A credential to look for when hiring a home inspector is membership in the American Society of Home Inspectors, known as ASHI. This credential indicates that the individual has completed at least 250 home inspections and passed a rigorous exam. ASHI members are also required to take continuing-education courses to keep abreast of new products, construction techniques, and research on building and product failures. Though some home inspectors and ASHI members specialize in new construction, buyers are better served by those who routinely look at both new and old houses. Such a person will know which items will cause problems in the future if not addressed immediately. Another less widely held credential to look for is membership in NABIE, the National Academy of Building Inspection Engineers. NABIE is affiliated with the National Society of Professional Engineers, and its members are licensed, professional engineers.

The working style of home inspectors can vary. Some provide a checklist of their findings, some write a narrative report, and some do a combination of both. Before hiring one, you should ask to see several of his reports to get an idea of what to expect. You should also ask how soon after an inspection you can expect to get the report. Some look at everything and some leave cosmetic issues like gauged floors, scuffed paint, and nail pops to the home buyers. They check appliances, the building systems—structure, plumbing, electric, heating and cooling—and the exterior of the house, including grading and paving.

Some inspectors charge by the hour and some by the size or price of the house. The inspection of the footings, foundation walls, and drain tiles, as well as of the insulation, will be short because there won't be much to see. But the pre-drywall inspections and the presettlement "punch list" can take three to four hours, depending on the size of the house.

Centex, Kaufman & Broad, and US Homes, three of the largest home-building firms in the United States, and many other builders welcome a home inspector as another set of eyes that gives a buyer a peace of mind. But not every builder embraces this idea, so you must discuss it before you sign a sales contract and include the details such as the number and type of inspections you want in a contract addendum.

You should also note that getting your home inspector there at the right time for each inspection is your responsibility, not the builder's. You need to monitor the progress of the house so you can tell the inspector when to come and take a look—nothing is more disheartening than to find that the foundations have been covered over with the backfill before the inspector had a chance to inspect them.

protectyourselffrom
constructiondelays

When you're flush with the heady decision to buy a new house, you're not entertaining the possibility that it won't be finished when the builder said it would. But your builder will allow himself plenty of time and then some to build your house. And this will be stated in the sales contract. Although the actual time required to build the house may only be four months, the builder will usually give himself a year to cover all possible contingencies. However, in some jurisdictions, a builder may legally give himself as long as two years or face no time limit at all. For most production builders, the delivery date stated in the sales contract is non-negotiable.

If you tailor the sale date of your present house to the builder's verbal promise of a delivery date of your new one, but the builder hasn't finished yet, he will consider this your problem, not his. If you are saddled with extra expenses for storage, temporary living quarters, and having to move twice, that's too bad.

The only way to avoid this scenario is to make a contingency plan *before* you sign a sales contract, either for your new house or your old one. "Put yourself in a position to stay in your old house until the new one is ready," advises Gaithersburg, Maryland, attorney Jim Savitz. "Add a provision to the sales contract for your existing house to delay settlement if your new one isn't finished. Otherwise, if you agree to be out by July 1 and then the builder says, 'August 1,' you are stuck."

One way to stay in your existing house is to sell it to your buyer as planned, but then lease it back for a specified period of time. If you want to do this, a residential lease-back agreement should be included with the sales contract, advises Los Angeles attorney Paula Reddish Zinnemann, who is currently the commissioner for the Department of Real Estate for the State of California. While such a lease-back proposal helps you, it can discourage potential buyers for your house, points out Miami attorney Dennis Haber. "People move because they have to move. Not too many want to buy your house and rent it [back to you]. They're buying because they want to move into it."

Counters Zinnemann, "This can be a question of 'what will the market bear?' If you have a buyer who won't accept a contingency relating to the possibility that your new house won't be ready, is there another buyer right behind him or her who will? It is also possible that the buyer of your old house could offer you such a great deal that it's worth a move to an interim place until your new house is ready."

If the move-in date is very important, another strategy is simply to buy a house that is close to completion. You'll have fewer choices, but it will be completed on time.

Even if a builder gives every appearance of refusing to negotiate on anything, the contract is not written in stone, and you can always ask. For example, you can add a clause stating that if the house is not finished by the builder's expected completion date, you as the buyer have the option to cancel the contract, getting back both your initial deposit and any additional deposit moneys given for options and upgrades. Since this could leave the builder with an unfinished house that he has to sell to someone else, he's more likely to agree if you do not select wild colors, unusual finishes, or anything else that will have limited appeal to other buyers.

At this point, you might well be asking: How long does it normally take to build a house and what factors can delay completion?

Although three or four months is the standard time frame for constructing a production-built house, if a market is very active, a builder may have a long list of houses to build before yours, as well as problems with labor and material shortages. The most common reason for delays, however, is the weather. The 120-day time frame already takes this into account, but if your new house will be built in an area with severe seasonal weather conditions, the builder might tack another two months onto his verbal estimates. The additional six months to a year or even longer that he builds into the sales contract is just added protection against any unforeseen contingency.

Besides the weather and the vagaries of the market, a builder's own circumstance can affect his ability to deliver a house in a timely fashion. Before you get very serious about a particular house and a particular builder, a few simple questions can help clarify when the house will be finished, and whether to move forward with the deal or move on:

- ◆ Have you built in this jurisdiction before? If not, there may be unanticipated delays because building-permit and inspection procedures may differ from what the builder is used to.

- ◆ Does he have a building permit for your house? If he does, he can start to dig the hole tomorrow. If he doesn't, there can be a significant delay, as some jurisdictions can take four to twelve weeks to issue a permit.

Once a sales contract is signed and the house started, buyers themselves can have a hand in causing delays. Deciding to alter a wall or add a closet can throw off the schedule; so can foot-dragging on items such as cabinet selections. Although most buyers assume these go in at the end, it still takes another thirty days to finish the house after the cabinets are installed.

While the builder protects himself in case of delays, he is as eager to finish building as you are. The clock on his construction loan starts ticking as soon as he starts digging. Any delays will cost him and eat into his profits.

third-party ten-year limited warranties

Many production-home builders offer third-party ten-year limited warranties on the houses that they sell. This can have a tonic effect on anxiety-laden buyers, about to make the biggest purchase of their lives. But with a careful reading of the fine print, you will realize that the emphasis should be on the "limited" aspect of these warranties, not the "ten years."

A quick look at the money numbers also indicates that these warranties won't cover much. For a $200 thousand house, a builder can pay anywhere from two hundred to fifteen hundred dollars for a limited ten-year warranty. Since the warranty has a "ten-year tail," as they say in the insurance business, it's clearly not going to cover much.

During the first two of the ten years, the builder is responsible for the warranted items. The warranty companies will step in then only if the builder refuses to make a repair, doesn't repair it to the buyer's satisfaction, or goes bankrupt. The warranty company becomes directly involved only in years three through ten.

Over the ten years, the coverage decreases dramatically and quickly. During the initial year, a long list of workmanship items such as leaking gutters, warped doors, and loose or buckling carpet is covered. In most states, the builder is legally required to warrant these anyway. The threshold for repair by the warranty company, however, is generally much higher than a builder's. For example, some warranties state that a drywall crack will be repaired only if it is more than 1/8 inch wide. When you realize that a crack this wide may be visible from twenty-five feet away, if the wall is a light color, you begin to understand what "limited" means.

During both the first and second years, certain parts of the mechanical systems such as air ducts, electric wiring, plumbing pipes, water supply, and clogged sewers are covered. For the entire ten years, only the failure of components with "major structural defect potential" deemed to affect the safety of the building occupants are included: roof-framing members, floor-framing members, bearing walls, bearing columns, headers or lintels above doors and windows, girders, load-bearing beams, and foundation walls and footings. Some load-bearing elements, such as roof sheathing and subflooring, are excluded because, contrary to what you might think, these are not considered *major* structural elements. Other elements that most buyers would consider integral to the house such as interior partition walls, doors, windows, drywall, and any type of exterior siding are also excluded because these are not load-bearing elements.

Even elements with "major structural defect potential" are not covered unless they pass the structural-defects test. Some of the warranties have criteria based on an "unlivable, uninhabitable" standard, rather than a precise measurement. The damage must:

1. occur to one or more of the specified-load bearing elements

2. be sufficient to cause the load-bearing element to fail

3. render the house unsafe and uninhabitable

These can be hard standards to meet. It can be difficult at times to discern if an element has failed, and "uninhabitable" can mean it must be condemned by a local jurisdiction.

Some warranties give precise warranty tolerances. Although this would seem to give the buyer more protection, it can actually end up protecting the builder and the warranty company more than the buyer, because the allowable tolerances, like the ⅛-inch-wide crack, can be to the far side of acceptable.

There are other aspects of the warranties that can further limit the protection offered. For example, the warranties clearly state that they cover only completed dwellings. "If a window leaks in the first year because the builder failed to install flashing or did it improperly, the warranty company may say that the house is not a 'completed building' and therefore is not covered," said John Nethercut, an assistant attorney general with the State of Maryland who handles consumer complaints about builder's warranties.

Given the obvious limitation of the warranties, what happens in practice? In the real world of home building, reputation and referrals of satisfied customers are everything. A reputable builder will repair items at lower tolerances than warranties may specify. For example, toward the end of the first year when the house has gone through a complete cycle of heating and cooling, many builders will repair all the visible hairline cracks in the drywall resulting from settlement or shrinkage of the wood framing. They know that if they fixed only those cracks that exceeded 1/8 inch in width, their buyers would be screaming. Likewise, warranties cite tolerances for bows of walls, but a reputable builder knows that if you can see it, you should fix it.

Clearly, the reputation of the builder is the best warranty of all. Richard Rivin, vice president of LIFE, INC., a Chesapeake, Virginia, construction and consulting firm that investigates building failures, says that in his experience, "Historically, a good builder is more important than the words in a warranty. But even with a very reputable builder you could still have trouble with one unit, a freak occurrence; just like with cars, you can always get the lemon." As one Maryland home builder puts it, "Some houses just have bad karma. We don't know what it is; all the houses were built the same, but something happened to one." In such an unhappy event, you need to know that the builder will stand by you until the problem is fixed.

A reputable builder will not only stand behind his product, he will go back and fix structural defects that occur after the warranty expires. To find out how firmly the builder you are considering stands behind his product, ask some of his buyers. If you want to be really thorough, visit a project that is four or five years old. Many of the original purchasers may have moved, but you should still be able to find enough of them to get an idea.

Since a reputable builder will often exceed and certainly match what is offered in the limited warranties, why do they offer them at all? In a few jurisdictions, they are required by law. But the more common reason is that the ten-year limited warranties are a good sales tool that can help calm nervous buyers. In some instances, builders offer them because the competition does. Unstated but certainly advantageous to the buyer: If the builder goes bankrupt, the warranty provides initial coverage for workmanship, materials, and mechanical systems and longer-term coverage for big-ticket, catastrophic structural failures.

Absent the ten-year limited warranty, the only warranty protection you have is the legally required one that in most jurisdictions is only twelve months (in some states, certain parts of the structure such as the foundations may be warranted for a longer period). If builder errors are not caught in the municipal building inspections, or by your private home inspector, or within the first twelve months, your only recourse may be to alert the local building department and hope that they can put "practical pressure" on the builder. If he is still active in your jurisdiction, he has an incentive to cooperate because the local building department issues the COs—the certificates of occupancy. Without a CO, a builder can't sell the house to you and get his money out. Absent this pressure, however, you can have a real problem.

This lack of consumer protection is yet another reason why dealing with a builder with a proven track record and a rock-solid reputation is so important.

buyer's remorse

After you've finally signed on that dotted line, you may find yourself nearly incapacitated with buyer's remorse—unremitting doubt that you will like the house, that you got a good price, that your friends and family will like it, that you will be able to sell it. Most people get over this and go on to enjoy the process, and experienced sales and buyer's agents can offer reassurance. But you may be one of the few who has a hard time trusting your judgment in making the biggest purchase of your life.

One solution for some buyers is rewriting the contract for a smaller house or cutting back on some of those pricey options. But some buyers just get completely derailed. When this happens, usually before the contract has been ratified—that is, signed and dated by all parties—some builders will return the deposit check upon meeting with the customer. They know from experience that trying to work with someone who is that unhappy is impossible for both parties.

Of course, you are not going into this with the expectation that you will become unglued when the contract is signed. Nonetheless, you should ask the sales agent what the builder's policy is regarding buyer's remorse, or discuss this with a buyer's agent if you are working with one.

In addition to the individual builder's discretion, new-house buyers in some states such as Maryland and Virginia can legally cancel their contracts under certain circumstances. In both states, if the property is within a development with a mandatory homeowner's association that all buyers are obliged to join, the builder must furnish buyers with pertinent and current association documents detailing all property restrictions (for example, no fence in the front yard) and regulations (for example, shoveling snow is the individual homeowner's responsibility). The buyers have a stipulated but brief period to review these documents. During this review period, they have the right to cancel their sales contract.

How do you find a buyer's agent? Some agents work exclusively with buyers. Most represent both buyers or sellers, but not in the same transaction. You can look in the Yellow Pages for a "buyer broker" who specializes in representing buyers, call a traditional real estate broker and ask for an agent who represents buyers, look on the Internet, or get names from friends and neighbors.

tipsfromthetrade: finding a buyer's agent

Since purchasing a new house differs significantly from a resale, confirm in that first phone call that the agent regularly works with such buyers. And since much of the agent's advice will be about resale issues, you also need to confirm that the agent regularly works on resales that are two to ten years old. Agents and builders both say that projecting trends farther than ten years is iffy. If you expect to be in your house longer than that, the resale aspect is less critical.

Finding a buyer's agent who has worked as an on-site sales agent for a builder and understands a builder's mindset is a definite plus. A credential to look for is ABR, Accredited Buyer's Representative. This means the agent or broker is a graduate of a certification program run by the National Association of Realtors.

Arrange to meet the agent at his or her office so that you can check out the support services as well as the agent. If the office appears disorganized and there's no receptionist to promptly answer the phone, the agent may not be able to give you the service that you need.

To gauge whether or not you and the agent are a good match, what questions should you ask? Meredith McKenzie, a Realtor in Los Angeles, California, for more than twenty years, offers these suggestions: "Your first question should be 'How long has the agent been in the business?' The more experience, the better; but agents generally agree that it takes at least two years to be effective. Next, ask how many buyer transactions the agent closed in the last six months, and of these how many were resales and how many were new houses? If you already know what area or builder you are interested in, ask if the agent has worked with builders in that area. If the agent says no, ask for a referral for someone who does. Since the agent makes money on a referral, he should be happy to give you one. Next, ask for a list of previous clients who bought houses within the last year and call at least three of them.

"When you talk with the former clients, ask them, 'Were you happy or unhappy? Would you choose this agent again?' The more specific you can be in your questions, the more you will learn about the level of service the agent provides, which is what truly differentiates one agent from another. For example, ask, 'Did the agent walk you through the paperwork and explain the loan process? Did the agent walk you through the sales contract? Did they bring up negotiating points? Did they help explain the financing terms and what other costs would be involved in the transaction, such as closing costs? Did they discuss other costs that you will likely incur in furnishing the house, such as window treatments? Did the agent accompany you to the builder's design center to help you pick out stuff? Was the agent there at the preclosing walk-through when you assessed the condition of the house and drew up a to-do punch list?'"

On this last point, McKenzie says that she always recommends that buyers hire a private home inspector for the walk-through, but he tends to focus more on the guts and structure while agents look at the practical and aesthetic. "Do all the doors and windows open and close? Is there caulk around the bathtub? You can't have too many eyes to look at a house, and we all have our blind spots."

Most buyer's agents request that their clients sign an exclusive agreement for a fixed period—usually sixty days—and often within a certain fixed geographic area. Many agents prefer a more formalized contract that also states that any houses shown to you by the buyer's agent must be purchased through the agent's broker to ensure that the agent gets the commission. The contract may also stipulate that if you visit a model home on your own and don't make clear that you have a buyer's agent (and hence the builder's sales agent won't honor your buyer's agent), you will owe your agent a commission if you buy a house from that builder.

Some contracts also address the possibility that you may not find what you want in the new-house market and decide to buy an existing house. If you elect to purchase one directly from the owner (otherwise known as a FSBO—a "for sale by owner" transaction), you will owe the agent a sales commission.

A buyer's agent may ask you to sign a contract on first meeting, but some prefer to sign a contract after an initial outing and a sense that a comfort level on both sides has been established. If the agent that you decide to work with requires a contract, read it carefully *before* signing.

sales contract

After a long and thorough search, you're down to the sales contract. You may be assuming that this is just a pro forma document because with the model there, you know what you are getting. But you would be wrong.

The production builder's sales contract reflects his emphasis on volume and speed. It is written so that the builder can build your house as quickly and efficiently as possible. If a decision has to be made on the spot, the builder wants to do it and move on without debate.

For example, if he must shorten up your garage by two feet so that your House B will fit within the required setbacks on your Lot 35, so be it. The contract will say that the house will be "substantially similar" to the model, but it will not define this precisely. Of course, the builder should tell you if he has to lop off two feet from the garage, but the contract is written so that he is not legally obliged to do so. If the garage dimension is especially important because lopping off two feet means your car won't fit, you need to explicitly state this in an addendum to your contract.

If a product that the builder would normally use is not available or no longer manufactured, he will want to replace it with something similar; if, for example, your chosen floor tile is unavailable, he will substitute what he thinks looks similar. This, of course, is a subjective judgment, and you may not like the substitute. The builder should tell you that he is switching tiles, but his contract will say he's not obliged to tell you anything. If you really care about the tile and want to be consulted about a substitution, you must explicitly state this in an addendum.

To clarify the meaning of "substantially similar," "the builder reserves the right to make substitutions of comparable quality," and many other phrases in the sales contract detailing exactly what the builder will and will not do, you need to engage a real-estate attorney who is experienced with production-builder sales contracts in your area. An attorney can also raise issues that are not in the contract, such as how to address the possibility that your house will be finished when it's too cold to pour the concrete for the driveway or install the landscaping.

You may resist the idea of an attorney review because you think it will be too expensive, and you'd rather put that money toward upgrading the carpet. However, a contract review for a production builder contract may cost less than you think. The attorney would charge for his time to review the contract, explain it to you, and compose appropriate addenda. When you contact an attorney who routinely reviews production-builder contracts, tell him who your builder is and ask what he usually charges for reviewing this builder's contracts. The attorney may already have worked with other clients of this same builder and be very familiar with the contracts, so his or her review may not take as long. On average, an attorney's review for a production-builder contract should be less than five hundred dollars, and some attorneys will reduce their fees for first-time buyers.

Much of the attorney's review will simply be explaining the terms of the contract, which can be confusing to the uninitiated. The willingness of the builder to make any changes generally depends on the state of the housing market, and the attorney will know this. When the housing market is hot, the builder won't be amenable to much. But even if you won't get many changes, demystifying the contract for yourself is critical, and your contract review will send a signal to the builder that you are a careful and conscientious buyer.

When the market is cold, everything is negotiable, but even then only up to a point. "There are limits on how much a builder will modify a contract," says attorney Robert

McNees of Carol Stream, Illinois. "A lawyer cannot impose terms that a builder won't accept. The goal is to preserve the transaction so that everyone gets what they want. The builder must have wiggle room or he won't enter into the contract."

Specific details of production-builder sales contracts may vary from state to state and jurisdiction to jurisdiction within a state, but as you go from one region of the country to another, the contracts are remarkably similar in certain respects. The listed seller may be a company you never heard of, the house you purchase will be only "substantially similar" to the model you studied so carefully, and no materials are specified.

whois**the**seller?

Many buyers are surprised to find that the name of the builder noted on their sales contract is not ABC Homes, whose name is prominently written on all marketing material and posted around the model house, but Little Pine Tree, a legally separate corporate entity.

The significance to a purchaser is that when the project is completed, the builder may fold his tent and disband the separate corporate entity, which can often be a limited-liability company, or LLC. Since your contract is with a firm that no longer exists, you may have a problem if you have a warranty issue. If you have a really big problem after the warranty has expired, effectively, you can't sue for damages. With a disbanded company, there are no assets and no one to collect from.

If ABC Homes is a reputable builder, the firm will stand behind its houses and address problems that affect appearance and resale potential or structural integrity, even though it is not legally obliged to do so. But "if ABC is on the contract, you are in much better shape to get it fixed. You should ask why they are not on the contract," advises Orange County, California, attorney Judith Deming.

"Unfortunately," adds Gaithersburg, Maryland, attorney Jim Savitz, "most builders who do this will not let you put their name back on. So besides asking why ABC's name is not on the contract, you need to check the local warranty laws and check for written evidence that the builder will still be responsible for problems. For example, in some jurisdictions, whoever pulls the building permit is responsible for the warranty work. If Little Pine Tree is not a licensed builder and ABC pulls the permit, then it will still have warranty responsibility. If the sales agent says, 'You can trust us to build a good house,' your position should be 'trust but verify.'"

This practice of listing a separate corporate entity as the seller varies from market to market. In some places all builders, large and small, do this. In others the large, national firms will put their name on the sales contract as the seller, but the small, local ones will not. And in a very few markets, almost no builders list a separate corporation as the seller.

whathouse**are**you**buying?**

Most sales contracts have words to the effect that the house that you are purchasing will be "substantially similar to the builder's model," but "construction of the house may have changes from the precise dimensions of the interior and the exterior." "Substantially similar," however, is not defined. All the lawyers said that you won't get the builder to qualify or quantify what precisely is meant by "substantially similar" or to modify the clause to say something like "the house should be 3,200 square feet within 1 to 2 percent as measured from outside to outside." But if a particular dimension is very important, for example your garage must be at least twenty-three feet long to accommodate your Chevy Suburban or the clearance when the garage door is open must be at least seven feet to accommodate your Ford Expedition, insist on adding this in a contract addendum, Savitz says. Likewise, if you have an unusual piece of furniture and require that the family room be at least fifteen feet wide as shown in the model, also note this in an addendum, he adds.

This part of the contract may also have a number of disclosure statements. Scott Jackson, an Orange County, California, attorney who prepares sales contracts for builders, advises buyers to read these carefully because "the disclosures describe what is and is not included in your home purchase. The basic home the builder is selling, typically, will not include all of the options and upgrades shown in the model homes. The model is not what the builder is selling. It is the 'potential' a buyer can realize if the buyer is willing to spend the extra money to purchase the upgrades shown in the model."

whatmaterials?

What materials is the builder using for your new house? At best, the sales contract will state that the materials, like the house, will be "substantially similar" to the model. The sales brochure will usually include a partial list that describes things only generically, for example, "vinyl siding." But as a buyer you need a very specific description—"Wolverine American Legend Double 4 Clapboard Siding, ALD4." The builder will have a detailed specification list that identifies the siding as well as every other material used in the house, and you should ask for this.

Depending on the market, the builder may or may not give you the detailed list. In Southern California, where buyers have been known to line up, "The sales agent in the model will not have this kind of information and, with a line outside, would be reluctant to give it, as would the builder. The best you can do is to look carefully," advises Newport Beach attorney James M. Parker.

But, McNees contends, "it's a good idea contractually to attach the specs. You want to make sure that everybody agrees what is to be done. The more specific, it's a better contract situation."

Moreover, most sales contracts for new houses are exclusionary—they exclude everything except the contract and what's attached to the contract—points out Alexandria, Virginia, attorney Beau Brincefield. He advises his clients to attach the detailed specification list, the elevations, and floor plans shown in the sales brochures, and any marketing materials to the sales contract and reference these in an addendum.

"If the builder says no, you can't put on a detailed spec list or plans, ask why not,'" Savitz urges. If the builder will not let you attach the spec list, floor plans, and other pertinent material, Savitz suggests creating a paper trail by sending the builder a certified letter with all these materials and a letter stating "'I bought the house from you relying on this material.' This puts the onus on the builder to reply if it's not true."

In Bloomingdale, Illinois, where attorney Terry Eland practices, builders routinely have a detailed plan and specifications on file that buyers can examine. He always requests that two copies of the plans and specifications be signed and initialed, with a copy given to the buyer to avoid any later confusion. Most builders will not agree to give the buyer the signed copy of the construction documents, and will only incorporate the documents by reference. Even if a builder does give buyers a signed set, Eland still advises buyers to go to the builder's office and study the plans and specs carefully, to make sure that they are getting what they think they are.

Many, if not most, of the details shown in the model are upgrades and will not be included in the standard house. Besides the more obvious ones such as crown moldings and chair rails in the dining room, the pocket doors and all the mirrors in the master bathroom may also be upgrades. This is one aspect of the sale where a buyer's agent can be particularly helpful, Eland says.

substitutions

A production builder's sales contract will state words to the effect that the builder "reserves the right to substitute materials or equipment of comparable quality (in builder's sole discretion)." Since the clock on the builder's construction loan is running while he's building your house, time is definitely money. The builder wants to adhere to a fast-paced schedule, so in theory the substitution clause is not unreasonable.

The builder, however, is the final arbiter of what constitutes "comparable quality," especially if he won't give you a detailed specification list to use as a basis of comparison. As a general rule, a reputable builder will inform his buyers when a major substitution is made (for example, vinyl siding is substituted for aluminum siding), but not when a minor one is, such as a different bathroom light fixture.

Ann Arbor, Michigan, attorney Sherry Chin says she always suggests that buyers add a clause stating that the buyers must be notified of *any* substitution, but in most cases the builder doesn't want to be bothered and won't agree. You may, however, get the builder to agree not to substitute a certain specific item, Savitz says. "If there's a particular item you can't live without, and without it you don't want the house, you may get the builder to agree on that one item. But you need to be very specific—for example, you want the exact same chandelier as shown in the model."

Substitutions can be problematic aesthetically, Eland points out. "If you are building a contemporary-styled house, you don't want colonial-styled cabinets in the kitchen." His solution is to modify the substitution clause to say that it will not apply to things with aesthetic value and that any changes in this regard, such as kitchen cabinets, other cabinets, flooring, and trim, must have purchaser's input and approval.

You also don't want the wrong color on the cabinets, so attorney McNees adds a substitution clause stating that the substituted item must also be of comparable color.

lotand**site**plan

The sales contract for a production builder will usually state that the location of the dwelling on the lot will be determined by the builder. Since he must conform to local setback requirements as well as existing lot contours, this is reasonable. But the builder may end up placing the house on the lot in a way that you won't like.

To prevent any unpleasant surprises on this score, however, you should state in a contract addendum that the contract will not be finalized until you have reviewed and approved the builder's proposed site plan. This is especially important if you want to build House C with a sunroom and deck on a lot where the builder intended to put House B, which has a radically different footprint. To get House C to fit may require only a simple reversal of the plan (putting the garage on the left instead of the right), but the plan reversal may produce unwanted results. You may lose that dramatic circular driveway you really wanted, or end up with an "unusual orientation," or even worse, lose the view from the family room that you paid a lot premium to get.

Even if you want to purchase House B on a lot where the builder intended to put a House B, the fine print of the contract can state that the builder reserves the right to reverse the plan. You should insist on an addendum stating that you have final site plan approval, no matter which plan or lot you want to buy.

Since the lots may vary in size or shape, the setback requirements may also affect the overall dimensions of the house or particular rooms, such as the garage. If a particular dimension, such as the length of garage, is especially important, you need to check this detail on the builder's proposed site plan.

Some firms require buyers to sign off on a proposed site plan before the firm will begin construction, but you should firm up the site plan *before* you sign the contract. If House C won't fit and that's what you want, you may have to pick a different lot or move on.

trees

The sales contract will likely state that the builder shall remove any trees on the lot that may interfere with construction, and that the builder is not responsible for any damage or destruction to any remaining trees. If trees are important, get the builder to walk the lot with you and mark the ones that will have to go, so that you will have an idea of what the lot will look like after the house is finished. When a lot is small, this is especially important because the builder has to have room for the construction equipment to maneuver, and will remove trees from a larger area than the house itself will occupy.

If you are choosing a particular lot because of its mature trees, bring in an arborist to help you assess the situation (for more on this, see Chapter 10). If you are paying a premium for trees that will be lost to construction, you may want to choose another lot or get the builder to reduce the price of this one.

If a large number of trees must be cut down and you want new trees planted after the construction is complete, include this in the contract addendum and be explicit, stating the number of trees, their species, and their maturity (this is usually stated in terms of their diameter). The builder may regard this as an option and charge you for it, but you may be able to make the case that they're a replacement for what he's cutting down, especially if he's charging extra for a treed lot in the first place.

deliverydate

The builder will give himself as long as possible and then some to get the house completed, in some markets as long as two years. When the market is very hot, you won't have any luck getting him to change the delivery date or even to add a clause that states that if the house is not finished on the promised date, you will be refunded your deposit money.

Even a builder who promises to deliver the house in 120 days will simply not allow himself to be penalized for not delivering the house on the promised date for delays due to weather, acts of God, or shortages of materials or labor. You can get tied up indefinitely, waiting for your house to be finished. If the interest rates go up while you are waiting, you may not be able to qualify for the mortgage, even though you qualified when you negotiated the sales contract. Should this happen, you will lose your deposit money as well as the house. This is simply a risk that a buyer of a brand-new house incurs, McNees says. The only thing you can do to protect yourself is "to keep your earnest deposit money as low as possible and not put everything on the razor's edge to buy the house."

You also need to develop a backup plan that will allow you to stay in your present house as long as possible. For more on this, see Chapter 11.

closing

Some sales contracts stipulate that the builder is required to give only five days notice of the date of settlement, at which time the buyer assumes ownership. You should insist on changing this to have adequate time to arrange for a move. Since the builder will be monitoring construction carefully, he will know the general date well in advance, and he should be willing to give at least fourteen days notice, but thirty days would greatly facilitate your move-in.

Before you sign those final papers and assume ownership, you may want a private home inspector acting in your behalf to do a walk-through and make up a punch list of all incomplete items that the builder must come back and finish. But, attorney Chin points out, typically the contract says the builder will do a final walk-through with the buyer. Some builders will balk at letting a private home inspector hired by the buyer do a separate inspection, so she always recommends that this be included in an addendum. Sometimes the builder wants to approve the inspector because he had a bad prior experience with an especially picky inspector, which is a reasonable condition.

If the weather is good, the punch-list items are usually minor. When the weather is bad, and it's too cold to pour concrete for driveways and sidewalks or install any landscaping, the unfinished work can be substantial. To ensure that the concrete work, which can affect the value of the house if left unfinished, really will be completed, some lenders require the buyers to escrow as much as ten thousand dollars. That is, the buyers must set aside ten thousand to pay for the concrete work. If the buyers don't comply, they won't get the mortgage and the house.

This possibility will not be stated in a sales contract. But attorney Eland said such a nightmare scenario can happen in his area with cold winters. He suggests adding a clause to the contract that the builder will put up escrow funds for weather-delayed items if the lender requires it. When alerted to the possibility that the lender's escrow demands could scotch the deal—if the purchasers can't come up with the money, the builder will be stuck with selling the house—most will acquiesce and agree to put up the escrow funds, he says.

Other than weather-related items, however, production builders will invariably refuse to escrow any funds for punch-list items because they know from experience that after the buyers move in, the punch list will lengthen, Savitz says. Most contracts also state that the buyer cannot delay closing over punch-list items.

Where it is customary for the seller to provide a title insurance policy, as it is in Michigan, Chin says the contract should require the seller to provide a title insurance policy in the amount of the final sale price. To get this, you may have to add an addendum. The title insurance will not necessarily protect the purchaser against construction liens (mechanic's liens) because most title companies exclude such coverage in new construction. In Michigan, the buyer has to look to the reputation of the builder on construction liens. In some states, such as Maryland, however, a production builder, not the buyer, is responsible for all the mechanic's lien waivers.

Before the buyer is required to close, the contract should also require the builder to produce written verification of approval by all governmental inspectors, and this may be another addendum item, Chin says. In Michigan, a certificate of occupancy is also required.

Many production builders will offer to pay some of the closing costs, but only if you use their preferred lender or title company. A builder's sales agent may assert that the builder's lender's rates are very competitive, but they may not be, and you should check the rates offered by other lenders. You may find that when you factor in the builder's incentives, he does offer the best deal. But if you could use his incentives with a different lender, you may get an even better deal. In an up market, a builder will insist that his incentives are not portable; in a down market, some builders will let you use their incentives with a different lender. To do this at closing, you must negotiate it at the time you sign the sales contract and include it as an addendum item.

Some builder's sales agents may assert that once you sign on with their lender you can't switch down the line if you find a better deal somewhere else that does not include the builder's incentives. If your initial decision to use the builder's lender is noted in the sales contract (which it often is), you may be contractually obligated to stay with the builder's lender. To give yourself the opportunity to switch, you need to include a clause in your sales contract along the lines of "The buyer will use the builder's lender if he can match the competitive mortgage rates the buyer can get elsewhere at the time of closing." By tacking on the added phrase, "Buyer's alternative financing will be at no added cost or risk to the builder," he will be more amenable to this arrangement. This will allow you do to some more mortgage shopping when your house is about 60 days from completion and switch (for more on this, see Chapter 4).

Some builder's contracts pass on costs to the buyer that are traditionally and sometimes legally the seller's expenses. An example in Michigan is the transfer tax, which is $8.60 per $1,000 of the purchase price (for a $200,000 house, this would be $1,720), a big, unexpected cost at closing. Typically, the builder's sales rep does not explain this to the buyer.

Another cost item that can be significant to the uninitiated buyer is special assessments, Chin says. Typically outstanding special assessments (for example, road improvements or sewer hook-up fees) are paid off at closing by the seller, but often the builder's contract passes these through to the buyers. If there is a five-thousand-dollar outstanding balance on special assessments, effectively the buyer is paying five thousand more for the house without realizing it. Again, the builder's sales rep often does not bring this to the attention of the buyer, and sometimes does not even know there are outstanding special assessments. If the buyer's attorney sees such a provision on the contract, the buyer may be able to negotiate it out. At the very least, the attorney can find out what the outstanding balance of special assessments is.

The buyers can be in for an even ruder awakening if the buyer's lender insists that the special assessments be paid off at closing, Chin adds.

The builder will say that the house will be clean when you take possession, but you want it professionally cleaned, especially if you have small children. You do not want any small pieces of anything on the floor, and you don't want dusty, dirty windows, bathrooms, or kitchen surfaces.

warranties

The best warranty is succinct and sweet. As attorney Chin puts it, "The best one reads, 'The builder will warrant against defects in workmanship and materials for three years.'" With most production-builder contracts, however, the warranty is quite lengthy and most of the description is disclaimers, stating what the builder will *not* do. Since a builder can try to disclaim what he is legally required to warrant, this is one place where a legal review is very helpful.

In some states, such as Florida, a builder is not required to warrant the house at all. It's purely voluntary. In other states, a builder is required to warrant the house for a specified period of time, whether he explicitly says so or not; this is called an implied warranty. The implied warranty in Michigan, which only applies to structural defects, runs for six years. In California, the implied warranty for structural defects is ten years. In Virginia, the warranty is broader. Both structural and workmanship items are covered, but only for one year; the foundation is warranted for five years.

In addition to the implied warranty, a builder may offer an express warranty, which can be whatever the builder says it is. Since this can vary from builder to builder, you should read this part of the contract carefully. For example, in Michigan a builder can offer an express warranty that is nontransferable, Chin says.

If the builder listed on the sales contract is a separate corporate entity or an LLC that was disbanded when the project was built out, you will have no warranty protection even if the state has an implied warranty law and the problem occurs during the time period when a warranty should still be in effect. "If in year nine you have a problem and the builder/developer is an LLC, he's long gone. The ten-year rule in California will help you if you use a well-known builder whose name is on the contract," attorney Parker says.

In some production-builder sales contracts, the builder expressly states or requests the buyers to initial a waiver of the builder's implied warranty. If such a clause appears in your contract, you should ask why. "If the house is well built, why does a builder need a waiver? If you use it as a defense, you must have felt there was a reason," Deming said. If the builder insists that you agree to the waiver, think twice about buying a house from him. If he's reputable, he shouldn't be asking you to sign away your right of redress if he doesn't deliver.

Many builders also include a third-party ten-year limited home warranty in their sales package. Unfortunately, a house can have problems that do not meet the warrantys' standard, but they make the house impossible to sell and reduce its asset value dramatically (for more on this, see Chapter 11).

gagrules

Some contracts specifically state that if you are unhappy with the builders, you cannot post signs in your windows or picket the sales office. If the builder insists that this innocuous clause remain, ask why. Rather than explicitly stating that you cannot post a sign complaining about the builder, the contract may simply say "no sign" or "no large sign" allowed. This stipulation may be stated in the Home Owner's Association (HOA) rules that you accept as a condition of the contract, rather than in the contract itself. This is one reason that you should read the HOA documents before signing the sales contract. Of course, the builder doesn't want to scare away new prospects with signs that malign him. But buyers who are driven to such tactics are generally not nitpickers complaining about paint drips. They are very distressed home owners with real problems.

litigationclause

In many states, attorney fees are not paid to either party as a matter of course; these must be written into the contract. Depending on the laws in the state where you are purchasing the house, the contract can explicitly state that if the buyer sues the builder, the buyer will pay all legal fees of both sides. You should change such a one-sided clause to read that the loser will pay all costs, or that each side will pay its own costs regardless of the outcome. If the builder won't budge on this, ask why.

Bear in mind, however, that if you end up locking horns with the builder, the cost to litigate will be huge. This is yet another reason to check the reputation and credibility of the builder before you enter into an agreement with him. Though legal fees can vary across the country, the cost for a simple trial without a jury can be as much as twenty to sixty thousand dollars. You will have to shell out all the fees yourself until a judge has ruled on the case, which could be several years. Even if you are clearly in the right, it may be less costly to eat the repairs, especially if you have to pay your own attorney's fees. If you ultimately are awarded $100 thousand but you have to pay sixty thousand dollars to an attorney, you aren't that much ahead.

Rather than go to trial, you may be better served by hiring a lawyer to negotiate a settlement. "Normally the issue is not the money, but results. The buyer wants the builder to redo the work and that won't cost so much," attorney Haber says.

Some sales contacts stipulate mandatory arbitration of any legal disputes between buyers and the builder. Arbitration used to be favored, but now it's not necessarily the case. Deming says, "Arbitration has been sold as quicker and cheaper than litigation, but usually a buyer will get a lesser award, so it's to the benefit of the builder, who worries that if there's a big jury trial, the buyer will get a big award. An arbitration judge can be a seasoned judge who won't get inflamed. In addition, if the buyers sign an arbitration clause, the builder may get up to half off his liability insurance rates. But if you arbitrate, it won't necessarily be less expensive for you because you still need to hire an attorney."

addendumitems

The addendum contains all items agreed to between you and the builder that are not in the body of the contract. Here are some examples of specific addendum items:

- Specific dimensions of specific rooms. For example, the interior dimensions of the garage must be at least twenty-three feet in length to accommodate your car.

- Specific items shown in the model. For example, the exact same chandelier as shown in the dining room, including manufacturer's name and item model number.

- Incorporation by attachment—you are attaching to the contract all plans, elevations, and descriptive material and a specification list as provided in the sales brochure, and, if possible, the builder's own detailed specifications and drawings that he is using to build the house.

- Substitution of any items of aesthetic value require your input and approval. For example, the kitchen cabinets, other cabinets, flooring, or any other substituted items must also be of the same color and quality as the originally specified and agreed-upon item. If a specific upgrade that you specify is not available and one of lesser quality is used, you will be notified and credited the difference.

- Proposed site plan for your house. The contract will not be finalized until you have reviewed and approved it. If you do not agree to the builder's site-plan proposal, you have the right to declare the contract null and void and your deposit will be refunded.

- Your lot selection will be subject to approval by a licensed landscape architect before the contract is finalized.

- If at the time you select a lot the landscape architect advising you determines that the slope of the finish grade may be less than 3 percent, closing shall be contingent on the builder's correction and the landscape architect's approval of the final grading of the lot.

- The builder agrees to minor modifications of the plan to facilitate buyer's landscaping plans. For example, adding a door to the breakfast area, relocating an outdoor air-conditioning condenser, widening the front walk to forty-eight inches, adding a second walkway from driveway to the front door.

- If you are purchasing a particular lot because of its mature trees, your lot selection will be subject to approval by an experienced arborist. If the builder will be cutting down trees that you want him to replace, explicitly state the number of trees to be replaced, their species, and maturity. If you want the trees to be planted in a certain place, state that you must approve the location of each new tree.

- Any verbal agreements made by the builder or his sales agent must be explicitly stated here. For example, the builder will move the doorway to the master bedroom one foot to accommodate your dresser. Or the builder will include as promised, without charge, the one-thousand-dollar upgraded bay window in the family room. If you get a lot of options, and the market is slow, a builder will frequently throw in a couple of extras.

- Terms for completion of work delayed by weather. If your house is completed when the weather prevents completion of all outdoor work, for example landscaping and pouring concrete, the builder agrees to complete the work when weather permits. If the lender requires an escrow amount for the concrete work and landscaping work before the mortgage will be approved, the builder agrees to escrow the required amount, which can be as much as ten thousand dollars.

- The house shall be professionally cleaned prior to closing.

- You will use the builder's lender if he can match the competitive mortgage rates you can get elsewhere at the time of closing; otherwise you will use a different lender.

- The builder agrees to let you use his financial incentives with a different lender.

- The builder agrees to let you use his financial incentives toward the purchase because you will not be using his lender. (For example you can use the $3,000 closing cost contribution toward a hardwood floor.)

- The builder's special assessment fees for road improvement, sewer hookup fees, and so forth shall remain the seller's responsibility and shall be excised from the closing costs due at closing. If you can't get the special assessment fees completely excised, state the reduced amount here. If you cannot get them even reduced, then explicitly state here what they are.

- The seller agrees to pay for a title insurance policy in the amount of the final sale price.

- The seller agrees to pay the transfer tax due at the time of closing.

- The seller agrees to pay for all special assessments, such as charges for road improvements, before closing. You as the buyer will not be responsible for these special assessments.

- At the time of closing, the builder will produce copies of all government inspections including the final certificate of occupancy for you to keep with your records of the purchase.

- The litigation clause will be revised so that either the loser will pay all legal fees or each side will pay its own fees.

- The contract will make no mention of a private home inspector. If you want one, you must state here that the builder agrees that you can bring your own home inspector onto the job site to inspect the work at specified times and at the end before the final closing. The builder may want approval over your inspector choice if he has had a previous unpleasant experience with an especially picky inspector.

Although it seems elementary, "Everything must be written down," says Orange County, California, attorney Judith Deming. If all the verbal agreements and promises given by the sales agent are not written down and included in a contract addendum, the builder is not legally obliged to honor those promises. "The builder may honor the agent's verbal assurances, but buyers risk that he won't if they don't insist on getting everything in writing."

Unfortunately, in Orange County, where Deming practices, "Buyers have been frantic and camping out all night to get a new house. There's a finite number of houses, and buyers are scared that they will miss out, that the interest rate will go up, so they throw caution to the wind. They drop their defenses and make concessions, and don't get everything written down."

Moreover, with so many buyers, agents do not always take the time to explain things carefully, Deming says. "Certainly not every builder and every sales agent misrepresent things, but buyers should be aware that in some sales environments, confusion abounds. What is in the basic house and what is an upgrade? Everything in the model may be an upgrade and only a 'shell house' is being sold, but this is not made clear to buyers. You sign for an upgraded tile. You may get lesser quality if the upgrade is not available. This may be known to the sales agent but not always made clear. If the agent deals with the buyers ten hours or one hundred hours, they're paid the same money, so some of them have no incentive to explain.

"After the basic contract is worked out, the buyers deal with a non–real estate professional who might say anything to finish the deal. They make promises that are not borne out in the paperwork, and buyers rely on this," Deming says.

tips**from**the**trade:**
verbal assurances
and agreements

sales contract

With a custom-built house, you get to pick out everything—the lot, the plan, the details, all the materials from the exciting big-ticket items like the kitchen cabinets to the little necessities like cover plates for light switches. Then you get the financing. You take out a construction loan, and you pay the builder in incremental amounts, called draws, as construction proceeds.

To ensure that the builder builds the house exactly as you specify and to address all the possible contingencies that might arise in the course of construction, you need a contract that spells out everything. With several hundred thousand dollars at stake, you shouldn't proceed on the strength of a handshake. The builder may have a contract that he's ready to pull out and have you sign. But to protect your interests, you should have the contract reviewed by an experienced real-estate attorney first.

If there's a dispute that stops the job, you're the one who's paying interest on the construction loan while it's being resolved. If your builder walks off in a snit, you're the one left holding the bag with $200 thousand already spent for a half-completed house. Getting someone to come in to finish will be hard, and the total cost will be much more than you planned on. Even worse, your builder's contract may obligate you to pay the forty- to sixty-thousand-dollar profit he would have realized on your $400 thousand house if he had completed the job. Or the builder stays on the job to the end, and then presents you with an unexpected twenty-five-thousand-dollar tab for the ten change orders plus the two thousand for "administrative fees for change orders" that was buried in his contract. Or you broke ground only to have the Home Owner's Association Architectural Review Board stop the job because you failed to get their approval before you started.

The cost for an attorney's review of a custom-home contract can range from about one thousand to three thousand dollars or more, depending on how many revisions the attorney needs to make. Unlike the consistency that characterizes sales contracts for production homes, custom-home contracts can be all over the map. In many cases, the contracts appear to be cobbled together from several documents. "They are often poorly drafted, inconsistent, vague, and almost always one-sided," says Ann Arbor, Michigan, attorney Sherry Chin.

Orange County, California, attorney Judith Deming says in her experience, "The builder's contracts are skeletal. I've never seen one end up as a final contract. They're more of a starting point. The contractor wants four pages; the attorney wants to expand it to cover every risk. Usually an attorney is brought in after the construction has started, when there's a dispute or a crisis. Every time you always wish you had drafted the contract initially so that it would have included a remedy for the crisis at hand."

Miami attorney Dennis Haber observes that the contract can be a good indicator of the business experience of the contractor. "You can have contractors with dirt under their nails who know how to put a house together, but they haven't thought through a good contract. A more experienced contractor will have a more comprehensive contract, and a less sophisticated contractor will have a less developed contract. Many times the contract can be wide open. They are full of holes for both sides; they're more like a 'handshake deal,' and that can be dangerous. The more holes there are, the more opportunity for both sides to get trapped by the vagaries and what the contract doesn't say."

The American Institute of Architects has a standard General Conditions of the Contract for Construction (A201–1997) and a Standard Form of Agreement Between

Owner and Contractor (A101–1997). These are not very widely used, however, because most custom-home builders have their own contracts. Haber recommends using the AIA contracts as the basis for drafting a sound contract because "they're more balanced and not designed solely from a builder perspective. They protect both sides, and it's designed with more sense of fairness."

If you're considering using the AIA documents for your project, Newport Beach, California, attorney James M. Parker offers a word of caution: Characterizing them as "one size fits nothing," he says, "They still need doctoring for your specific situation with amendments and attachments."

The four areas of a custom-home contract that the attorneys say cause the most problems for owners are allowances, change orders, construction delays, and, surprisingly, what exactly will be built. There are other contract issues as well that should be addressed.

whathouse**are**you**building?**

Since there is no model home to use as a reference, the plans and written specifications must be extremely thorough and include a detailed generic description of standard building materials—for example, the subflooring shall be four-by-eight-sheets of 3/4-inch, tongue-in-groove, exterior-grade Douglas fir plywood. Where relevant, the brand and model number of every item should be included. When the house is finished, you should be given all the warranty materials, including proof of purchase.

The more detailed the specification, the better and the less chance of being upset later, Chin says. But, she points out, "You must know what is being identified. It's time-consuming and there are no shortcuts. If you don't take the time to familiarize yourself with the fixtures and features that the builder plans to install in the master bathroom, you may be disappointed at what gets installed."

Unlike a production-built sales contract, you can insist that your custom-built contract include a clause stating *no substitutions of any kind* without your prior written assent.

When you finally reach agreement on the plan and specifications, two copies of the final version must be dated, signed by both you and the builder, clearly labeled "Final Plan" and "Final Spec," and referenced in the contract. Otherwise, you can end up in a "we agreed to eliminate this; no I didn't" argument at the job site.

This admonition might seem a statement of the obvious, but in the course of deciding what you will build, the specifications and plans will get revised and marked up many times. The "final" part of the designation is especially critical. If you simply number the plans and sign the last one, it could be the wrong one. "You can decide that the seventh version was too expensive to build, so you sign version six, and the carpenter who is not primed to look for final anything goes to the office and gets plan five," explains Bloomingdale, Illinois, attorney Terry Eland.

At the end of the job, you will also need a set of "as built" plans which will incorporate all the major and minor changes that will invariably be made as the house goes up. "The house may look like the drawings, but it's not," Parker points out. Should you make any repairs or decide to renovate some years down the line, the "as-builts" will be a critical piece of information, and the person who eventually buys your house will also want them.

owner'sresponsibilities

Typically, owners verify the location of the lot lines and the setback requirements and easement locations, if any, and they usually get the surveyor's stakes in place for the lot lines and the four corners of the house. However, this should be spelled out in the contract.

Other owner responsibilities:

◆ *Setbacks.* You have to verify the setback requirements of the developer as well as with the local jurisdiction. The developer's may be stricter. For example, the local municipality may require only a fifty-foot setback from the street, but the master deed of the community where you want to build may stipulate seventy feet.

◆ *Unforeseen circumstances.* Who will pay if rock is discovered after you start excavating? Nearly all custom-builder contracts will stipulate that if a soil problem is discovered after the construction starts, it will be an extra cost. To avoid this headache, get soil borings before you buy the lot.

◆ *Building permit fees.* Who will get them and who will pay the fees? In some jurisdictions, the person who pulls the permit has the warranty responsibility. If you get the building permit, you may get the builder off the hook for warranty work. You also have to stipulate who will set up temporary utility service and who will arrange and pay for such things as sewer-connection fees and water-tap fees. Some of these fees can be quite high—the sewer-connection fee, as much as eight thousand dollars. If you don't spell out who will pay the fees in the contract, it will be an issue later on.

◆ *Architectural review board approval.* Some subdivisions or planned communities require that all owners submit their building plans to an architectural review board for approval, prior to construction. If you start to build without going through this step, you could be faced with an injunction to stop the job. Your contract should state who will be responsible—you or the builder—for getting the plans approved.

- ♦ *Environmental controls.* If you are building in an area with strict environmental controls, you may also have to pass muster with the oversight agency. If you are building on the coast of California, for example, "the California Coastal Commission will make you jump through hoops," attorney Deming says.

structuralengineer**review**

Before you sign off on the final plans, get the foundation plans and specifications reviewed by a structural engineer and make your final approval of the plans contingent on his approval, attorney Chin urges. In most jurisdictions, a structural engineer's review is not required for residential construction. But if your foundation fails, she points out, the effects on the very expensive house you're building can be catastrophic.

The structural engineer may find the builder's foundation plan to be satisfactory or he may suggest some simple tweaking such as bringing in different material to use as backfill because the dirt at your site may not be suitable (backfill is the dirt that's put back against the outside of the foundation walls). If you have the time and money, Chin recommends that you get the entire set of plans reviewed by a structural engineer.

allowances

Rather than specifying many items that often are a matter of personal taste such as carpets and floor finishes, cabinets and countertop materials, light fixtures, and appliances, a custom builder will allocate a fixed dollar amount in the budget—an allowance—and leave it to the buyer to choose the item. The problem comes when the dollar amounts are inadequate. "If the allowance is not hammered out in advance, it gets people in trouble. This is why houses never cost what owners expect," attorney Haber says.

To correlate quality level with price, however, you have to go out and price things before your contract is finalized. This means more than just a few phone calls. You need to go to several stores and look at different products for all the allowance items.

Then you have to know which prices the builder is quoting—a builder's discounted wholesale price or the full retail price? You also have to verify how the builder is accounting for the labor cost to install the allowance item. Is it included in the price of the house or in the allowance? If it's the latter, you will end up with less money to spend on the items, resulting in lesser quality than you expect.

Clearly, the more items that you can select and price out before the contract is finalized, the better off you are. But many people lack the confidence to make a selection on the basis of only a few floor tiles or a small sample. They must get into the project and see something before they can pin down the floor tile, for example. If you don't feel comfortable picking out items well in advance, it's all the more important to know prices and quality so that you get allowances that are adequate.

Should your taste prove to be more modest than you anticipated and you don't use all the allowance allocated, your contract should state that you will be credited with the difference. If you exceed the allowance, the contract should state that you will pay at the end of the job.

When building a custom house, if you are not working with an architect, it is often advisable to bring in an interior designer while the house is being built to help in the selection process, Chin says. While this is an added expense, it makes the overwhelming selection process much easier and can save money in the long run by avoiding major mistakes by the typical consumer's inability to visualize from small samples of materials such as flooring.

changeorders

Invariably, as the house goes up and owners finally begin to see what it will look like, they want to change things. But, the lawyers say, you must nail down the cost of the change order first.

Do not make a change unless you can agree on what is to be changed and the corresponding cost. This must be in writing, and both you and the builder must sign. "Don't make a change on a 'handshake,'" McNees advises. Otherwise, you could face thousands in extra charges at closing and end up with headaches, like the builder having estimated that it would cost eight thousand dollars to finish the basement but it turned out to be fifteen thousand.

Typically a builder will charge you two to three hundred dollars in "administrative fees" for each change order. And the builder is not obliged to honor your request for the change if he doesn't want to. As to the cost, you are at his mercy. If the change is minor, such as moving a door, the additional cost should be paid for at the end of the job. But if the change adds a substantial amount of money to the job, the builder may ask to be paid for the change on the spot. Within the contract, you need a formula addressing this.

Besides the cost, a change can also delay construction. "One hundred percent of the time, if there's a delay in completion, the builder will say, 'Well it's your fault because you made so many changes.' To avoid any misunderstandings, the contract should stipulate that every change order include the price and the added construction time, if any, and it must be signed by both parties," Savitz says.

constructiondelays

"When you build a new house, the only two things you can count on are that it will cost more than you expect and it will take longer than you expect," Parker says. In Deming's experience, the culprit is the weather. "No matter how tightly the builder coordinates his subs, you cannot count on the weather. In one case, a ten-year rain (an exceptionally heavy storm that occurs on average only every ten years but in this case it happend twice in one rainy season) washed the building pad out twice and delayed construction four months. It was very costly and beyond anyone's control." Construction delays can also be stressful. "It tests a marriage very harshly."

How should the delays be addressed in the contract? Most of the lawyers say that builders will refuse to accept a financial penalty for lateness, but Savitz has a carrot-and-stick approach that he says has usually been accepted: If the house is finished early, the buyers will give the builder a bonus. If the house is finished late, the builder pays the interest on the construction loan that the buyers are paying. "Your position is, 'I carry the loan on this property. When will you complete the job?' Give a little wiggle room. If the builder says eight to ten months to finish, penalize in the eleventh month and require the builder to pay one-half of the construction-loan interest. In the twelfth month, the builder pays all the interest. I have had great success with this because the builder wants to get in and out. If you push the penalty far enough in the future, you can get it accepted."

privatehome**inspector**

Before the bank okays a draw—that is, a payment to the builder—it will send out an inspector to check that the work has been done. For your own protection, though, all the lawyers say you should have your own private home inspector monitor the job. Since his primary goal will be to catch mistakes very early on so they can be corrected with minimal cost and hardship, you should arrange to have him visit the site on a weekly basis and include this provision in the contract. These weekly visits would be in addition to the major inspections that you should have a private home inspector perform at critical points in the construction. (For more on this, see Chapter 11.) If you have an architect, you can have him be your regular inspector, but the architect may not be willing to take this on.

qualityissues

Though quality is a legitimate concern, attorney McNees says it is too subjective and too hard to define to be included in a contract. "I don't write it in. You can assess progress—an item is in or it's not. You can say there will be no more than two inches deviation from the plan. As for quality, you better make certain you have a custom-home builder with a proven track record. Check his references. Is he a 'subs love him and will follow him anywhere' type of builder? Double-check with people who have bought houses from him."

Haber agrees that quality per se is impractical to define in a contract. But, "The more detail that you include in the contract documents, the less room for ambiguity in how the house is built and what materials are used, and the more likely your expectations will be met. A military spec is detailed to the nth degree. Carrying it that far for your house would be very expensive, but the more detail you provide in the contract in the way of drawings and written specifications, the more clarity there will be in the results."

regularmeetings

If you are not actively involved during the construction of your house, monitoring its progress and attending weekly meetings at the site with your builder, you will invariably have more complaints later, Haber says. You should include regular weekly meetings as a condition of the contract; if you can't be there, pay someone else to be.

whatif**the**builder**quits?**

Typically, a custom-builder contract will say you can cancel at any time but you must pay for lost profits—that is, *all lost profits*. If your contract was for $400 thousand and he stood to make forty to sixty thousand dollars at completion, you must pay this plus the charge for the work done. However, you may have canceled the contract because the work was subpar. In that case, Savitz says your position should be that you will compensate him for the work done, minus the cost to correct his mistakes, and no profit will be given.

If the builder cancels without cause—that is, for no reason—then your position should be that you will pay him for the work completed but no profit. If you cancel for no cause, your position should be that the builder will get his profit proportional to the amount of work completed. If he completes 50 percent, he gets 50 percent of his anticipated profits.

Chin includes a clause stating that if the builder defaults, the owner can fire him, hire someone else to complete the home, and the builder owes the owner the difference between the balance owed in the original contract and the final cost to complete construction.

whoowns**the**plans?

If you go directly to a custom builder instead of hiring an architect, the builder will likely supply the plans himself. If the job stops and you have to get another builder, you want the right to use the plans to complete the house with someone else. Should this happen, you need an "assignment of the plans and specifications." If the plans are copyrighted, you may not have the right to use them without permission.

lien release and payments to subcontractors and suppliers

In some states, such as Maryland, the production builder is responsible for mechanics' lien waivers—release forms signed by *all the subcontractors and all their suppliers* attesting that they have been paid for services rendered in the construction of your house. With a custom-built house, however, you are responsible for these. Not only do you have to get one from each and every subcontractor and his suppliers, you also have to get lien waivers from the subcontractors who will be on the job for several weeks, such as the framers, and from their suppliers who will be making numerous deliveries of materials, *each and every time they are paid.* Otherwise, a subcontractor or a supplier may be entitled to place a lien on your house, and you can end up paying for the same service twice.

"It's a pain in the neck to get a release of lien, but you need it. If you pay for the foundation and the builder goes to Las Vegas and doesn't pay his foundation sub, you can be stuck paying twice," Savitz says. In some jurisdictions, a builder is required to give you a list of all people who will be paid five hundred dollars or more so that you can track all the payments. If this is not required in your area, Savitz suggests that you stipulate that such a list be provided in your contract: this is often called a sworn statement.

Even if you get all the waivers taken care of, you can take your shoe box full of receipts down to the title company and they can say, "I'm still not satisfied" and deny you extended title insurance. Without this, you are not protected from subcontractors and material suppliers filing a lien against you within a certain fixed period after the house is completed.

To make the lien chore easier and to eliminate the possibility that the title company won't accept all your hard work, Eland suggests making all your payments through the title company. "Let them review the lien-release forms, authenticate them, and take the risk that someone will come back and demand payment. It may cost you about a thousand dollars to get this service, but it's definitely worth it. I suggest that the contract state that the parties will set up a construction escrow with the title company who will make all payments. The builder won't care and probably prefers it."

In some places, though, a construction escrow account with a title company may not be workable. For example, in the Washington, D.C., area, framing crews commonly drive a hundred miles to the job site from Pennsylvania every day. They would be unwilling to go anywhere extra to get paid. Nonetheless, an experienced attorney should be able to create a solution to the lien waiver requirement that requires less work for you.

escrow

A production builder will not let you escrow any funds to ensure that the work will be completed. A custom builder will. Typically, the holdback is 10 percent. At the final walk-through when you draw up a punch list of all items to be completed, the contractor will price out the cost to complete each one. To ensure that he will complete the work, your contract should stipulate that you will retain 150 percent of the cost of each punch-list item and pay only when it's completed. For example, if the builder says it's eight thousand dollars to complete the driveway, you should hold back twelve thousand. When all the punch-list items are completed, you will pay the balance, if any, that is left in the escrow account.

drawschedule

The builder wants to be paid as he completes each phase of the work, but the lender may not agree to the builder's draw schedule. For example, the builder wants to be paid ten times in the course of the job, and your lender usually draws checks only five times. You must coordinate the two and incorporate the draw schedule into the contract. Many builders state that if you don't pay them on a timely basis, usually ten days after they submit the bill, they will penalize you.

financing

The builder will make the contract contingent on your getting financing. He will usually give you thirty to forty-five days, and he won't break ground until you get the financing or sell your house to get the cash. If you are still operating on allowances when you apply for financing, and don't know exactly how much money your house will cost, adding another 10 percent to cover the strong possibility of cost overruns is a prudent move. Even if you have no allowances, a contingency fund to cover unforeseen events is still a good idea.

warranties

Most builders will not warrant for longer than they are legally required to do so, which is typically one year. For some part of the house such as the foundation, some jurisdictions require a longer warranty. For example, Virginia requires a home builder to warrant the foundation for five years. Some custom builders also offer third-party ten-year limited-warranty policies, but the coverage is very limited (see Chapter 12).

hazardous materials

Some jurisdictions now require that a builder certify either that he doesn't know if there are any hazardous materials or certify what if any hazardous materials are used in construction. Besides this, many building codes now require the builder to install a passive radon device. You should also ask your local building or public-health department what, if any, environmental issues or hazards exist in your area. If you think they would affect your house, you should address it in your contract. (For more on radon, see Chapter 14.)

other red flags

If you want to buy a lot in a subdivision where the developer has not yet completed the roads and other infrastructure, you should not settle—that is, pay for the lot—before those items are completed. To ensure that all the promised improvements are put in, some local municipalities require the developer to bond over money. But, McNees warns, "If all you are operating on is the developer's word it will be done, you're very much unprotected if you buy a lot without all the improvements in place."

addendum items

This is the place to include any items that are not already addressed in the contract. For example, if you hire an arborist to develop a staging plan that designates where the builder can stockpile his material and keep his equipment so as to protect your trees, you would reference it here. Since your attorney may draft your entire contract rather than modify the builder's, your addendum list may be very brief.

tips**from**the**trade:**
dispute resolution

No one goes into a home-building project expecting any problems, and if you have good plans and specs, there's less chance of any earth-shattering disputes. But the possibility is always there, so you need to anticipate it in your contract. One place where you can get into trouble is when the lender's inspector and your inspector disagree. Attorney Savitz explains: "If the lender's inspector comes out and says, 'Here's a defect you must fix,' the builder will fix it. If your inspector or architect finds a defect, but the lender's inspector says it's okay, then you have a problem. You hope that you can keep on building while you try to resolve the disagreement, but the job may come to a grinding halt. If arbitration is your only option, you pick an arbitrator, the builder picks one, then you and the builder select a third. And then you schedule and hold the arbitration hearing. The job will be halted for a minimum of three months, and it could stretch out for as long as nine." During this time you will be paying the interest on your construction loan. Though arbitration is billed as being quick and easy, "It's just as costly and time-consuming as if you went to trial."

Rather than leaping directly to arbitration when you and the builder lock horns, Savitz recommends an intermediate step that he calls the "designated professional" approach. Prior to construction, you and the builder together select a qualified architect or engineer, a designated professional, to serve as the person to whom all disputes will be submitted. If you or your inspector (or architect if you have one) ask the contractor to correct something and he objects, you can submit your disagreement to the designated professional, who will promptly resolve it. His decision is binding on both you and the builder. If the disputed issue exceeds ten thousand dollars, either side can appeal the decision by submitting it to outside arbitrators.

Savitz's qualifications for the designated professional: The person must have ten years experience in new-home construction, be recognized as ethical and reputable, and have had no employment by either party for the last two years or be unable otherwise to act with true independence. The most important thing in choosing the designated professional, however, is that you get a person who can make a decision that both sides will accept, Savitz stresses. It doesn't always have to be a person with no relation to either side. If either the buyer or the builder has an architect, "Usually the owner and builder will agree that the architect who designed the house will be the final arbitrator of any dispute." If neither side has an architect, they fall back to finding an outside designated professional.

Savitz avoids using the word *mediator* in the contract because "if people see this in the contract they think it's a dispute resolution, but it's not. A mediator tries to get the parties to agree, but he can't dictate a resolution."

chapter fourteen

Construction

considerations

The nuts and bolts of a new house—the structure, the heating and cooling, the lighting and all
the other systems—are without a doubt the
least interesting and least sexy aspects of the
purchase. But in one way or another, they all
relate to your personal comfort and ultimately
how well you will enjoy your new home. If the
heating and cooling system isn't delivering, for
example, you'll be miserable, no matter how
great the design or the view is. If you can't tell
the navy blue blazer from the black one in your
closet because there's no light in it, you may

find yourself at that important meeting slightly mismatched. And if you're already planning out how you will be working in your home office, how will you get high-speed data access for your computer? And how about the other computers in the house for your spouse and your kids?

Before you finalize the deal, spend some time mulling over the nuts and bolts. You don't have to be a journeyman electrician to figure out your lighting needs, or even handy around the house to learn the pertinent questions to ask of your builder. Knowing something about how houses are built will help you know what you are looking at when you visit the site. If you climbed all over new construction as a kid, you're in for a shock—the building principles are the same, but most of the materials have changed. The main structural framing material is wood, but not like any that you remember seeing. Don't mistake different for cheaper—many people have a tendency to think that all old houses are well built and new ones not so well built. In fact, for the most part, new houses are better built than most were in Grandma's day or in your own childhood, and new houses are certainly more energy efficient.

buildinggreen

When a home-building firm characterizes itself as "green," what does this mean? The short answer: It builds a house that is more environmentally benign. The longer answer: After observing the environmental effects created by building tens of millions of houses, some home builders, manufacturers, architects, and engineers decided to rethink every step of the entire process, from what kind of roof shingle to use to how to dig the hole. The new paradigm is generally referred to as "building green." Its three areas of emphasis are:

1. energy efficiency

2. healthier indoor air

3. resource conservation, both in the selection and manufacture of construction materials and in the operation of the house itself

Initially, builders who subscribed to the green idea were a tiny minority. But the concept has gradually moved from the fringe to the mainstream. US Homes and Centex Homes, two of the largest home-building firms in the country, are now actively developing green programs in some of their divisions.

The numbers and facts that have led to this rethinking are compelling. According to the National Association of Home Builders, a two-story, 2,085-square-foot-house requires 13,127 board-feet of framing lumber. This is the equivalent of about 2,500 eight-foot-long two-by-four wood studs. If laid side by side, the amount of sheathing, exterior siding, roofing materials, insulation, and interior drywall required would cover three quarters of a football field. When these amounts are aggregated across all the single-family detached, single-family attached (town houses), and multi-family housing unit starts in the United States (more than 1.6 million in 1999), the amount of construction materials used in the home-building industry is staggering, and the potential environmental impact of all this activity is worth considering.

Not merely acres but square miles of forest are cut, and huge amounts of energy are expended, in the manufacture of wood, vinyl, and the many other products used in home building. The energy consumed in the manufacture and construction process is a one-time cost, but once the house is finished, the energy requirements to heat and cool it are ongoing.

Concerted efforts to make houses more energy efficient have in turn created another environmental problem: indoor air quality. To reduce heating and cooling loads, houses have become more airtight. But less incoming fresh air has meant that occupants are exposed to greater concentrations of volatile organic chemicals—generally referred to as VOCs—that off-gas from many building materials.

All those exterior surfaces created in a new housing development—roofs, driveways, sidewalks, and streets—also have an environmental impact. The rain that was once absorbed into the soil now runs off and has to be absorbed somewhere else. In addition, the rainwater now carries fertilizers and other sediments that have to be removed before the water can pass without harm into local streams and groundwater.

The easiest piece of building green for the public to grasp and builders to act on has been energy efficiency, and simple modifications can have a big effect. For example, about 25 percent of the energy used to heat and cool a house can be lost through leaky air ducts. Sealing metal ducts with liquid mastic rather than tape, which can eventually disintegrate, keeps the air in the ducts.

Improving energy efficiency is not just a matter of substituting one material for another, but rethinking the entire delivery system for heating and cooling in a house. When the furnace is moved from a far corner of the basement to the center, the duct runs can be shorter, the air doesn't have to be pushed as far, and the furnace can be smaller and cost less.

Modifying the heating and air-conditioning system can benefit indoor air quality as well. Installing return air ducts in every bedroom rather than one in the hall for the entire floor will provide better air quality as well as a better supply of warm and cool air to each bedroom.

Energy is also the easiest aspect of a building-green program to evaluate because it's measurable; evaluating the "environmental goodness" of a material is fuzzier.

And exhaustive, because a green-building product check-list includes a thorough examination of its entire life-cycle.

Few buyers ever wade this far into the details, but if you want to, these are the questions to ask:

◆ Is the item made of a material that is renewable such as wood, or non-renewable such as oil?

◆ How much energy is expended in the extraction and manufacturing processes?

◆ How much energy is expended to transport it to the site?

◆ How durable is it?

◆ At the end of its useful life, can it be recycled?

◆ How much does it cost and will you buy it? Will you reconsider if it is twice the cost of the less benign material?

The answers will not be the same for every buyer or builder. For example, vinyl siding manufactured to look like clapboard is an oil-based product; on the other hand, it's not affecting the diminishing supply of old-growth lumber as real redwood or cedar would. It also has a long life, is reasonably priced, and, of even greater interest to most home owners, it's very low maintenance. When all these considerations are factored in, most green builders would give it the green light, though some would not because highly toxic dioxin is a by-product of the vinyl manufacturing process. For this same reason, some home builders in the green movement won't tolerate anything vinyl, including windows, flooring, decking, and railings.

not**grandma's**house

Whether your builder is green or not, he will use some green components. The most common one is engineered wood, which is used in the structural framing. On first encounter, you are likely to think that engineered wood is a cheap substitute for real wood and further proof that the house will not measure up to Grandma's—a benchmark standard that most people apply to new houses in the belief that older is better, an often debatable point.

Engineered wood does look different, with large chunks of wood that appear to be randomly mixed with brown gook and pressed into sheets like plywood, or strange-looking floor joists that are shaped like steel I-beams. It may look cheap, but it's more expensive, better quality, and more environmentally benign than dimensional, sawn lumber that comes straight from the tree.

Those randomly placed chunks are actually thousands of strands of lumber that were precisely shaved off a log, coated with wax and resin, aligned to provide maximum structural strength, and shaped variously to be a beam, column, subfloor, sheathing, or joist. Home builders like engineered wood because what you see is what you get. It is very stable, whereas dimensional lumber often warps, cracks, twists, or checks, causing nail pops and other problems for both builders and homeowners as it goes through heating and cooling cycles. Environmentalists also like engineered wood. It is made from poplar and aspen, species that many loggers call "weed trees" and consider useless. The aspen tree even regenerates itself. You cut it in the fall, and the roots send up new growth in the spring. And engineered-wood products can be made from small trees. A two-by-twelve-sized engineered-wood floor joist can be made from trees that are only six inches in diameter, but a two-by-twelve-inch dimensional, solid wood requires a tree with at least a twelve-inch diameter.

Although an entire house can be framed in engineered wood, it's still more cost effective to use dimensional lumber for some parts of the house such as wall studs, and nonwood materials for others.

The one engineered-wood component that nearly all production builders do use, however, is the floor joist, to support the floors. Most builders call it a TJI or an I-joist. This is one structural component that you should pay particular attention to because the size and spacing of floor joists, whether they are I-joists or dimensional lumber, in combination with the subfloor sheeting, will determine "floor performance" and whether or not a floor will vibrate excessively.

From the street, the most noticeable item on a new house going up is the sheathing—four-by-eight-foot sheets of varying materials that enclose the stud walls and roof trusses and prevent the house from being blown over by the wind. For a production-built house, the roof sheathing will invariably be an engineered-wood product called oriented strand board, or OSB. The wall sheathing may also be OSB, but usually only on higher-end houses because there are cheaper alternatives. Asphalt-impregnated fiberboard—made of recycled newspapers and recovered wood chips—is the lowest-priced sheathing available in most markets (you can recognize it by its characteristic black color). The most widely used wall sheathing among production builders is laminated fiberboard, which looks like masonite. Plywood is the most expensive type of sheathing, and is found only on very high end production-built and custom-built houses.

Buyers who venture inside a house that's still at the framing stage are most likely to be walking on OSB subflooring, though some builders still use plywood.

indoorairquality

A sure path to energy efficiency is eliminating air leaks. If you cut down the amount of air that has to be heated and cooled, you cut your utility bill substantially. But plugging up all those air leaks means less fresh air inside, and this has brought on other problems.

Americans move on average every five years, but many people stay in the same house for decades. And you may be one of them. Thus it's only prudent— if a mite disheartening—to make some allowances for your old age as you plan your new house. This may be a hard pill to swallow if you're one of the aging baby boomers who brought us sex, drugs, and rock and roll. But universal design features that accommodate the needs of any physically challenged person can be so seamlessly incorporated that only your builder will know the difference. Most can be inexpensively done during initial construction; but waiting until you need them often means costly remodeling.

will you still live there when you're 64?

Zeroing in on specifics, here are fifteen modifications suggested by accessibility expert Rick Millard of Richmond, Virginia. Many of them, such as lowering kitchen wall cabinets, will make a new house easier for a person of any age to live in.

1. doors. Install a thirty-six-inch door for all openings so that all rooms, including walk-in closets, are accessible to someone in a wheelchair or a walker. Millard says that a wider door should run about five to ten dollars more than the typical twenty-eight or thirty-inch interior-size door that most builders use. Whenever possible, provide lever-type door handles, which are easier to use.

2. hallways. Three feet is wide enough for a wheelchair to pass through going straight, but a forty-two-inch width will feel more comfortable. To make a ninety-degree turn into a doorway in a wheelchair, a hall width of four feet is required. Doorways that are angled at forty-five

degrees are easier for a person in a wheelchair to pass through.

3. stairs. In most jurisdictions, current building codes for new houses mandate a stair with a seven and three quarter-inch riser and a ten-inch tread. But one with a lower riser and a wider tread is easier to use and a person is less likely to trip. Millard recommends a seven-inch riser and an eleven-inch tread at a minimum, but a six-inch riser and a twelve-inch tread is even more user friendly. Three feet is the standard width for a staircase, but a stair lift can be more easily added later if the stairs are four feet wide. He also recommends railings on both sides of the staircase and lights in the stairwell that illuminate the treads.

4. light switches. A rocker type switch can be easily operated by someone with arthritis. A switch that is forty-eight inches above the floor or lower will be easier for someone in a wheelchair and small children to use.

5. electric outlets. These should be no lower than eighteen inches from the floor so that taller people don't have to bend down so far. This is also easier for a person in a wheelchair to use.

6. bathroom grab bars. These may not be needed for years and can be installed on an as-needed basis. The important first step during construction is to have the proper wood backing installed and a type of shower or tub unit that can be modified easily. A builder-grade fiberglass tub or shower unit is generally not adaptable. Millard recommends choosing a unit with a flat wall design that can be reinforced.

7. **bathroom toilet.** An eighteen-inch-high toilet rather than the standard fifteen-inch-high one will be easier for an older person to use. The higher toilet will cost more, though Millard notes that as demand increases, the cost of the higher toilet is going down. Ask for a toilet with the trip lever (toilet handle) on the open side of the room.

8. **showers.** A roll-in shower with a seat that a person in a wheelchair could use might add as much as a thousand dollars to the cost of the house. If this is a consideration, make sure that the seat is near the shower controls, so that the shower can be used in either a standing or a sitting position.

9. **kitchen wall cabinets.** Lowering the wall cabinets from the standard eighteen inches above the counter to fifteen inches will make the second shelf accessible for everyday use for most people. Some small appliances that people like to store on the counter in the space between the countertop and the underside of the wall cabinet are higher than fifteen inches, so measure yours before doing this.

10. **kitchen counter height.** Varying the counter height will make the kitchen an easier place for taller adults and shorter children to work in. Raising the dishwasher so that the counter above it is at bar height (forty-two inches) provides a taller person with a more comfortable work space. It also means that the tall person or someone in a wheelchair doesn't have to bend over so far to load the dishwasher.

11. **kitchen base cabinets.** For a person in a wheelchair to be able to use a cooktop and a sink, a recessed area must be provided underneath and the counter height must be no higher than thirty-four inches. Such an arrangement can also benefit anyone who spends a long time chopping and peeling at the sink or cooking foods that require constant stirring and wants to sit down while doing this. If the kitchen is big enough, an alternate possibility is to add an island work center with a vegetable sink and put the under-counter opening there.

12. **kitchen aisle width.** A width of forty-two inches instead of thirty-six allows several people to work in the kitchen at the same time; it also allows someone to get around a person in a wheelchair. A forty-eight-inch width is even more comfortable.

13. **kitchen counters.** When they are rounded at the edge instead of square, no one will bump into them when, for example, they are bringing groceries into the house. Using a contrasting color for the edge band of the counter can be a nice detail, and it will provide a visual orientation to the workplace.

14. **windows.** A cranking, casement-type window is easier to open than the standard double-hung type used by most builders. Casement windows are more expensive, but Millard points out that you don't have to install them everywhere.

15. **entries into the house.** At least one level wheelchair-accessible entry, preferably in the garage, eliminates the need for construction of an elaborate, unsightly, and costly ramp later.

Anyone who has ever lived or been in a house and felt the floor or chair they were sitting in shake as another person walked by knows that this can be extremely annoying. Many buyers assume that vibrating floor problems are handled by building-code requirements. But the codes address joist sizes, spacing, and spans only as these affect safety, not comfort. A floor can be very safe but still vibrate.

Conventional wisdom among builders holds that the spacing between the joists is a major factor affecting the vibrations or bounciness of a floor. But the critical factor is the depth of the joist, not the spacing, says Frank Woeste, a professor of engineering at Virginia Tech in Blacksburg, Virginia, who has studied floor-performance issues.

Field-testing the floors in the builder's model can be informative, but the only way to know how your floor will perform is to test a floor in a finished house that replicates as closely as possible what you intend to buy. A house that differs from the model in seemingly minor ways such as carpeting instead of hardwood floors can have significant differences in floor performance. Increasing the floor span to get a slightly bigger room can also produce negative effects, Woeste says. "In one instance a friend added a bay window to a dining room that increased the span by two feet, and the vibration is awful. You sit at the dinner table and when someone walks through, your bottom shakes."

Floors can vibrate at many different frequencies, but when these are in the range of eight to ten cycles per second—the number of times the floor goes up and down in one second after someone hits a joist with

VOCS

One of the first problems to be identified was elevated concentrations of volatile organic compounds in the air. Commonly called VOCs, these compounds are used in the manufacture of the many synthetic building products used in most new houses today, including carpeting, flooring, paint, cabinetry, countertops, and the structural framework itself. Hundreds of off-gassing VOCs have been identified, but the one that has captured the most attention is formaldehyde. It is a potent eye and nose irritant and causes respiratory problems. It is also classified by the U.S. Environmental Protection Agency as a probable human carcinogen.

In response to the concerns raised by health officials and the public over the last fifteen years, manufacturers of some building materials and furnishings have altered their chemical formulations, significantly reducing the amount of VOCs off-gassing from their products. But a brand-new house will still have a significant amount of VOCs in the air, because the rate at which the VOCs off-gas is highest initially. This phenomenon accounts

their foot or drops something on the floor—most people will feel them, some more than others.

When field-testing for floor vibrations, Woeste suggests putting the member of the household who is most sensitive in the center of large rooms and then walking around them briskly as if walking on a giant tick tack toe board. If the stationary person feels vibrations that are annoying, second thoughts on the house may be in order.

Woeste also recommends the "heel drop test" for dining areas. With the sensitive person sitting in a dining chair, the other person should rise up on his toes and then drop his heels to the floor. If the seated person can feel the chair shaking, this may also be objectionable.

In many areas of the United States, notably in Southern California, Texas, and Florida, houses do not have basements, and the first floor is built on a slab. So vibrating floors in the main living areas will not be a problem, but you still need to check the second-floor rooms. Many building codes allow a builder to assume there will be less furniture and less weight on floors used for sleeping rooms. But a floor built for a lighter load will be more flexible, and floor vibrations can be even more of an issue, Woeste warns.

To test the second floor for vibrations, have one or two people walk around the second floor while a third watches and listens from below for audible footsteps and shaking ceiling fans and light fixtures. If you plan to have an exercise room upstairs, try to mimic the repetitive movements you will make on exercise equipment while your observer below is still taking note.

Waterbeds on second floors can be problematic because they are frequently much heavier than standard beds. If you have one, you need to find out exactly what it weighs and ask the builder for the live load standard that he used. You may find that your bed is too heavy to be supported adequately.

for the "new house smell" that most buyers experience. Delaying a move-in and airing out a house by opening all the windows and running all the exhaust fans will be of benefit, even if this is done for only two days, advises John Girman, director of the Center for Analysis and Studies for the Indoor Environmental Division of the U.S. Environmental Protection Agency.

Continuing to keep the windows open and ventilating the house for several days to several weeks, if weather permits, can also be beneficial, adds Al Hodgson of Lawrence Berkeley National Laboratory in Berkeley, California, who has been studying indoor air quality for the last eighteen years.

After the first month or so, the rate at which the VOCs off-gas may fall off, but Hodgson's research indicates that the phenomenon will continue at a slow and steady pace for months or even years. Hodgson measured the indoor air quality in eleven new but unoccupied houses one to two months after their completion; some were monitored over a period of about nine months. Overall he found that the concentrations of VOCs in the houses were not alarming, although the concentrations of some compounds were high enough to produce an odor. The levels of formaldehyde were too low to have a smell, but high enough to cause discomfort in some individuals.

Buyers can reduce VOC levels at the outset by their selection of finishes. Hodgson's research has shown while carpets are generally low emitters of VOCs, a reasonable quality, medium-grade, nylon, certified-green-label carpet may emit less than the basic-grade carpet that most builders offer as standard. Installing the carpet with tack strips instead of an adhesive eliminates a potential VOC source altogether. Synthetic-fiber padding emits less than the rebonded padding that most production builders provide.

Hodgson's " certified green label carpet" refers to the green and white Carpet and Rug Institute emission test sticker found on carpeting that meets their emission standard. Their testing program was established after sensational stories about "killer carpets" appeared in the early nineties. In a New England lab, mice were exposed to carpet samples and subsequently died. Scientists in other labs including the EPA were never able to replicate these results, and the reason for the mice's demise remains unclear.

After the Carpet and Rug Institute started its carpet-testing program, it raised the emission standards, which has further reduced carpet emissions. Even so, carpeting can still have an odor that makes people think that they are being exposed to something awful, Hodgson observes.

Vinyl flooring is a stronger emitter than carpet, but it too should not be a cause for concern, Hodgson says. The oil-based alkyd and water-based latex paints used in most houses are another source of VOCs. The alkyds, which create a harder, more washable surface, are usually used for bathrooms, kitchens, and the trim around doors, windows, and baseboards. They produce a terrible smell and emit hundreds of VOC compounds, but these are almost entirely dissipated after about forty-eight hours, says John Chang, of the EPA labs in Triangle Park, North Carolina. The latex paints have a different smell and emit only four or five VOC compounds, but these continue to off-gas for days and weeks after the paint is dry. Low-VOC latex paints are now available, but some of these emit formaldehyde, and buyers should check the paint emission data.

In some cases, products that were considered to be low emitters are turning out to be a significant source of VOCs when viewed in the context of the whole house. For example, formaldehyde and other VOCs given off by the oriented strand board or plywood used for the subfloor in most new houses today are low when calculated on a square-foot or a per-piece basis. But Hodgson's research shows that when the total area of the subflooring in a typical house is taken into account, it can be a significant VOC source, and that the overlying carpet and carpet padding are not effective barriers.

Other research in indoor air quality has focused on the problem of underventilation. Until the last twenty years or so, mechanical engineers could reasonably assume that between air leaks and occupants opening the windows, everyone was getting plenty of fresh air. But as houses have become tighter, less outside air is penetrating through air

This naturally occurring radioactive soil gas is found all over the country, and prolonged exposure to it has been shown to cause cancer. After extensively surveying the country, the U.S. Environmental Protection Agency created a radon map of the United States, dividing it into three zones of predicted average indoor radon levels. State and county boundaries are delineated on the mapping, which is posted on the EPA website (see Resources). In addition to the overall country-wide map, you can click to blow-up maps of each state.

is **there** radon **in** your **new** house?

If you plan to build a new house in Zone 1 or Zone 2, the EPA recommends that you incorporate passive radon-mitigation features. You may not need them, but this cannot be predicted with any accuracy before a house is built. Moreover, you can't rely on the measurements taken in the new house on the lot next door, because radon levels can vary over very short distances, even between adjacent town houses.

The simplest method for radon abatement in a new house and one recommended by the EPA is called "subslab depressurization," a long name for a simple modification to the basement or first-floor slab of your house. Depending on the local code requirements, your builder may already be doing this. The EPA estimates that the added cost may be as much as three to five hundred dollars, but it may be less.

After your house is completed, you can then measure the radon level in it. If this is above four picocuries per liter, the EPA recommends that you contact a professional radon-mitigation service to add the rest of the system, which may cost up to five hundred dollars more. A credential to ask for when seeking a mitigation service is membership in the National Environmental Health Association (NEHA).

leaks in the exterior and with air conditioning, no one opens the windows in the summer anymore.

To rectify this situation, the American Society of Heating, Refrigerating, and Air-Conditioning Engineers (ASHRAE) proposes that mechanical ventilation be required in all new houses, as it is in most commercial and office buildings. The engineers have not dictated how this should be accomplished, and the desired ventilation rate varies with the size of the house and the number of bedrooms. For a 2,400-square-foot house with four bedrooms, for example, the proposed rate would be .35 changes per hour. At this rate, all the air in the house would be replenished every three hours.

Some home builders have suggested that ASHRAE's ventilation proposal could add fifteen hundred to six thousand dollars to the cost of a new house, but ASHRAE's proposal could be easily and inexpensively done. One continuously running 100 cfm (cubic feet per minute) bathroom exhaust fan that is exhausted to the outside would do the job for a 2,400-square-foot house; this modification would cost only seventy-five to one hundred dollars more than the exhaust fan and venting that the builder would already be installing in the bathroom, says Max Sherman, also of the Lawrence Berkeley National Laboratory, who has studied indoor air for twenty years. Putting a smaller, continuously running fan in each bathroom is a more expensive solution, but it would distribute the fresh air more evenly.

The ASHRAE proposal includes a sound recommendation for the continuously running fan because occupants turn fans off when they're too noisy. The dedicated exhaust fan should have a sound level of one sone or less so that it won't disturb a household at night when the ambient noise level is low.

Relocating the air-handling unit from the garage to some other place in the house would also improve indoor air quality, Sherman says. When houses do not have basements, the air-handling equipment is often put in the garage. Unfortunately, the ducts for the system often leak, so that if a car engine is left running for any length of time, homeowners can unwittingly introduce carbon monoxide into their living areas.

biologicals

When your mother admonished you to pick up, dust, vacuum, and join in her semiannual cleaning frenzy, she wasn't just being a stickler for order. Clean houses are healthier, because biological contaminants such as molds and dust mites are far less likely to get a toehold and multiply.

What's the big deal about molds? Although much about molds is still unknown, research has shown they can affect human health, explains Sandy McNeel, of the California Department of Public Health. The susceptibility of individuals varies, but some people who live in houses with extensive mold growth can develop persistent flulike symptoms; others develop mold allergies that cause classic hay fever symptoms such as runny noses and itchy eyes. It is not yet known if molds can cause asthma to develop, but mold can bring on added attacks in people who already have it. Some molds produce a chemical that can be irritating to the eyes and throat, and some produce toxins that can, on rare occasion, produce symptoms such as diarrhea, headache, and vomiting.

When mold grows, it releases spores into the air. Adult exposure is almost entirely limited to inhaling the spores, but children and toddlers can get rashes and eye infections from skin contact with mold in carpets. Mold spores are ubiquitous. They can't be kept out of a house. They can exist in any climate, even one as arid as Arizona or Nevada. When building a new house, however, you have the opportunity to incorporate several strategies that can help to keep them at bay.

With sufficient moisture, molds can grow on almost any building material, so the first line of defense against them is moisture control, advises Richard Shaughnessey, an indoor-air-quality and mold expert at the University of Tulsa. The substantial amount of moisture generated in bathrooms, kitchens, and laundry rooms should be eliminated by venting it to the outside. Most builders are required to supply exhaust fans in these areas, but some vent the moisture into an attic or a crawl space, where mold can germinate and reenter the house.

When you visit builders' models, look for the exhaust outlets on the outside of the house. Stove exhausts should go to the outside, but often they do not, and dryers exhausting into wall cavities are not unheard-of. The builder may say all the exhausts are vented to the outside, but you should verify this.

While you're outside, check that the grade slopes away from the house. Not only can water penetration damage the foundation, it can get into the basement and provide mold sustenance.

On your tour, turn on all the exhaust fans to see how noisy they are. Builders often install inexpensive ones that are so noisy that household members don't turn them on. When you finally settle on a house and a builder, consider upgrading the fans to get quieter ones that will be used.

Good ventilation with a constant replenishment of fresh air will help to keep down molds as well. An ultraviolet lamp that kills spores and other bacteria can be added to the air-handling system, but indoor air experts including Shaughnessey question its effectiveness. Though the light may reduce the number of mold spores, dead spores are just as allergenic and they can still cause adverse health effects, he says. Installing a high-efficiency air filter that removes the spores altogether is a more sensible strategy. The air-filter systems installed by most home builders are not very effective, catching only about 7 percent of the particulate matter. An electronic air filter will zap about 80 percent of it, including minute, micron-sized particles. The only catch is that you have to clean it periodically, but maintenance is required with any air-filter system.

Then there's source control. Most mold spores enter your house on your shoes. Catching them at their point of entry with a "walk-off mat" and a hard but easily cleanable flooring surface by the front door will keep their numbers down. Taking shoes off will also help. Wall-to-wall carpeting can harbor mold spores, dust mites, and other biologicals, especially if the indoor air is very humid or if the carpet gets wet. Reducing the amount of carpeting by installing hardwood floors or ceramic floor tile with area rugs will eliminate much of the area where these biologicals can thrive.

The least appealing aspect of mold control, which applies to both old houses and new ones, is the regular maintenance part. Not only should the air filters on the furnace be regularly checked and cleaned, so should the coils on the air-handling systems and the drain pan that is located just below the coil unit on your air handler. If this pan doesn't drain properly, mold can grow, and the mold spores can be distributed throughout your house through the ducts. The drain pan under the frost-free refrigerator should also be checked regularly to make sure that it isn't blocked.

In temperate climates, basements tend to become damp and moldy in the summer. Using a dehumidifier to remove moisture from the air will hold down mold growth, but vigilant maintenance is a must, Shaughnessey cautions. Otherwise, the humidifier itself can become a reservoir for mold. The pan where moisture collects must be emptied regularly; if a hose is connected from the pan to a drain, it must be periodically checked.

Humidifiers that add humidity to heated spaces in winter can increase human comfort levels, but maintenance is an issue with these as well. If they're not vigilantly maintained and cleaned, they can cause adverse health effects. A room humidifier must be cleaned every few days, not every few weeks or months. Humidifiers can be installed on furnaces, but these must also be vigilantly maintained; otherwise, mold will grow and air blowing through the duct system will disseminate it through an entire house.

windows

These days nearly everyone wants living spaces that are flooded with natural light, and most new houses, whether traditional or wildly contemporary, have big windows. Getting ones that are energy efficient is a must. Otherwise those sun-bathed interiors can become an architectural albatross—expensive to heat and cool and still too hot, too cold, or too drafty.

The first thing to check on a window, energy-wise, is the "U-factor," a measurement of the rate at which heat passes through a window. The lower the U-factor, the better. But it's more important in places with cold winters and large temperature differences between indoor and outdoor temperatures.

The U-factor is dramatically reduced when a second layer of glass is added to create an insulated air space between the panes. In most parts of the country, many home builders have already taken this step. The U-factor can be reduced even further, however, if the air space between the panes is filled with argon, an inert gas, and the inner side of one of the glass panes is coated with a low-emissivity (usually called low-e) material. The low-e coating also keeps the heat where you want it—inside during the winter and outside during the summer—and reduces the flow of UV rays that fade carpets and furniture.

It's relatively easy to get information about the energy efficiency of a specific window and to compare energy efficiencies between different windows, thanks to the work of the National Fenestration Rating Council (NFRC). This private, nonprofit organization runs a testing and certification program for measuring energy performance in windows. Before the NFRC program was established, there were no industry-wide standards, making accurate comparisons nearly impossible.

Eight states—Alaska, California, Florida, Massachusetts, Minnesota, Oregon, Washington, and Wisconsin—now require that all windows sold within their jurisdictions be tested and rated through the NFRC program. Fifteen other states—Georgia, Idaho, Indiana, Louisiana, Maryland, Nebraska, North Carolina, Ohio, Oklahoma, Rhode Island,

South Carolina, Utah, Vermont, Virginia, and West Virginia—reference NFRC in their building codes, so most window manufacturers certify products sold in those states. After a window brand has been tested and certified, an NRFC sticker stating the results must be posted on every window sold.

The NFRC data on energy performance for all windows tested through their program is posted on its website (for more information, see Resources).

In addition to posting a U-factor for each window listed, about half the NFRC window ratings also include a solar heat gain coefficient (SHGC), a measure of how much solar heat passes through a window. Since solar heat streaming through the windows accounts for about half the heat buildup in a house where cooling is the major concern (for example, in Florida) the SHGC can be a critical factor when choosing a window in those areas.

When comparing the ratings posted on NFRC's website, however, you will find that within a given category, most of the windows have a similar profile for energy efficiency. Since there are substantial price differences between windows with similar ratings, what else differentiates them and what should you look for?

The first thing is additional testing from other certification programs. The American Architectural Manufacturers Association (AAMA) and the Window and Door Manufacturers Association (WDMA) each run a testing and certification program for structural properties, air and water penetration, and forced entry of windows. A window that qualifies for the AAMA or WDMA designations will have a permanent sticker in the window jamb and often a temporary sticker on the window pane.

Another window rating program is run by Energy Star, a public/private-sector program jointly sponsored by the U.S. Department of Energy and the U.S. Environmental Protection Agency. Unlike NFRC's program, Energy Star's correlates energy efficiency with climate and rates windows accordingly. The three Energy Star designations are N for northern climates where heating concerns predominate, S for southern climates where cooling is the primary concern, and C for central climates where both heating and cooling are considerations.

A critical difference between windows that does not show up in any testing program, however, is the warranty. If your builder is using a window made by a manufacturer that you have never heard of, and it is one that does not participate in any certification program (a likely possibility since only about 30 percent of the nearly one-thousand window manufacturers in the U.S. participate), the warranty may be the only way that you can judge the window's quality.

Most firms warrant their glass units and nonglass parts separately. Industry leaders such as Andersen, Pella, Hurd, and Marvin offer ten years on the nonglass parts, but differ on the glass. Hurd offers a lifetime warranty on the glass, but limits its coverage to 50 percent after ten years. Pella and Andersen warrant the glass for twenty years, Marvin for ten.

Your windows will be energy-efficient if they have dual glazing (two panes of glass), a low-emissivity (low-e) coating on one of the glass surfaces, and argon gas between the panes. But these energy savings features add to the cost. By going one step further and tailoring the energy efficiency of your windows to your climate, you can reap the energy and comfort benefits without over spending to get them. A window that works in Vermont with its frigid winters and mild summers is overkill in a mid-Atlantic state like Virginia. And in regions like Florida where cooling is the main concern, a window that works for Vermont would be inappropriate.

If you live in a place with a climate like Vermont's, get windows with the lowest U-factor you can afford (the U-factor is a measure of the rate at which heat passes through a window). By adding a third pane of glass or a storm window combination, for example, you can bring the U-factor down to as low as .21 to .25. If your new house will have large, south-facing windows that will get plenty of direct sun, get a *hard* coating low-e glass with a high solar heat gain coefficient (SHGC) of .55 to .60 (the solar heat gain coefficient is a measure of how much solar heat passes through a window). With a hard low-e coating and a high SHGC, you may get enough solar heat coming through the windows to justify a smaller, less expensive furnace.

Should you live in a place with cold winters and hot summers, you need a different strategy. Instead of the hard coat low-e glass that is recommended for Vermont, you need a *soft* coat low-e glass with a SHGC of .40 or less to keep out the summer heat. You won't get the free solar heat in the winter, but your house will be cooler in the summer. Since cooling costs are generally about three times heating costs, you'll still come out ahead. If your winters are really cold—say you live in Minneapolis—you should get a U-factor at least at low as .40, but the lower the better. If your winters are merely cold as they are in the mid-Atlantic region, a U-factor of .40 will be adequate.

Where the weather is hot and hotter, you want to keep heat out of the house all year long. Since solar heat pouring in through the windows accounts for as much as 50 percent of the total heat load on houses in these areas, you need a window that will reduce this unwanted solar heat. The lower the SHGC, the better. In Florida, for example, a SHGC of .40 or below is preferable. For hot and hotter climates, the U-factor is not so important because the problem is not heat loss (heat going out of the house) but heat gain (heat coming into the house).

Air infiltration can also be a troublesome issue with windows, though much of this is attributable to the installation of the window and not to the window itself. A window with the WDMA or the AAMA certification sticker will have an air infiltration rate of .3 or less. This will work in most areas, but in places with cold and winter gales, a lower air infiltration rate of .10 is preferable.

Some warranties are fully transferable to subsequent owners, but many limit coverage to the original purchaser. The worst ones cover the frame but not the glass, "like a car with no warranty on the engine," observes Dariush Araster of the Windows and Daylighting Group at the Lawrence Berkeley National Laboratory in Berkeley, California.

If the energy efficiencies, certifications, and warranties for the windows you are considering are similar, the choice my come down to price and appearance. The two most commonly used framing materials are vinyl and wood, which are about equal in terms of energy efficiency. Though many people think that wood is inherently superior to vinyl, it can be a nightmare to maintain, requiring repainting every two to five years. To avoid this, the extra cost of an exterior vinyl or aluminum cladding for a wood window is worth every penny.

Though you may be apprehensive about vinyl window frames, their quality has vastly improved over the last ten years. The first vinyl windows made fifteen to twenty years ago did have problems with yellowing, cracking, and warping, but the formulations for the vinyl have been changed and these problems are no longer an issue, several manufacturers said. One thing to note, however, is that a vinyl window with a welded frame and sashes will be stronger and more durable than a cheaper one in which these are mechanically joined.

Aluminum is still the least expensive framing material available, but aluminum is an excellent conductor and aluminum frames channel indoor heat straight into the great outdoors in the winter. They should be avoided in areas with cold weather. In warm areas aluminum frames are acceptable, though not optimal; if used, the frame should have a thermal break.

heatingandcooling

You want your new house to be more energy efficient. A more expensive, more efficient gas furnace could be a sensible choice if you will use it eight or nine months of the year. You could also argue for a more expensive, more efficient air conditioning unit even if you will use it only three months of the year, because electricity costs more than gas and because the pollution created by the electric generating plant contributes to the depletion of the ozone layer. But to make a sizable dent in your energy consumption and utility bills, you need to look at the entire heating and cooling system, not just the two biggest pieces.

For example, in most houses the ducts that carry the conditioned air leak at their connection points. On average, about 25 percent of the energy used to heat and cool a house is wasted in this way. When the unsightly ducts are put in an attic or a crawl space, a common practice in much of the country, this leaking air is lost to the great outdoors. Thanks to the laws of thermodynamics, additional heat or cold is lost through duct walls.

Even worse, some of the air may not be ducted at all. In some areas it's a common practice to route the air back to the heating or cooling unit through wall cavities between wood studs and the space between floor joists. Sending all the conditioned air through ducts and sealing them with mastic (a gray or white goopy paste) is the obvious first step. Duct tape, as it turns out, is ideal for the quick fix or the emergency repair (every family should toss a roll in the trunk before leaving on any vacation), but lousy when used for its stated purpose. Other types of tape are available but researchers in Florida and the Pacific Northwest have found that most tapes fall off in a few years' time. An added benefit to sealing the ducts properly: the time to cool down a house that has been empty all day can be reduced by more than one hour.

The next step is moving ducts out of the attic or crawl space and into the conditioned envelope of the house, thereby capturing that otherwise lost air. Since many people don't like the aesthetics of this solution—furred-out ducts running along the ceiling line could derail plans for crown moldings—another possibility is to leave the ducts where they are, but seal up and insulate the attic or crawl space so that it will be inside the thermal envelope of the house.

This is easier said than done, however. Sealed-up, unvented, and fully insulated attics and crawl spaces contradict established building practices that are more than a hundred years old, and most building codes do not allow it. A number of intrepid and persuasive builders and researchers in Nevada and Florida fought city hall and succeeded in building the sealed-up, fully insulated attics, but this approach has yet to catch on. Another attic strategy now being tried in Florida is to box in and insulate a small portion of the attic and put the ducts in there.

If you live in an area where the furnace, air handler, and ducts are put in a basement, you can avoid the attic/duct headache. In this case, the air leaking from the ducts will find its way back into the living areas above; but the rooms that are farthest from the furnace may be uncomfortable. Sealing and insulating the ducts, which is not commonly done when they are in a basement, will help ensure that the air is more evenly distributed.

The outside air coming into the house through the walls also affects energy consumption. When this air infiltration is excessive, it causes the furnace or air conditioning to run unnecessarily, which runs up the utility bills. All those points of entry need to be plugged. Even when they are, heat can also pass through the wall itself. A good insulation to slow this process is essential. The insulative property of a material is measured in R-values—the higher the R number, the better. But, insulation is most critical when there is a large difference between the indoor and outdoor temperatures. Wall insulation is critical in areas with cold winters, but attic insulation is critical everywhere in the country. In the summer, the temperature in most attics can reach 140 degrees while the temperature in the air-conditioned space below is 75 degrees.

The most commonly used insulation materials in houses are rolled fiberglass batts and blown-in cellulose. Builders generally prefer the batt type because it is much faster, and therefore cheaper, to install. The fiberglass batts are unrolled, placed between the wall studs, and stapled in place. The cellulose is blown into the cavities between the wall studs after a netting has been stapled in place. The cellulose is made from recycled newspapers—about 460 copies of the Sunday *New York Times* would supply the cellulose needed to insulate a two-story, 2,400-square-foot house.

Fiberglass and cellulose work equally well at slowing down the flow of heat through a wall, but the cellulose will also help plug up all those air leaks because it fills in around all the irregularities between the wall studs such as outlets, water lines, and gas pipes. For this reason, weatherization experts tend to favor cellulose.

Heat can also pass through the windows, so getting windows that suit your climate is also essential. Even the roofing material and color will affect the heat load in the house below; in the deep South, as near to white as prospective buyers can stand and tile if they can afford it is the best.

When you address all the other things in your new house that will affect how much energy is needed to heat and cool it and finally get back to the furnace and air conditioner, you should be pleasantly surprised. In all likelihood, you will be able to purchase less expensive ones than would ordinarily be installed in a smaller house because you've reduced the heating and cooling loads. When your new system is up and running after you move in, you'll find that it is significantly less costly to operate. Even better, it will deliver a noticeably higher level of comfort than the one in your house now because the heating and cooling will be more evenly distributed throughout the house.

Such a comprehensive and systematic approach to heating and cooling has been advocated for at least twenty years by building science engineers. But it has finally captured the imagination and attention of home builders through the Department of Energy's Building America program. Started in 1996, this program has two ambitious goals:

1. Devise strategies that will make new houses 30 to 50 percent more energy efficient than conventionally built ones.

2. Accomplish this through a series of tradeoffs and substitutions so that the dollars saved by some of the changes will cover the added cost of others.

In the past, energy efficiency has been a hard sell because it nearly always made houses cost more. Few people got very pumped up about a more efficient furnace, and buying one only made financial sense if the buyers planned to be in the house five to ten years, long enough to exceed the "payback period"—the length of time required for the savings on the utility bills to equal the extra money spent on the furnace. Immediate tangible benefits—a much greater level of comfort because the house was evenly heated and cooled—were often unrealized because the rest of the heating and cooling system was unchanged.

Change comes slowly to the home-building business, and it will be years before Building America's or Energy Star Homes' systematic approach to heating and cooling become the norm everywhere. In the meantime, here are some questions to ask and things to look for as you tour models or a custom builder's finished houses.

questions to **ask** your **builder** about **heating** and **air** conditioning

1. **Who designed the heating and cooling system?** You need an experienced mechanical engineer, not a heating and cooling contractor who did it on the fly. A poorly designed system can produce uneven air distribution (some of the rooms are too hot or too cold), unhealthy indoor air (some rooms get too much fresh air and others not enough), and unwelcome noise (poorly installed and/or wrongly sized duct work).

2. **Who is doing the work?** In some areas, the heating and ventilating contractor will subcontract out different parts of the installation work. With several different crews doing the work, quality control is hard to maintain.

3. **Is the entire heating and cooling system ducted?** If some of the return air is sent through wall cavities and spaces between floor joists instead of through ducts, the inefficiencies will be worse. If the builder uses ducts everywhere, but these terminate in a plywood box at the air-handling unit, there will be excessive leakage.

4. **Are the ducts sealed, and if so, with what?** If you're buying a new house in Florida the builder is required to seal the ducts, but this is not a standard practice everywhere so don't assume that the builder is doing it. Mastic, a gray or white paste, is a better sealing product that can last indefinitely, but many installers prefer to seal the duct joints with tape because this is faster. Unfortunately research has shown that most tape falls off in a few years' time. Even with a good seal, the ducts will still leak some.

5. **Where are the ducts located?** When the furnace and the air handler (the fan that blows the hot or cold air though the house) are in the basement and the ducts leak, some of the leakage will find its way back into the living areas above, but the rooms that are farthest from the air handler will be uncomfortable. Sealing and insulating the ducts, which is not commonly done when they are in the basement, will help insure that the air is more evenly distributed throughout the house.

When the ducts are in a crawl space or an attic, they are separated from the house by an insulation barrier so none of the leaking air can be recaptured. Sealing the ducts will help; so will insulating them. But even when the ducts are insulated, energy loss through the duct walls will still be incurred. This loss will be greater in the attic, especially in the summer.

Most of the heat in an attic comes from the sun beating down on it. In hot climates where the sun beats down all year long, installing a radiant barrier to reflect a good portion of the solar heat back outside is sensible. The most cost-effective radiant barrier material is aluminum foil, which can be laminated to the backside of the roof sheathing. This adds about $150 to $250 to the cost of a one-story, 2,000-square-foot house, but this extra cost can be offset by the savings gained in purchasing a smaller air conditioning unit than would normally be required.

6. Where is the air handler? This is the fan that sends the hot and cold air through the ducts. In some regions, it is routinely put up in the attic space; in others it is put there only in larger houses that require two heating and cooling zones. Either way, this location will cause additional energy losses, which can range from 10 to 25 percent of the total consumed to heat and cool a house, not to mention the difficulty in servicing the air conditioning and changing the filters if you have to go up into the attic to do this. The obvious solution is to bring the air handler down and put it in a closet inside the conditioned space.

7. Does the duct system have dampers, and if so, are they accessible? Dampers are metal plates installed inside metal ducts that can be rotated to adjust the airflow to different parts of the house. They give you some control over the temperature of individual rooms. If you are looking at model houses, ask the sales agent to show you where the dampers are located. If the builder doesn't install them, the manual type is not a costly upgrade. With the round flex-ducts used in attics, however, dampers are not an option.

8. Where are the returns located? The returns are the openings for the ducts that carry the air back to the air handler where it is recooled or reheated and then recirculated. In many new houses today there is only one return on each floor. This works fine when all the interior doors are open; when they're closed, you can have problems. Some rooms will be too cold and others too hot. And to make up for the air that can't get out of the room with the closed door, the return will suck in air from outdoors or the garage; in hot, humid climates, this will bring in unwanted humidity.

The cheapest solution is to undercut each door so that air can pass underneath when it's closed. A more expensive solution, but one that affords more privacy, is a transfer duct that takes the air from each room to the hall where it is picked up by the return. The most expensive solution, but one that affords the most comfort, is a return in every room. Few builders do this because it almost doubles the cost of the duct work and can add three to four hundred dollars to the cost of the house.

Another potential problem with a return is its size. If the return is not big enough, it will make a lot of noise as it tries to suck in air. Not only is this irritating, it also shortens the life of the air-handling equipment. If the air handler is not running when you are in a model or a finished house, ask to have it turned on while you stand by the return and listen. You can also get noise in the supply ducts so you should listen to them as well.

9. **Was the mechanical system tailored to the orientation of each new house in a subdivision, or calculated for the worst case and then installed in all the houses?** If the calculations are based on the worst-case scenario, the system may be oversized for your house. The oversizing will cause the equipment to cycle on and off constantly, which will shorten its useful life. Even worse, your discomfort may be acute. During the cold months the furnace will be constantly overshooting the temperature setting and turning itself off. You will be either too hot or too cold. The rooms which are the farthest from the furnace will be the most uncomfortable. During the hot months, the air conditioning will cycle off before the humidity has been removed. The air will be cool, but you will feel clammy, as if you were in a cave.

If the major living areas of your house face east or west—the worst-case scenario—and this was not taken into account when the system was designed, you will be uncomfortable to miserable, especially if you live in an area with a humid climate such as Houston.

10. **What kind of windows is the builder using?** If he is using ones with two panes of glass and a low-e coating that is appropriate to your climate, the problems associated with orientation can be greatly reduced, if not eliminated. Windows with the low-e glass can add four to five hundred dollars or even more to the cost of the house, but this extra cost can often be offset by downsizing the air-conditioning unit.

11. **Does the builder offer additional windows as an option?** In many cases, a buyer can add as many as six or eight windows to a production builder's standard floor plan. This may greatly enhance the interior spaces, but it also adds to the heating and cooling load, so ask if the mechanical system has been appropriately modified.

12. **If you are buying the end unit in a row of town houses, the house will have a large exposed end wall. Was the mechanical system designed to take this into account?** If your heating and cooling system is the same size as the interior unit next door, you will be very uncomfortable, especially if your end wall faces east or west.

13. **Does the builder offer a whole-house exhaust fan?** When the outside temperature cools off in the evening, you can open your windows and bring this cooler air into the house, cooling it off for the night and reducing the use of your air conditioner.

14. **Does the builder offer a ceiling fan?** With air movement, you can be

comfortable at higher room temperatures. For every degree that you raise your room temperature above 75 degrees Fahrenheit, you will save 10 percent of the cooling cost; set your thermostat at 77 and you will save 20 percent.

15. **Does your builder offer an upgrade for the air-conditioning unit?** All builders are required to install an air-conditioning unit with a 10-SEER rating, but a 10-SEER unit is likely to be bare-bones, builder-grade quality. Upgrading to a 12-SEER unit will give you one that's better made, more durable, has a longer warranty, and is less costly to operate.

16. **Does the builder offer any choice on roof color or material?** In a temperate climate, the color of the roof is not so important, but in the South it can make a significant difference in the heating load on your house. Lighter is better and white is best. Florida researchers have shown that a white asphalt shingle can save 8 to 10 percent of cooling energy; a white barrel tile or white metal roof can save about 15 to 20 percent of cooling energy. Before you invest in a white roof, though, you need to check with the Home Owner's Association, as

some have strict rules on roof colors and materials.

17. **Where are the filters located?** All hot-and cold-air systems have filters that must be periodically changed or cleaned. When the filter is at a return grille, this is easy, but if the filter is in the attic or somewhere else that may also be fairly inaccessible, this becomes an odious chore that is often left undone. When you're looking at the model, ask the sales agent to show you where the filter is and judge for yourself how often you will change it. You should also ask if any filter upgrades are offered. Standard issue in a production house will almost surely be the "dollar filter" type that only removes the largest dust particles—7 to 10 percent of what comes through the ducts. The electronic type removes about 80 percent of the dust that comes through. Between these two extremes are several intermediate grades. Because some of the filter upgrades are sizable and can affect the installation of the air handler, you need to discuss any filter upgrades with the builder and his heat and air-conditioning contractor before the sales contract is finalized. A good choice for most houses is the one-inch-thick disposable pleated filter which sells for about $10 and fits most filter grilles.

Energy efficiency is a much easier sell when buyers pay only a minimal extra amount and get greater comfort and savings from day one. That is the genius of the Building America program, and it has made energy savings a win-win proposition for both buyers and builders. Pulte Homes in Las Vegas, for example, has found that with the Building America systems approach, the buyers of one of their 2,400-square-foot houses save about $660 a year on their heating and cooling bills, compared to what they would be paying in a conventionally built house. The added cost to get the savings and comfort is about $1,000.

Since each part of the heating and cooling system is interrelated, and many other things in a house can also affect it, a multi-discipline approach is essential. Each of the five national teams fielded by Building America includes home builders, architects, building system engineers, mechanical engineers who specialize in heating and cooling, tradesmen, and product manufacturers.

As the building scientists and energy gurus predicted, the Building America teams have found that surprisingly simple changes can make a big difference in energy consumption. For example, when the building frame is thoroughly sealed and caulked and the drywall is glued and screwed, the amount of air infiltration can be reduced by as much as 50 percent. In one project the thermal envelope of the house was so energy efficient, the hot water heater provided both hot water and heat.

The Building America teams—each with a slightly differing approach—have built prototypes, tested them, modified them, and retested them. Some of the strategies were too costly for mass application, but the prototypes that met all the criteria are now being built in subdivisions across the country and more prototypes are on the drawing board or in the testing phase. By the end of 2001, Building America anticipates that 5,800 houses will have been built through their program. Although this number is small, the hope is that Building America's successes will be adopted by non-participating builders.

Energy Star Homes is another program designed to increase energy efficiency in new houses. Unlike Building America's industry-wide team approach, Energy Star's is targeted at individual builders (for more information, see Resources). If you can't find a builder in your area that participates in either program, you can still ask any builder that you are considering about duct sealing, duct location, windows, air infiltration, and insulation. (For more information on the Building America program and the Energy Star Homes program, see Resources.)

lighting

No doubt you are eagerly anticipating the first night in your new house. But as you prepare your first dinner or spend your first evening in the family room, you don't want to make the disheartening discovery that the lighting is grossly inadequate. Even worse, if you wait to address this problem until after you move in, you will find that adding lights then will be much more costly than doing it while your house is under construction.

How could you overlook something as central as lighting? If you visit the model only during the day, you won't think about it; that's why it's *essential* to visit at night, when lighting inadequacies are often glaringly apparent. Another problem is that few builders are knowledgeable about lighting, so they rarely offer anything beyond what's required.

In this respect, Ann Arbor, Michigan, theatrical lighting designer Gary Decker had an unusual advantage when he purchased a production-built house and modified his builder's standard package. But all of the lighting changes that he made in his new house were modest ones that you can do as well. For example, he increased the number of ceiling fixtures in his long second-floor hallway from one to three.

For his own house and most residential applications, Decker says, you need two kinds of lighting—task and ambient. Task lighting is brighter and more intense, and is required for performing specific tasks such as reading. Ambient lighting, which is much less intense, provides general room lighting. Task lighting is usually provided by table lamps; ambient lighting, by ceiling or wall fixtures.

For some tasks, however, table lamps are not the solution. To get adequate task lighting in a kitchen, for example, you have to build it in. Most builders provide a light over the sink, so trying to see if you really got the dirt off the plate is not difficult. But many food-preparation tasks such as chopping and mixing are done away from the sink. Under-cabinet lights will supply adequate task lighting, but most production builders do not offer these even as an optional upgrade. If your builder won't install the lights, ask if he will install the wiring so that you can add them after you move in. Most under-cabinet lights are fluorescent, but the color of halogen lights is more pleasant, and this type of fixture can be directed exactly where you want it.

Many households with children also use the kitchen for non-cooking tasks, such as homework. Hanging a half-globe fixture about thirty-six inches above the breakfast table will provide ample light for reading and writing. With the addition of a dimmer switch, you can lower the lighting for meals.

For general lighting in the kitchen, most builders install a single ceiling fixture, but the lighting is usually very uneven as you go from one end of the room to the other. A few strategically placed recessed cans, which most builders offer as an option, will distribute the light more evenly. Another solution is track lighting, which can be installed after you move in, but this can looked cluttered if the kitchen is not large.

Another room where task lighting is essential but a lamp is out of the question is the bathroom. Many builders provide overhead lighting above the sink, but this creates shadows on your face, and makes putting on makeup almost impossible. Theatrical lights on three sides of the mirror will give the most even wash of light, but a band of six to eight lights across the top is a reasonable compromise for most people.

For general ambient lighting, most buyers assume that the builder will provide a ceiling fixture. He will, but only when the code requires it—in bathrooms, the kitchen, and laundry and utility rooms. In other rooms, including bedrooms, builders are required only to install a switched outlet; that is, a switch that is connected to an outlet and turns on a lamp. If you want an overhead light in each bedroom, you will have to request this too. Adding a theatrical touch to the master suite in his own house, Decker put the builder's standard dining-room chandelier in the master bedroom area.

Another often overlooked lighting need that Decker now regrets not getting for himself is closet lights. In most jurisdictions a builder is required to provide one for the walk-in closet in the master suite, but you should get them for all the closets, he advises. Otherwise you'll find yourself, as he often does, burrowing around in the dark for missing shoes and umbrellas, trying to distinguish dark clothing items, and searching for matching towels in the linen closet.

Ambient lighting for two-story spaces, especially large family rooms, can be problematic. Most builders offer recessed cans, but they're hard to change when the ceiling is seventeen feet off the floor, and they're also ineffective. When a recessed fixture is this high, it delivers only a quarter as much light at floor level as it does when it is only eight or nine feet from the floor. You'll see well enough to move about the room, but you won't have enough light to read by. Wall-mounted sconces placed seven or eight feet off the floor are easier to change, but they still won't provide enough light for reading. For this, you'll need table lamps.

When recessed cans are placed in a ceiling that is only eight or nine feet above the floor, however, they can provide both task and ambient lighting. For a fourteen-by-twenty-foot family room with a fireplace and bookcases at one end, seven cans on two switches should work well. Put three cans at the fireplace end on one switch and four cans on the other switch, spaced so that they would wash the walls evenly.

By varying the type of recessed can used, you can create other lighting effects. In the family room, for example, a can with an eyeball placed above the fireplace would direct light to a picture hung over the mantel.

A fourteen-by-twenty-foot family room with an eight- or nine-foot ceiling is also big enough to install track lighting and not have the space look cluttered. If you opt for track lights, you can create a variety of lighting effects, and you can direct the light exactly where you want it to go.

outlets

Lighting is not the only electrical issue for many new home buyers after they move in. So are outlets. Though some people plan everything down to where they will put each chair, table, and lamp, very few of these conscientious buyers carry the planning through to the very last step—plugging the lamp or coffee maker into the wall. Only after they move in and search for the outlet do they realize the closest one is on the other side of the room. And adding outlets afterward can add up, says Ann Arbor, Michigan, electrician Marj Schloff.

The no-outlet-where-you-need-it problem shows up most often in large family rooms, where people tend to group furniture in the center of the room rather than against the wall. After they've finally put the furniture in place, the new owners find there's no outlet nearby. The only alternative to an unsightly cord running across the rug, which can also be a trip hazard, is installing a floor outlet. But if the electrician has to cut a hole in the nice brand-new carpet without damaging it, and then cut a hole in the floor for the outlet box and run the wiring, the job will cost twice what it would have if this had been done during construction.

If the ceiling in the family room is low enough, you can dispense with table lamps and floor outlets altogether and rely on ceiling fixtures. But adding overhead fixtures later can easily be two to four times what it would have been if the fixtures were installed before the drywall went up.

Building codes usually dictate the location and spacing between wall outlets in a kitchen, but this can put the outlet in the wrong place. You have to move the appliance to the plug each time you use it or end up with a lot of unsightly cords running along the backsplash. Envisioning how you will use the kitchen and exactly where you want the outlet for the coffee maker or mixer at the time the outlets are installed is hard, Schloff acknowledges, because the house is at the framing stage and all you see are two-by-four-inch studs. Before trying to do this, she advises buyers to study the kitchen and outlet locations where they live now. Then have the builder mark the studs where the appliances and sink will be. With these benchmarks in place, deciding where to put the outlets will be easier. Since getting the kitchen outlets exactly where you want them will take the electrician longer, you will most likely have to pay extra for this. But the ease with which you can work in your new kitchen is worth it, Schloff says.

Planning ahead for exterior lighting will avoid headaches later, especially during the Christmas season. Although some buyers request wiring for outside security lights, no one ever thinks about hanging Christmas lights outside until the holidays arrive. Adding wiring expressly for this during construction will make this task much easier and avoid dangling cords everywhere. If you like to put lights along the eaves just below the roof line, add wiring and an outlet there.

If you're worried about resale and think that you should get whirlpool jets for the master bath but know that you will never use them, and don't want to spend the twenty-five hundred dollars needlessly, Schloff suggests installing only the wiring and leaving it up to subsequent owners to install the jets and motor if they wish. This will cost only about two hundred dollars. However, some building officials do not like wiring that is not hooked up to anything, so you need to check out this possibility with your local building department first.

wiringforthefuture

"Wiring for the information age" is probably high on your must-have list. Beyond knowing that you want it, though, you may not know what this means or even the nature of the problem with the wiring in your existing house. You just know the symptoms—interminable waiting to get on the Internet, interminable waiting to download material, and telephone gridlock. For much of the day in many houses, trying to make a phone call can be an exercise in frustration. A computer modem for accessing the Internet has tied up one line, a fax machine another. A spouse working out of a home office commandeers a third one during business hours, and teenagers can tie it up at night. The final kicker—the phone company wants a fortune to add any more.

Simply diagnosed, the problem is woefully inadequate phone and cable wiring, and it can be solved in a new house in a single stroke called "structured wiring." Using phone and cable wire with much greater capacity than what you have now and networking them from a central hub, you can access the Internet instantaneously (this is real liberation), and have four or more phone lines selectively ring at different locations in your house.

With structured wiring, you can also set up a video network that allows you to share one VCR or DVD among all the televisions in your house, and a computer network that allows you to share expensive equipment such as a printer/scanner. Plug a security camera into the network and you can see who is at the front door or what the kids are doing in the backyard via a screen in your basement office.

Some other advantages of a wired network are still in the future, but not very far. For example, when the next generation of kitchen appliances becomes available, plugging one into a structured wiring network allows manufacturers to diagnose mechanical problems from afar and dispatch a service man with the appropriate parts. Of greater interest: When a wireless webpad is added to the next-generation refrigerator door, you can scan in food items as you run out. The list can be tallied at your local grocery store and your larder restocked with a regular weekly delivery.

As you might suspect, with a structured wiring network, the type of wiring used and its installation is critical to success. The phone and high-speed Internet connection wiring must be a category 5 unshielded twisted pair of "cat 5 utp" (currently, standard phone wire is category 3). The video wiring must be broad band RG6 coaxial cable tri- or quad-shielded. Most cable companies now install this, but not in a structured wiring configuration.

Conventional phone and cable wiring is strung continuously from outlet to outlet through the house, but the wiring for a structured wiring network must emanate from a central control panel with a separate wire going to each phone and video outlet. This wiring configuration is usually called a home run or a star. This upgraded, high-capacity wiring is sensitive; bend it too much or inadvertently add a few kinks during installation and the performance will be affected.

Five national firms, OnQ, Home Director (a spin-off from IBM), Lucent (a spin-off from AT&T), UStec, and Leviton specify and in some cases actually manufacture the new-generation cat 5 and RG6 wiring, which they sell along with the other components of the system. Working nationwide with their distributors, these firms also train installers. The wiring and other equipment that these five firms sell is similar; of greater importance to consumers is the training of the person installing it. Make sure that he or she has been trained and certified by one of the five and that *the system itself* is tested and certified after its installation.

Most of the firms that actually install the equipment are small and locally owned. Verizon Communication (formerly Bell Atlantic Ready), a subsidiary of Verizon (formerly Bell Atlantic Communications, which merged with GTE), is as yet the only company that installs residential structured-wiring networks on a large scale; it now operates in forty-four states.

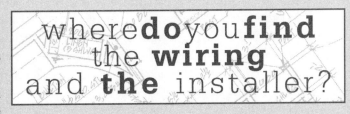

What are home builders offering? In the Washington, D.C., area with its high-tech industry and sophisticated clientele, a number of the large national builders include a structured-wiring network package in their base price, and the smaller builders offer it as an option. Elsewhere in the country, builders are familiar with the concept of structured wiring, and many currently offer it as an option. But nearly all agree it will be routine and expected by buyers everywhere before long. (For information on how to find an installer and on the firms that manufacture equipment, see Resources.)

Installing a structured wiring network correctly requires specific training and equipment even for people who already are experienced (and where required, licensed) in low-voltage electronics, as this field is professionally designated. Though the term *low-voltage* may not be familiar, the actual trades included in it certainly are: installers of telephone and cable systems, home theaters, surround sound, and security systems.

The most important first step in setting up a structured wiring network is getting the wires into the walls and multi-media outlets (an outlet with jacks for phone, Internet access, and cable) into the major rooms of your house. As you may eventually purchase one of the kitchen appliances that can be wired into the network, you should install an Internet outlet by the stove and refrigerator. Everything else including linking the computers or the televisions can be added later, but adding the wires and outlets later will cost about four times as much as doing it during the initial construction when all the walls are open.

The wiring used in structured wiring systems today will eventually be superseded by something even better and faster. To install it relatively easily and cheaply when the time comes, installers advise "future proofing" your home network with a cheap, low-tech solution: a two-inch plastic plumbing pipe that runs from the hub (usually in the basement or utility room) to the attic space under the roof. From the attic, an installer can easily drop new wires into the second-floor rooms below; new wiring for the first-floor rooms can be run up from the basement. If you plan to finish this area, ask an integrator (as installers of structured wiring systems are frequently called) where to locate ceiling access panels. If your basement ceiling will be nine feet high, consider a drop ceiling with a panel that can be easily removed to install new wiring.

How much does the structured wiring cost? The firms that install these systems generally offer basic and upgraded levels of installation. The lowest-priced basic level usually includes a central hub, three to six multi-media outlets, and one or two additional phone outlets. Most important, it gets the basic wiring into the walls. The next upgrade usually includes additional multi-media outlets so that you get one in each major room plus the video network, computer network, and wiring for one or two security cameras. This would cost about two thousand dollars for a 2,500-square-foot two-story house.

roofing
asphalt shingles

If you're buying a production-built house, the chances are close to 100 percent that the roof will be asphalt shingles, the most cost-effective roofing material currently available. The builder will ask you to pick one from a selection of colors and grades displayed on sample boards. But if you're like most people, you'll find it hard to imagine what a few pieces of asphalt-encrusted shingles will look like fifteen to thirty feet off the ground and replicated two thousand times.

It's much easier if you start with the big picture. When you pull back for that big pan shot, you'll see that the slope of the roof is its defining characteristic. As a Tampa, Florida, roofer succinctly puts it, "Low slope or high slope, it's a night-and-day difference." If the slope of the roof on your new house will be shallow—18.5 degrees or less—the roof will not be a strong visual element. Looking at it from the ground, you'll see the leading edges of the shingles and their overall color more than the shingles themselves or their pattern. Picking a good-quality shingle that keeps out the elements without going overboard on looks is a reasonable strategy.

But given the housing styles that are popular today, it's more likely that the roof on your new house will have a much steeper slope and be a prominent architectural feature. If you're considering that perennial favorite, the Cape Cod, half the front elevation will be roof. The shingle pattern will be very visible, and the roof itself will be the first thing those resale buyers will see as they drive down the street toward your house, so give some thought to the roof's appearance. For resale, looks count.

In the world of asphalt shingles, there are two types, "three-tab" and "dimensional," (also called "architectural" and "laminate"). A three-tab shingle has two notches cut into the lower edge so that when it's laid on a roof it looks like three smaller shingles. Seen from below, three-tab shingles have a very distinguishable repetitive pattern. This type of shingle costs less than a dimensional type, but its precise pattern requires more time to install. Thus it is less favored by roofing crews, who are usually paid by the number of shingles they install, not by the hour. For a shallow-pitch roof, however, the three-tab is a reasonable choice.

A dimensional, or laminate, shingle has extra pieces of shingle laminated to it that give the appearance of thickness and texture when seen from below. There is no discernible shingle pattern, so it can be installed more quickly than the three-tab type. Besides the shadow line created by the added thickness of the extra pieces, most manufacturers embellish this with artificial shadow lines created by artful placement of colored granules.

The thickest and most expensive dimensional shingles, which usually carry the designation "forty-year shingles," often have two artificial shadow lines plus an overall subtle texturing of the shingle. The "thirty-year" dimensional shingle generally has only one fake shadow line, less subtle blending of the granule colors, and the shingle is not as thick. The least expensive, "twenty-five-year" dimensional shingle, which many production builders offer as standard, has a less pronounced shadow line, and its thinner shingle creates less of a three-dimensional effect. To give consumers more choices, some shingle manufacturers also sell a less expensive three-tab textured shingle with a fake shadow line.

When viewed up close on a sample board, only the shingle manufacturer's artifice will be apparent. To get an idea of what the shingles will look like when viewed from afar, you need to find a finished house with a roof that has a similar size and slope.

The other consideration when choosing an asphalt shingle is longevity—how many years can it shed water and keep the rest of your house dry? Assuming that the roof has an adequate slope and is installed properly, this will depend on the local climate and how much asphalt—the key water-proofing ingredient—is on the shingle.

Shingles were once differentiated by weight, which indicated the amount of asphalt in the shingle. About twenty years ago, as more and more manufacturers switched to making shingles with fiberglass cores that did not require as much "black gold," they began to categorize shingles by their projected years of useful life. Since there is no industry-wide standard for what constitutes "forty-years," "thirty-years," and so forth, this designation has been left to individual manufacturers to determine.

In the absence of manufacturing precision, some explanation of asphalt shingle mechanics may be helpful. The key factors are time and temperature. The hotter asphalt becomes on your roof and the longer it stays hot, the shorter its useful life will be. A shingle in Phoenix will not last as long as one in Detroit. Even seemingly benign weather will heat up a roof. When the air temperature is a mere 75 degrees, the roof surface can easily reach 140 to 160 degrees.

The heat causes the asphalt to expand; the hotter it gets and the longer it stays hot, the longer it will be in a "stretched" position. When the sun goes down, the asphalt contracts back into its original position. Besides shortening its useful life, the heat causes the asphalt to soften and slide. If applied to the shingle in its pure form, it would slide off into the gutters on the first warm day of spring. To prevent this, inhibitors are added to the mix to raise the asphalt's "softening" temperature.

The UV rays of the sun are problematic as well, attacking the asphalt and causing it to become brittle and cracked. The granules—those pulverized stones or glazed ceramic pieces that give a shingle its color—function as a UV umbrella to shield the asphalt from the sun.

Eventually, after several thousand heating and cooling cycles, the asphalt loses its ability to contract back into its original shape and the granules start to fall out, exposing the asphalt underneath to the sun. (This is why power-washing an asphalt-shingle roof to remove dirt and mildew is a bad idea—the force of the water will pry off the granules and greatly shorten the life of the roof.) The roof will start to look scuzzy. It may be several years before it actually begins to leak, but once a roof starts to look bad, most homeowners decide to replace it, observes Tom Bollnow, technical director for the National Roofing Contractors Association.

How many years does it take for a roof to look bad? Climate clearly affects how long a given manufacturer's "twenty-five-year" shingle will really last; so will its color. Across the southern half of the United States, with longer summers and more intense sun, dark shingles will absorb more heat and age faster than lighter ones. In the northern half of the country, color is less significant, says Greg Malarkey, senior vice president of Malarkey Roofing Company, an asphalt-shingle manufacturer in Portland, Oregon.

Most manufacturers extend the life of their shingles by adding more asphalt. The Malarkey firm prolongs life by adding a filler ingredient that makes the asphalt rubbery and increases the number of times it can expand and contract before the granules start to fall out.

Since the staying power of the granules is a critical factor, a quick but telling test no matter where you live is to run a quarter across the granules on a builder's sample. If a lot of granules come off, it's not a great shingle, and you should question the quality of the other materials the builder is using.

The core material in the shingle can affect its longevity. In the northern areas of the Midwest and New England and Canada, which experience extreme freeze-thaw conditions, some roofers prefer an older style asphalt shingle with an organic mat core instead of a fiberglass one because they feel it lasts longer. Elsewhere in the country, less expensive fiberglass shingles are used almost exclusively. Of these, the twenty-five-year dimensional fiberglass shingle is the most commonly used.

What do roofers say about longevity of the twenty-five-year shingle? When queried, the answers included eighteen years in Houston (high humidity and petrochemical air pollution speed up the aging process); eighteen to twenty years in Tampa, Florida (the intense sun tears up the materials); twenty years in Washington, D.C.; twelve to seventeen years in Ann Arbor, Michigan ("if you're lucky, but with some brands that are a heavier weight, you can get seventeen to twenty years"); and in areas with benign climates such as the Pacific Coast near San Luis Obispo, California, fiberglass shingles "really will last out their full twenty-five years."

Before you pick shingles, consult with several local roofers and building-supply stores. Then factor in how much you want to pay for longevity and how much for looks. You may not get as many years of life from the shingles as the manufacturer suggests, but the look of a more expensive shingle may not cost as much as you think. The difference in the cost of a square of the twenty-five-year dimensional shingle and a square of the forty-year shingle is only about twenty-five dollars (a square is one hundred square feet; all roofers calculate roof area in squares). The roofer would add on a "profit and overhead" figure for the more expensive shingle, but the cost of the labor and the other materials such as nails and roofing felts would be the same.

tile

Roofing tile is the most durable choice of all. It is manufactured in a variety of shapes and is made of various materials including red clay, cement, concrete, and a composite material made of Portland cement and wood fibers. Although the tiles are what you see—and what accounts for most of the cost of a tile roof—the underlayment is the critical element in waterproofing. If it is not installed properly, the useful life of your "lifetime" tile roof will be greatly reduced. Moreover, repairing leaks will be expensive, because the tiles and the wooden strips they are nailed to must be removed before you can get at the failing underlayment.

To ensure that you get as many years from the tiles as the manufacturer suggests, roofers recommend that two layers of thirty-pound roofing felt be used under the tiles (one roll of forty-five-pound felt will suffice in some areas). Since many production builders routinely use one layer of fifteen-pound felt for asphalt shingles, you need to make sure they ratchet this up for a tile roof.

As a rule, concrete tiles are less expensive than clay ones, but in some areas such as Florida, regular maintenance costs should be factored in. If concrete tiles are not cleaned regularly, fungi may turn them an unsightly dark black.

All tiles are heavier than asphalt shingles and some, such as concrete, can weigh four to six times as much. The heavier weight requires more roof framing and a stronger foundation to support it; both of these factors will add to the cost of a tile roof.

After the devastation of Hurricane Andrew in 1992, Florida building codes required that roof tiles be carefully fastened down. As the slope of the roof increases, more elaborate and more expensive fastening is required, which also adds to the cost of a tile roof. The building codes in other hurricane states, such as Texas, also require special roof fasteners for tile.

slate

Highly durable, slate is the most expensive roofing material available, often costing eight to twelve times as much as the highest grade of asphalt shingles. Slate also weighs much more than the asphalt shingles, and the roof framing and bearing walls will have to be beefed up to support it. The additional framing requirements will, on average, add about 10 percent to the cost of a slate roof.

Slate is graded for hardness. The hardest grade may last as long as 75 to 150 years, often outlasting the building it was installed on. If the slate is carefully removed before the wrecker's ball starts to batter away, the slate can be reinstalled elsewhere.

Slate is quarried in Vermont, Pennsylvania, and Virginia. The most expensive and durable is Buckingham slate from Arvonia, Virginia. If you need to replace a slate piece fifty years from now, the company will send you a replacement slate quarried from the same vein as the original piece and it will be a perfect match. Slate from Vermont and Pennsylvania is generally not as hard, and some of the slate from these quarries will fade over time, a phenomenon called weathering. All American-quarried slate is graded for hardness and durability. The best and hardest slate carries the S1 designation; an S2-graded slate will not be as durable. Slate from Vermont, Pennsylvania, and Virginia all carry the S1 designation but of these three, Virginia Buckingham is the hardest.

Imported roof slate from Asia and Europe is now available in many markets. The imported slate is often "soft," meaning it will break more easily during installation, and the color may also fade quickly. If your builder suggests using it (some of the imported slate is much less expensive than American-quarried slate), ask to see the specification and grading information. Some of the imported slate, such as Spanish Del Carmen, does carry the S1 grade, the designation given to top-quality American slate, but most of it does not carry any grading designation at all. If you are going to the extra expense of adding additional framing material and paying a very large labor premium to have the slate installed, you should go the distance to ensure that you are also getting a good product.

Another point to consider with slate is that you will need ice guards, often called snowguards, to protect your gutters and yourself. Slate has a slick surface, and snow will slide off easily. If the snow falls off all at once, it will take your gutters with it. If it falls at the moment you walk out your front door, you could be seriously injured. For a large house, snowguards can add fifteen hundred to two thousand dollars to the cost of the roof. Copper gutters and downspouts always complement a slate roof, but this could be another five to eight thousand for a large house.

wood

Cedar shakes and shingles add cachet to many houses, but the quality of cedar now available for roofing materials is not as good as it was thirty to forty years ago, and the roofs will not last as long. Cedar also presents other problems. It some areas of the country, including Southern California, wood roofs are banned as a fire hazard. In other areas, such as Florida, algae and bugs make a cedar roof impractical; in Southeast Texas humidity extremes will shorten the useful life of cedar.

Cedar roofing is available in either shakes or shingles. The shakes are handsplit on the exposed side to give a rough-textured appearance and smooth sawn on the underside. The shingles are sawn on both sides. In either case, you should insist on a #1 blue label grade. It will be more expensive than #2 grade, but the top grade will last longer because it will be free of knot holes and have a tighter grain. If your builder only offers a less expensive #2 grade, you should seriously reconsider with this caveat: #2 grade western red cedar is equal to #1 grade blue-label eastern white cedar, which is often called "extra." Even with #1 grade, roof pitch and climate will have a major effect on how long the roof will last. Though the manufacturer may suggest that these will last as long as twenty or twenty-five years, you should consult with a local roofer.

As with roof tiles, cedar roofing has special underlayment requirements. It must be installed over wooden battens (strips of wood) or over a special mesh to ensure that the cedar is adequately ventilated. The mesh is a recent innovation and it's faster to install, but some roofers are skeptical about its efficacy.

ecoshake

Manufactured by Re-New Wood in Wagoner, Oklahoma, the Ecoshake shingle is made entirely of recycled materials. One half is wood scrap; the other half is post-industrial flexible vinyl scrap purchased from factories manufacturing garden hoses, vinyl flooring, shower curtains, automobile bumpers, and other vinyl products. The Ecoshake resembles a cedar shake roof in texture, but it has a fifty-year warranty and a Class A fire rating (the highest fire rating you can get for a shingle); it is impervious to bugs and moisture; and it can withstand wind speeds up to 110 miles per hour. Of greater interest if you live in an area where hail is a problem, the Ecoshake is hail-resistant. Hail can break both cedar shingles and shakes and asphalt shingles. Ecoshakes cost about three to three and a half times as much as the highest grade of asphalt shingles, but only about twice as much as the #1 blue-label red western cedar shakes they are manufactured to replace.

metal

Standing metal seam roofs have become increasingly popular with the revival of the front-porch and Victorian-styled houses. This type of roof can also be installed on a roof with a lower pitch than is possible with a shingled roof, so it is often used for the roof of the increasingly popular front porch, even when the rest of the house has asphalt shingles.

The most expensive metal used for roofing is copper. It weathers to a light green and requires no painting, ever. A variety of other roofing metals are available, but be fore-warned: If you use the least expensive non-galvanized metal, it will require frequent repainting. Many production builders use this type of metal roofing for a bay window.

roof slope

Roofers express the slope in twelfths—for example, 4/12. That is, for every 12 units across, you go up 4. The minimal allowable slope for a shingled roof varies with climate, and is generally stipulated in a local building code. In some places it's as low as 3/12 (14 degrees), but most roofers aren't comfortable going below 4/12 (18.5 degrees), and they often prefer more than this because with more slope the roof will drain better and the shingles will last longer. For example, in Florida, where the annual rainfall is high, 5/12 (23 degrees) is the preferred minimal slope. In Michigan, where it snows a lot, 4/12 is considered minimal.

As architectural styles have changed and the roof has become a prominent feature, many new houses have a roof slope of 6/12 (27 degrees) or even 7/12 (31 degrees). You should note, however, that as a roof slope increases, a roof becomes more expensive because:

- a steeper-pitched roof has more roof area to cover and requires more shingles and other roofing materials

- a steeper slope is harder to work on, so labor costs will increase; above a 7/12 slope, special equipment is required to install the shingles

- the steeper-pitched roof also requires more framing materials to support it

roofing system

The shingles are only the outermost layer of a roofing system. The other components include felt underlayments, which are rolls of black paper laid under the shingles; ice guard, a special material installed at the roof perimeter and around chimneys and skylights to prevent ice dams and leaks during the winter; and flashing, or metal strips that are placed alongside skylights and chimneys and in the valleys where two slopes meet to prevent water from seeping in.

If all the parts of a roofing system are not installed properly, the expected life of the shingles can be seriously compromised, sometimes by as much as 50 percent. (The structure under the shingles can also be compromised if they are not installed properly.)

gutters

Roof gutters are not required for a roof to function; their purpose is to channel the runoff water so that it doesn't damage the exterior walls or the foundation below. Various metals can be used for gutters, but the most cost-effective type is factory-painted aluminum. With aluminum, the joints cannot be soldered; they must be riveted and caulked. As long as this is done properly, the gutters should be trouble free; the obvious way to check is to simply observe them during a rain. Aluminum comes in varying gauges—some production builders use a thinner .027 gauge, but you should insist on a heavier .032, because over time you will be resting ladders against your gutters to clean out leaves and other debris that will collect in them.

Many builders put a plastic splash block at the base of the gutter, but roofers generally prefer a five-foot extra length of gutter at the base to carry the water away from the house. A better looking but more expensive solution is to encase the base of the gutter in a plastic sleeve that channels the water into a buried plastic drain pipe that carries the water away from the house.

During the housing search, you're likely to focus on what you can see, not on what you can hear. So you may not notice any irritating sounds until the house is built and you move in. At that point, a solution is often expensive or impossible. Even more disheartening, in many cases, the problem could have been easily and inexpensively addressed during construction.

tips**from**the**trade:**
acoustics

The best way to avoid such an unhappy outcome is to listen carefully as you look and to plan ahead, says Chris Savereid, an acoustical consultant with Acentech in Cambridge, Massachusetts. Before you think about noise inside the house, check the surrounding environment, advises Savereid, who's gotten more than one phone call from a distraught home owner who moved in and then discovered his house was in the flight path of an airport.

The three most common external sources of unwanted noise—highways, airports, and trains—are pretty hard to miss. The problem is that the time of day, or the day of the week, when the noise is greatest may not be the time that you look at the house. For example, Saturday afternoon and Sunday morning are low-traffic periods at many airports. In some instances, owners realized that the backyard would be noisy, but didn't anticipate that it would be so audible in the house. After verifying the existence and location of any potential noise source in the area, make arrangements to visit the site and the model house when the sound is loudest, even if this means going at night.

As more developers tackle urban infill sites that can be in or near industrial zones, industrial noises from factories or a constant stream of diesel trucks passing by can be an issue. Even the sound of children on the playground during school recess is not for everyone. You should also note that "acoustically unacceptable" can be a very subjective judgment; what bothers one person may not disturb another, so you need to test for yourself.

If you find the noise is objectionable, the obvious solution is to look somewhere else. If for some reason the airport or the diesel trucks cannot be avoided, you can reduce the sound inside the house by modifying the doors and windows, but you won't eliminate it completely. Savereid, who has worked on noise-mitigation projects in residential areas around airports all over the country, says the most effective results were achieved by modifying the doors and windows. He recommends adding a storm window to create at least a two-inch air space between the glass surfaces, and heavier exterior doors that are 1¾-inch solid wood plus a solid storm door to provide the two-inch air space.

Focusing on the house itself, the noise issue with town houses is sound emanating from the other side of shared walls, specifically the low-frequency, deep-bass rumblings of the neighbor's favorite rock band. To see if this will be a problem in a place that you are considering, have a friend or spouse play a tape recorder in a unit next door and see if you can hear anything. Since most townhouse projects have at least two adjacent furnished models, such a field test should not be difficult.

With a detached single-family house, the noise issue is sound generated from within. When you're looking at furnished models, turn on your tape recorder or portable television and then walk through the house, noting how the sound carries. Savereid again urges buyers to plan ahead and think about the likely activities of their household. If you have music lovers or an aspiring rock star, for example, get them to agree to restrict their music making activities to one room. With a few sound-isolating modifications, you can keep most of the sound contained within it.

First, install batt insulation—the same material used in outside walls to reduce heat loss in winter—in the walls and ceiling of the room. Several manufacturers now make an "acoustical batt insulation" specifically for sound-deadening purposes. Savereid says that independent tests suggest that it will produce slightly better results for mid- and upper-frequency sounds such as speech and song lyrics, but it won't help much with the rumbling base.

Next, add an extra layer of gypsum board to the walls and ceiling inside the room itself and to the shared walls of any adjacent rooms. Then install a solid-core door, rather than the hollow-core ones that most builders use for interior rooms. The builder may resist adding the second layer of drywall because it will affect how he usually finishes doors and windows. To get his agreement, you will need to pay for nonstandard door and window details as well as the cost of the extra drywall and the labor to install it.

Locating the music/media room in a part of the house where noise is less of a problem—rather than next to the master bedroom, for example—and surrounding it with neutral room functions such as bathrooms and closets also helps, Savereid says. Bear in mind that some plan configurations can produce unpleasant acoustics. For example, an open floor plan with few walls and no doors will make the house feel bigger, but the noise will go everywhere, and acoustical privacy will be nil. "The absence of doors plus lots of hard surfaces—walls and ceilings—means there will be little chance of acoustical privacy unless the house is very large. If acoustical privacy is important, you need to look for a house with contained spaces and plenty of doors you can shut," Savereid advises.

"Acoustically acceptable" can also vary with circumstance. A living room with an eight-foot ceiling and carpet is fine when only three to five people are talking. But the same room with twenty people talking will be unpleasant. If you entertain a lot, some sound-absorbing treatment will make a noticeable difference—on the ceiling in the living room, in the kitchen where guests invariably congregate, and in the dining room. The spaces will seem less chaotic, and carrying on a conversation will be much easier. If you have a large, two-story family room, loud music will boom all through the house unless you add sound-absorbent material on the ceiling. The sound won't disappear entirely, but "it may not bug you as much," Savereid says.

The simplest and most inexpensive way to treat a ceiling is to install the same acoustic tile used in many offices. Since most home owners raise aesthetic objections to this solution, Savereid recommends ceiling-mounted fiberglass panels that are covered with perforated metal panels or a breathable fabric that complements the furniture, carpets, or curtains. For a more contemporary look, the fiberglass panels can be faced with stained- or painted-wood slats.

Although the fiberglass-panel solution may sound exotic, you can get them at any lumberyard and cover and install them yourself. If you want the fabric look, the only trick is making sure that the fabric is breathable so that the sound energy can pass through and be absorbed by the fiberglass. Another possibility for ceiling-mounted sound absorption is a one-inch-thick white fiberglass panel that can be installed in the recesses of a coffered ceiling. Once installed, it looks like plaster.

The finish materials in a space will also affect its acoustics. Change the carpeting in a family room to wood or sheet vinyl and the space will seem noisier because of increased footfalls, dropped objects, and furniture scraping.

Kitchen appliances, especially dishwashers and range hoods, can produce irritating noises. Setting the dishwasher on neoprene cushions and encasing it with batt insulation will deaden the sound of a builder-grade dishwasher, but getting a quieter, albeit more expensive, model is easier. Savereid advises prospective house buyers and remodelers to go to an appliance store and listen to various models on display. Some range hoods are so noisy that homeowners would rather live in a house full of cooking smells. To avoid this dilemma, get a quieter, more expensive range hood, but not one so quiet that you forget it's on and don't turn it off.

Some noise problems, such as a partner's snoring, can be improved, but not entirely eliminated, Savereid notes. With snoring, the source of the noise is too close for sound-absorbing carpeting, bedding, or curtains to have any effect. Two strategies that might work are blocking the sound with earplugs or masking it with a white-noise machine.

resources

chapter one: the big picture

stylistic overview:

website:

www.dreamhomedesignusa.com and click to "period design"

books:

American House Styles: A Concise Guide, by John Milnes Baker, A.I.A., W.W. Norton & Company, New York, 1994.

Buy a House Without Losing Your Assets, by Ron Dickson, self-published. To order, contact the author, 2487 Brawley School Road, Mooresville, N.C. 28117 (704) 664-4157 $25.00 prepaid.

Build It Right, by Myron Ferguson, Home User Press, Salem, Oregon, 1997.

Creating the Not So Big House, by Sarah Susanka. Taunton Press, Newtown, Connecticut, 2000.

The Healing House: How Living in the Right House Can Heal You Spiritually, Emotionally, and Physically, by Barbara Bannon Harwood, Hay House, Carlsbad, California, 1997.

House, by Tracy Kidder, Avon Books, New York, 1985.

The Most Beautiful House in the World, by Witold Rybczynski, Penguin Books, New York, 1989.

The New House Buyer's Guide, by Martin Turk, Groom Books, Alexandria, Virginia, Revised edition, 2001. To order, contact the author at (703) 941-0100, ext. 158.

Norm Abram's New House, by Norm Abram, Little Brown & Company, Boston, 1995.

The Not So Big House, by Sarah Susanka, Taunton Press, Newtown, Connecticut, 1998.

Your New House, by Alan and Denise Fields, Windsor Peak Press, Boulder, Colorado, 1999.

chapter three: how much will it cost?

The ANSI square-foot standard, ANSI Z765–1996, can be ordered from the National Association of Home Builders Research Center for $20.00 plus $4.00 shipping and handling fee (800) 638-8556.

chapter four: financing

websites:

The three national credit reporting bureaus can be reached at:

Experian (888) 397-3742, www.experian.com/consumer/index.html or
www.creditexpert.com.

Equifax (800) 685-1111 or www.equifax.com or PO Box 105873, Atlanta, Georgia 30374–0256.

Trans Union (800) 916-8800 or www.tuc.com or PO Box 200, Chester, Pennsylvania 19022.

The FICO website includes information explaining the Fair, Isaac and Company credit scoring model: www.fairisaac.com/consumer. To get your own FICO score, as calculated by Equifax, www.myfico.com or through Equifax at www.equifax.com.

Fannie Mae and Freddie Mac have websites: www.fanniemae.com and www.homepath.com and www.freddiemac.com.

Mortgage information websites: www.mortgageripoffs.com and www.americanhomeowners.org.

Numerous lending institutions have websites with detailed mortgage information and mortgage calculators. Here are two: www.homeloancorp.com and www.bankone.com.

books:

Taking the Mystery Out of Your Mortgage: What Desktop Underwriter Analyzes in Your Loan Application, a free Fannie Mae booklet available through Fannie Mae Consumer Resource Center, (800) 7FANNIE or (800) 732-6643.

Buy Your First Home, by Robert Irwin, Second Edition, Dearborn, Chicago, 2000.

Home Buying for Dummies, by Eric Tyson and Ray Brown, IDG Books Worldwide, Foster City, California, 1999 Edition.

How to Buy and Sell Your Home Without Getting Ripped Off!, by Patricia Boyd and Lonny Coffey, Dearborn, Chicago, 2000.

100 Questions Every First Time Home Buyer Should Ask, by Ilyse R. Glink, Three Rivers Press, New York, 2000 Edition.

Power Tips for Buying a House for Less, by Robert Irwin, McGraw-Hill, New York, 2000.

chapter five: the production-built house

websites devoted to new house sales:

www.homebuilder.com (nationwide data base)

www.HousingGuides.com (select metropolitan areas around the country)

www.NewHomesDirect.com (nationwide data base)

www.NewHomesGuide.com (Washington, DC–Baltimore area only)

www.NewHomesNetwork.com (nationwide data base)

chapter six: the custom-built house

websites:

The American Institute of Architects, aiaonline.com, lists members by state and city who do residential work; you can also call (800) 242-3837 to get a referral.

Home Plan Services. There are at least 100 plan services. These are four of the better known ones:
www.caddhomes.com (800) 722-2432
www.designbasics.com
www.homestyles.com
www.stephenfuller.com (800) 274-2444

books:

Design Considerations for a New House: Home Design Handbook, The Essential Planning Guide for Building, Buying or Remodeling a Home, by June Cotner Myrvang and Steve Myrvang, Henry Holt & Company, New York, 1992.

Raising the Rafters: How to Work with Architects, Contractors, Interior Designers, Suppliers, Engineers, and Bankers to Get Your House Built, by Stephen F. Collier, The Overlook Press, Woodstock, NY, 1994.

chapter seven: the kitchen

The "miracle corner," the swinging-tray mechanism for a blind-corner cabinet condition, is made by Hafele, a German company, and used by a number of custom cabinet makers in the U.S. For more information, contact the U.S. office for Hafele, (800) 423-3531.

websites:

General information about cabinets and cabinet certification testing procedures administered by the Kitchen Cabinet Manufacturers Association, www.kcma.org, (703) 264-1690.

General information about kitchens and kitchen design, National Kitchen and Bath Association, www.nkba.org.

Almost every cabinet manufacturer has a website.

stock cabinets used by many production builders:

Aristokraft, www.aristokraft.com

Cardell, www.cardellcabinets.com

Merillat, www.merillat.com

Wellborn, www.wellborncabinet.com

widely used semi-custom cabinets:

Amera (made by Merillat), www.merillat.com

Kraftmaid, www.kraftmaid.com

Decora (made by Aristokraft),www.decoracabinets.com

Brookhaven (made by Wood-Mode), www.wood-mode.com

wine storage specialists:

www.vintagecellars.com, (800) 876-8789

www.wineappreciation.com or info@wineappreciation.com, (800) 231-9463

composite countertop materials:

Crystalite, www.crystalite.com

Silestone, www.silestoneusa.com

Zodiac, www.zodiac.com

these two sites have information on maintenance and stain removal for stone countertops:

Fred Hueston's National Training Center for Stone and Masonry Trades, www.ntc-stone.com

Stone Care International, www.stonecare.com

solid surface materials:

Avonite, *www.avonite.com*

Corian, *www.corian.com*

Fountainhead, *www.ftnhead.com*

Gibraltar, *www.wilsonart.com*

Sorrell, *www.formica.com* and click to Sorrell

plastic laminate:

Formica, www.formica.com

Nevamar, www.nevamar.com

Pionite, www.pionite.com

Wilsonart, www.wilsonart.com

kitchen appliances:

websites:

The Energy Star Program rates both dishwashers and refrigerators for energy
efficiency, www.energystar.gov.

Consortium for Energy Efficiency also rates refrigerators and dishwashers,
www.ceeformt.org.

Consumer Reports website lists their reports that rate kitchen appliances,
www.consumerreports.com.

Every appliance manufacturer has a website. Each site will have a complete list of
all appliances offered and many of them have features that allow you to make
cost comparisons between appliances with different features. The prices listed
are "suggested retail price," but the appliance business is very competitive and
sales are frequent. Most retailers will match the prices offered by competitors.
Some sites and other resources also include useful consumer information:

books:

Consumer Reports Annual Buying Guide, published by Consumers Union,
Yonkers, NY.

Consumer Guide to Home Energy Savings, by Alex Wilson, Jennifer Thorne, and
John Morrill, American Council for an Energy Efficient Economy, Washington,
D.C., 1999 Edition.

chapter eight: other rooms

websites:

General information about bathrooms and bathroom design, National Kitchen and Bath Association www.nkba.org.

The Energy Star Program rates clothes washers at www.energystar.gov.

The Consortium for Energy Efficiency rates clothes washers for both energy efficiency and water usage, www.ceeformt.org.

chapter nine: flooring

websites:

Carpet and Rug Institute, general consumer information about every aspect of carpeting, www.carpet-rug.com or (800) 882-8846.

Nearly every carpet manufacturer has a website.

laminate flooring manufacturers:

There are a number of companies that manufacture laminate flooring. These three are described in the text:

Formica: www.formica.com

Pergo: www.pergo.com

Wilsonart: www.wilsonart.com

composite decking made from recycled wood fibers and recycled plastic:

Boardwalk: www.certainteed.com; click to "outdoor living products"

SmartDeck: www.smartdeck.com (This is linked to the parent company's website, USPlasticLumber.com)

Trex: www.trex.com

recycled plastic:

Carefree: www.carefree-products.com (This is linked to the parent company's website, USPlasticLumber.com)

Virgin vinyl:

Brock Deck: www.royalcrownltd.com

EverNew: www.certainteed.com, click to "outdoor living products"

Kroy: www.kroybp.com

chapter ten: the lot

websites:

Locating a registered licensed landscape architect: Contact the American Society of Landscape Architects (800) 787-2752 and ask for the phone number of the local chapter in your area. Call the local chapter to get names of members who do residential work. For general information about this organization and profession, check their website, www.ASLA.org.

To locate a consulting arborist in your area, check the website of the American Society of Consulting Arborists, www.asca-consultants.org or contact them in Rockville, Maryland, at (301) 947-0483.

To find a Certified Arborist in your area, check the website for the International Society of Arboriculture (ISA), www.isa-arbor.com or contact them in Savoy, Illinois, at (217) 355-9411.

chapter eleven: the purchase

websites:

To find a private home inspector through the American Society of Home Inspectors, check its website, www.ashi.com, or call its toll free number (800) 743-2744. In addition to the ASHI credential, home inspectors in fifteen states are required to be licensed, certified, or registered. Detailed information is available on the ASHI website.

Another professional organization of home inspectors is the National Academy of Building Inspection Engineers or NABIE. A much smaller organization, it is affiliated with the National Society of Professional Engineers. To find a private home inspector through it, check the NABIE website, www.NABIE.org.

chapters twelve and thirteen: production-home and custom-home sales contracts

books:

Brincefield's Guide to Buying a Home: The 21 Biggest Mistakes People Make When Buying a Home, by James C. Brincefield, Jr., self-published, Alexandria, Virginia, 1993. To order a copy, call (703) 836-2880 or buy online at www.brincefield.com.

Crumbling Dreams, by Ruth S. Martin, M.C., Lakeside Press, Cleveland, Ohio, 1993.

chapter fourteen: construction considerations

bouncy floors:

For more information on floor vibrations and rules of thumb for joist spacing, see "Beyond Code: Preventing Floor Vibrations," by Woeste, F.E. and Dolan, J. D., Journal of Light Construction, 17(1): 69–71 or http://www.jlconline.com/jlc/archive/framing/floor_vibration/index.html.

indoor air quality:

website:

Radon: The U.S. Environmental Protection Agency's radon maps of the U.S. designate predicted average indoor radon levels for every state and county is listed at its website, www.epa.gov/iaq/radon.

books:

The Healthy House, by John Bower, The Healthy House Institute, Bloomington, Indiana, 1997.

The Healthy House Answer Book, by John and Lynn Marie Bower, The Healthy House Institute, Bloomington, Indiana, 1997.

Residential Indoor Air Quality and Energy Efficiency, by Peter DuPont and John Morrill, American Council for an Energy Efficient Economy, Washington, D.C., 1989.

windows:

websites:

The National Fenestration Ratings Council (NFRC) data on energy performance for all windows tested through their program is posted on its website, www.nfrc.org, and published in three volumes available for $60.00 by calling NFRC at (301) 589-6372. Note that double-hung windows, the most common type used in residential construction and what you are most likely to use on your new house, are listed as vertical sliders.

For general information on windows, check the website for the Lawrence Berkeley National Laboratory in Berkeley, California, www.efficientwindows.org.

For information on energy-saving window strategies for 48 U.S. and four Canadian cities, check "window selection" at www.efficientwindows.org.

To cross-reference window type with framing materials, climatic region and manufacturers that participate in the Energy Star Windows Program, check "windows" at www.energystar.org.

books:

Residential Windows: A Guide to New Technologies and Energy Performance, by John Carmody, Stephen Selkowitz and Lisa Heschong, W.W. Norton & Company, New York, 1996.

heating and cooling:

websites:

Building America Program, to locate a builder who participates, check its website, www.eren.doe.gov/buildings/building_america/index.html.

Energy Star Homes Program. To qualify for the Energy Star designation, a builder's houses must be 30 percent more energy efficient than the Model Energy Code requires. To insure that the completed houses meet this standard, they must be tested and certified by an approved third party. Builders can use a variety of strategies to achieve this goal, and the Energy Star program promotes many of the same energy-saving measures that Building America does. To locate a builder who participates in the Energy Star Homes Program, check its website, www.energystar.gov and click on homes. Many of the builders are small, but some divisions of the larger, national firms including Centex, Brookfield, Beazer, and Ryan are also involved.

Two other websites that have useful information about energy efficiencies in housing: The Lawrence Berkeley National Laboratory in Berkeley, California, http://duct.lbl.gov, and Florida Solar Energy Center, www.fsec.org; browse the homes and buildings pages.

residential lighting:

books:

Home Lighting, by the Editors of Sunset Books and Magazines, Menlo Park, California, 1999 Edition.

structured wiring:

websites:

These five firms sell the equipment and train and certify installers. You can get a dealer referral by calling them directly or checking their websites:

OnQ Technologies: www.onqtech.com or (800) 321-2343

Ustec: www.ustecnet.com or (800) 836-2312

Home Director: www.ibm.com/homedirector or (800) 426-7144

Lucent Technologies: www.lucent.com/netsys/homestar (800) 344-0223, ext. 8001

Leviton: www.levitontelcom/com (800) 722-2082

These two firms install the systems and can be contacted directly:

Verizon Connected (formerly Bell Atlantic Ready): www.bacccsi.com or
(888) 947–3782

Digital Interiors: www.digitalinteriors.com

Two professional organizations for installers whose membership indicates an
installer is involved in this industry and keeping up with its frequently changing
technology:

Building Industry Consulting Services International or BICSI, www.bisco.org
(800) 242-7405.

Custom Electronic Design & Installation Association, CEDIA. To get a referral to a
member in your area, check the website, www.CEDIA.org, or (800) 669-5329.
The website also has general consumer information.

Smart Homes for Dummies, by Danny Briere and Pat Hurley, IDG Books, Foster
City, California, 1999.

acoustics:

websites:

For general information about acoustics, check "tech information" at Acentech's
website, www.acentech.com.

For the name of an acoustical consultant in your area who does residential work,
check the Yellow Pages or contact the National Council of Acoustic Consul-
tants in Springfield, New Jersey, at (973) 564-5859 or e-mail them at
info@ncac.com.

roofing:

websites:

Every manufacturer of roofing materials has a website.

books:

Roofing and Siding, by the Editors of Sunset Books and Magazines, Menlo Park,
California, 1999 Edition.

*The Slate Roof Bible: Everything You Want to Know About Slate Roofs Including How to
Keep Them Alive for Centuries,* by Joseph Jenkins, Chelsea Green Publishing,
White River Junction, Vermont, 1997.

two periodicals for general readers with information on green building and energy efficient construction:

Environmental Building News: The Leading Newsletter on Environmentally Responsible Design and Construction, published monthly, www.BuildingGreen.com or (802) 257-7300.

Home Energy, bimonthly, www.homeenergy.org/ or (510) 524-5405.

books that cover residential construction more broadly:

Building Your Own Home: An Insider's Guide, by Carol Smith, Home Builder Press, Washington, D.C., 1996.

How Your House Works, by Dan Vandervort, Ballantine Books, New York, 1997.

Understanding House Construction, by John A. Kilpatrick, Home Builder Press, Washington, D.C., 1993.

The Walls Around Us: A Thinking Person's Guide to How a House Works, by David Owen, Vintage Books, New York, 1992.

The Well-Built House, by Jim Locke, Houghton Mifflin Company, Boston, 1992.

glossary

A paper: A mortgage loan given at a lender's best terms and lowest interest rate.

batt or batt insulation: Rolled fiberglass insulation.

base price: The price for a standard production house without any options or lot upgrades.

blind corner: The area under a countertop where the two legs of an L-shaped counter intersect. It cannot be accessed unless a special cabinet is used.

bridge loan: A short-term loan that allows buyers to borrow against the equity in their existing house before they have sold it in order to close on a new house.

building green: An approach to construction that emphasizes energy efficiency, healthier indoor air, and resource conservation both in the selection and manufacture of materials and in the operation of the building itself.

cans: A light fixture that is recessed up into the ceiling.

cat 5 utp: Category 5 unshielded twisted pair wiring used for high-speed Internet connections.

change orders: An order for an item that was not in the original contract with a builder. It will be an added cost to the homeowner.

closing costs: The fees that a lender requires at the time a mortgage is assumed. Closing costs range from about 1 to 5 percent of the mortgage amount.

collector lot: A lot in a subdivision that collects the rainwater runoff from several adjacent lots.

composite countertop: A countertop material that looks like granite but is actually made of quartz particles mixed with an epoxy or acrylic binder.

composite wood: An outdoor decking material made of recycled wood fibers and recycled plastic.

credit score: A score used by lenders to determine a loan applicant's credit worthiness.

crown molding: Wood strips shaped in various rounded profiles and installed at the ceiling line to add a decorative detail. A single crown molding is only one piece of wood; a triple crown molding has three pieces of wood and is more elaborate.

custom builder: A home builder who builds one-of-a-kind houses, using either a plan provided by the client or one from his own portfolio. The builder builds on the client's lot and his price includes only construction.

design/build: A custom home builder who offers design services.

developer: The person who buys the raw land, subdivides it, and sells lots to home builders. Some developers are also builders.

dimensional lumber: A sawn piece of lumber that comes straight from the tree and is cut to standard sizes used in residential construction.

dimensional shingle: An asphalt shingle that appears to be three-dimensional when seen from the ground below.

eave: The edge of a roof that overhangs the wall below.

elevation: The exterior side of a building.

elevation drawing: A picture of the exterior of a building.

empty nesters: A couple with adult children who no longer live at home.

engineered wood: Structural framing members made by shaving thousands of strands of lumber off a log, coating them with wax and resin, aligning the fibers to provide maximum structural strength, and shaping them to be variously a beam, column, joist, subflooring, or sheathing.

engineered-wood joist: A roof or floor joist that is shaped like a steel I-beam, but made of wood. The two chords at the top and bottom may be solid wood or laminated (layers of wood that are glued together). The web between the two chords is made of engineered wood.

equity: The difference between what you paid for a house and its present market value.

felt: See *Roofing felt.*

FICO score: A credit score based on your credit records and calculated using a statistical model designed by Fair, Issac & Company in San Rafael, California. The FICO score is used by lenders to determine your credit worthiness.

flashing: Strips of metal used around door and window openings, along walls and everywhere the roof plane intersects another plane (chimneys, roof vent, skylight, another section of roof, etc.) to prevent moisture penetration.

footer: A foundation footing.

Footing: The base of the foundation; to spread out the total building load, it is wider than the foundation wall above it.

foundation: A wall made of concrete or concrete masonry units that carries the building loads above it down to solid soil. To spread out the total building load, the base of the wall, called a footing, is wider.

framing: The structure that both supports and encloses the house. In most residential construction the framing is primarily wood and includes wood studs, roof trusses or roof joists, floor joists, subflooring, and roof and exterior wall sheathing. The framing rests on the foundation.

gable: The triangular end of a roof.

galley kitchen: A kitchen with a single aisle and counters and appliances to either side.

glazing: Glass areas; either doors or windows.

grade: Ground level.

green: A material or method of construction that is more environmentally benign than a standard building material or building convention.

ice dam: An ice build-up at the edge of a roof that prevents melting snow from draining into the gutters; in extreme cases, the melting snow leaks into the living spaces below.

I-joist: Another name for an engineered-wood joist.

integrator: An installer of a structured wiring network.

inventory house: A production-built house that is finished or under construction, but not yet sold.

joist: The framing member that supports the floors and the roof when roof trusses are not used.

junk fees: Extra fees a lender tacks onto his closing costs to make more money on the loan.

lease-back: An arrangement whereby a house is sold and then the seller leases it back from the buyers for a specified period.

lock-in: A mortgage lender's commitment to a specified interest rate, provided that the loan is closed within a fixed period.

low-e: Low emissivity. A low-e coating is added to window glass to make the window more energy efficient. The coating helps to keep the heat inside in winter and outside in summer.

master planned community: Another name for PUD (see below).

mechanic's lien: A legal claim on a property by those who perform work on it or furnish materials. In the case of a new house, all laborers and suppliers are entitled to attach a mechanic's lien against the owner if they have not been paid.

ogee: A wood trim piece with an S-shape profile, commonly used as part of a wall base or a crown molding.

option: An upgrade offered by a builder of a production-built house.

oriented strand board: Four-by-eight sheets of engineered wood commonly used for subflooring and for exterior wall and roof sheathing.

origination fee: A fee charged by a mortgage lender and included in the closing costs. It is usually 1 percent of the mortgage amount.

OSB: Oriented strand board (see above).

pile: Carpet fibers.

point: 1 percent of the mortgage amount. Points, which are calculated to the nearest eighth, are charged by nearly all mortgage lenders and included in the closing costs charged at the time a buyer assumes a mortgage.

production builder: A builder who offers a limited number of floor plans and optional upgrades for a fixed price and who sells the lot as well as the house. Most build on lots that are subdivided by a land developer, and most will make only minor changes to the floor plans that they sell.

PUD: Planned unit development. A very large housing community that usually includes a mixture of house types (single-family houses, town houses, and condo apartments). Each house type will be offered in varying sizes and prices by several builders. Amenities generally include recreational facilities such as tennis courts, swimming pools, jogging trails, tree stands, and open green spaces. The size can vary from as small as two hundred acres to as large as several square miles.

RG6: Coaxial cable tri- or quad-shielded; it is used for the video and cable wiring portion of a residential structured wiring network.

recessed cans: A light fixture that is recessed up into the ceiling.

R-factor: A measure of the rate at which heat passes through a building material. The higher the R figure, the slower that heat can pass through it, and the more energy efficient it is.

roof deck: The roofing surface created when four-by-eight-foot sheets of plywood or oriented strand board are nailed to the roof joists or trusses. The underlayment and finish roofing material are attached to the roof decking.

roof truss: Wood trusses used to support a roof.

roofing felts: Black, asphalt-impregnated paper nailed to a roof deck for temporary waterproofing and as an underlayment before the shingles are installed. The felts are designated by pounds, as in "30-pound felt."

SEER: Seasonal Energy Efficiency Rating, a rating system that is used to indicate the energy efficiency of central air conditioners and heat pumps operating in their cooling mode.

semi-custom builder: A builder who sells a limited number of floor plans but who is willing to make substantial changes to meet buyers' needs.

SHGC: Solar Heat Gain Coefficient, a measure of how much solar heat passes through a window.

sheathing: Four-by-eight-foot sheets of plywood or OSB that are nailed to the wood studs and roof trusses to enclose the house and give it structural stability. Wall sheathing can also be less expensive sheets of laminated fiberboard (looks like masonite) or asphalt-impregnated fiberboard.

site superintendent: The person at the job site who has the day-to-day responsibility for overseeing the construction of a house.

slope: A vertical drop in feet per hundred horizontal feet. A 1 percent slope drops 1 foot over a distance of 100 feet.

soffit: The underside of a roof that projects beyond the wall below.

solid surfacing material: A synthetic material used to make countertops. It can be either solid acrylic or an acrylic/polyester mix.

spec or specifications: A detailed written description for each item used in the construction of a house.

stand-alone subdivision: A subdivision that has only one type of house rather than a mixture of house types and few if any amenities. The houses are usually built by only one builder.

structured wiring: High-capacity phone and cable wiring networked from a central hub. The network allows high-speed data transmission, multiple phone lines, and networking of computers.

stud: A two-by-four-inch by eight- or nine-feet piece of wood that is used to frame walls in residential construction.

subfloor: Four-by-eight-foot sheets of plywood or OSB that are nailed to the floor joists to create a floor. The finish flooring material—carpet, hardwood, or whatever—is laid over the subfloor.

swale: A shallow ditch that carries surface water runoff.

tear-down: A house of relatively little value that is purchased and then torn down so that a new and usually much larger house can be built.

TJI: A floor or roof joist made of engineered wood that is shaped like a steel I-beam.

tract builder: A builder who builds houses on tracts of land, subdivided into lots by a developer. Most tract builders prefer to be called production builders.

trim: Wood that is installed around window and door openings and at the base of walls to cover over structural framing and drywall edges and create a finished look.

U-factor: A measure of the rate at which heat passes though a window. The lower the U-factor, the more energy efficient the window.

underwriting: The process of evaluating a mortgage loan application.

VOCs: Volatile organic compounds, which are chemically unstable and off-gas from many building materials.

window treatments: Blinds, drapes, or louvers added to a window to provide privacy. These are usually provided by the homeowner, not the builder.

wood stud: A piece of wood that is two by four inches by eight or nine feet that is used for framing in residential construction.

index

acknowledgments

Just as a house requires the effort of many people, so does a book. I am the author, but I have gotten a lot of help along the way.

In the year that it took me to write *The Brand-New House Book*, my husband, Steve, and my daughters, Daisy, Shelley, and Claire, have been supportive and encouraging, even when this meant missed family trips and seemingly endless days and nights working. As I got to the final crunch and my computer started to give out, Shelley provided critical assistance.

My agent, Loretta Fidel, arranged for a contract with Three Rivers Press. My editor there, Chris Pavone, provided critical guidance as to what readers need to know and kept me from going overboard on the details. My sister Gwenda Blair and Steve read early drafts and gave useful feedback. Mortgage broker Lonny Coffey provided me with lots of background on financing and reviewed the chapter on financing. Attorneys Jim Savitz and Sherry Chin shared their advice on sales contracts and reviewed those chapters. The following experts shared their advice and also reviewed relevant portions of the manuscript: arborist and attorney Dennis Yniguez; architects Carl Hunter and Norman Smith; attorneys Beau Brincefield, Judith Deming, Terry Eland, Dennis Haber, Scott Jackson, Robert McNees, John Nethercut, James Parker, and Paula Reddish Zinnemann; building-failure consultant Richard Rivin; buyer's agent Meredith McKenzie; golf-course architects Bill Newcomb and Cal Olson; heating and cooling specialist Subrato Chandra of the Florida Solar Energy Center; indoor-air-quality experts Max Sherman, Al Hodgson, and Iain Walker of the Lawrence Berkeley National Laboratory; kitchen and bath designer Carolyn Thomas; landscape architect David Foote; private home inspector Skip Walker; real estate appraisers William C. Harvey and Martha Heric; roofers David Harlow and Chuck Wagner; stone-care expert Fred Hueston; and structural engineer Frank Woeste.

The book is based on "Housewatch" columns written for *The Washington Post* and "Your New Home" columns written for Inman News Features, and nationally syndicated in newspapers and on websites.

I started writing for the *Post* in 1994 at the invitation of Ken Bredemeier, who was the real-estate editor. It was a first; at that time the *Post* was the only daily in the country that offered regular advice to buyers of brand-new houses, about to make the largest purchase of their lives. I also received tremendous support from David Ignatius, then the finance editor; Bob Kaiser, then the managing editor; and Len Downey, the executive editor. Nancy McKeon, Ken's successor, and Maryann Haggerty, now the *Post* real-estate editor, have also been very supportive of the "Housewatch" column and my decision to write this book. Many people in the Washington-area home-building community became invaluable and informative sources, including Russell Arkin, Bill Berry, Jim Boyd, Tom Bozzuto, Charlie Browning, Bob Burdette, John Cowles, Tom Dean, Chip Devine, Larry

Dobson, Rhonda Ellisor, Jeff Gray, JD Grewell, Chip Gruver, Peter Gulick, Bill Harvey, Bob Hubbell, Bob Jordan, Sandra Kessler, Jim Kettler, Pat Kolinsky, Tom Kreutzer, Rick Kunkle, Steve Perlik, Jody Pilka, Anna Pitheon, Steve Porten, Betty Quirk, Michael T. Rose, Guy Semmes, Ted Visnic, Allan Washak, and Bob Youngentaub.

Local and national government officials who provided timely help and information include Jim Collins, Willy Furr, Paul Lynch, Eric Mays, George Rose, Ray Scott, Stan Waldeson, Randy Wyrick, and Sophie Zager.

Gopal Ahluwalia and Betty Christie of the National Association of Home Builders always provided prompt and useful information. Ken Sugarman, Bill Froberg, and Anna Pitheon of the Myers Group provided statistical information, which I usually needed in a hurry.

Members of the Washington-area design community who remain important sources include Larry Bassett, Jim Bingnear, John Colby, Randy Creaser, Bill Devereaux, Win Faulkner, Susan Gulick, Sami Kirkdil, Chris Lessard, Roger Lewis, Margaret Rast, David Reddick, Ronda Royalty, Debbie Saling, Norman Smith, Bill Sutton, and Carolyn Thomas.

In 1996 Brad Inman invited me to be a syndicated columnist with Inman News Features and write for a national audience. Dick Barnes, now the managing editor for Inman and then the real-estate editor of the *Los Angeles Times* has been a great support as well as the first editor to take my syndicated column. Cory Anders, former real-estate editor of the *San Francisco Examiner*, was another important early supporter.

In the five years that I have been writing for Inman, I have developed a national network of experts including Rich Bartlett, Boots and Gary Baumbaugh, Barry Berkus, Lonny Coffey, Judith Deming, Lita Dirks, Terry Eland, Frank Fanto, Vince Ghiloni, Leon Goldenberg, Dennis Haber, Paul Heilstadt, John Henry, Carl Hunter, David Johnston, Carson Looney, Meredith MacKenzie, Nadav Malin, Robert McNees, Murray Milne, James Parker, Randy Reinhart, Richard Rivin, Ron Resch, Turko Semmes, Will Snyder, Lee Wetherington, and Alex Wilson.

This is a lengthy list, but, in fact, these are only some of the people who have been helpful to me. In addition to them, 457 other individuals contributed to the reporting of the columns that form the basis of this book, and more than 200 others helped with columns that were not included. Because of space constraints, I am unable to thank each person by name, but I wish to express my appreciation for all the assistance that has been so generously extended to me.

Of course, even with all this help, errors are possible and I am solely responsible for the contents of this book.

Katherine Salant
Ann Arbor, Michigan